Successful Project Management

Applying Best Practices and
Real-World Techniques with
Microsoft® Project

BONNIE BIAFORE

Published with the authorization of Microsoft Corporation by:

O'Reilly Media, Inc.
1005 Gravenstein Highway North
Sebastopol, CA 95472

Microsoft Press titles may be purchased for educational, business, or sales promotional use. Online editions are also available for most titles (*http://my.safaribooksonline.com*). For more information, contact our corporate/institutional sales department: (800) 998-9938 or *corporate@oreilly.com*.

1 2 3 4 5 6 7 8 9   M   6 5 4 3 2 1

Microsoft, Microsoft Press, the Microsoft Press brand, Access, Enterprise Project Management, Excel, Exchange Server, Office, Outlook, PowerPoint, Project, SharePoint, Visio, Windows, and Word are either registered trademarks or trademarks of Microsoft Corporation in the United States and/or other countries.

This book expresses the author's views and opinions. The information contained in this book is provided without any express, statutory, or implied warranties. Neither the author, O'Reilly Media, Inc., Microsoft Corporation, nor their respective resellers, or distributors will be held liable for any damages caused or alleged to be caused either directly or indirectly by this book.

Acquisitions and Development Editor: Kenyon Brown
Production Editor: Teresa Elsey
Editorial Production: Octal Publishing, Inc.
Technical Reviewer: Ciprian Adrian Rusen
Illustrator: Robert Romano
Indexer: Angela Howard
Cover: Karen Montgomery
Composition: Nellie McKesson

978-0-735-64980-4

Acknowledgments

PUBLISHING A BOOK is a project, and for *Successful Project Management*, I was fortunate to work with a team that has the can-do attitude that every project manager dreams of.

My thanks go to Kenyon Brown, the acquisitions and project editor, who shepherded the manuscript through several iterations; Nancy Sixsmith, the copy editor; Sumita Mukherji, the production manager; and Angela Howard, the indexer, for polishing the manuscript to the pages you're reading now.

I also want to thank the reviewers who made sure that I was clear; provided useful information; and, most important, didn't make things up. For sharing his uncanny project management sense as well as his sense of humor, I thank my friend, Bob McGannon. I also thank Ciprian Rusen for his thorough technical review and valuable suggestions.

In this edition of the book, I have included best practices generously offered by project managers from a variety of industries. I learned a lot from their experiences and suggestions, and, even better, have made some new friends. I would like to introduce you to these contributors:

Max Dufour is a principal with SunGard Global Services. He has been managing global projects for more than 10 years with a focus on strategy formulation, operational effectiveness, risk management, and corporate social responsibility. He holds an MBA from Duke University, has a BA from Northeastern University, and is a PMP.

Jeff Furman (*www.jeff-furman.com*) has 15 years experience as an IT project manager and is author of *The Project Management Answer Book* (Management Concepts, 2011). He teaches PMP prep and Train-the-Trainer courses for the Microsoft Certified Trainer and CompTIA CTT+ certifications.

Tres Roeder is founder and president of Roeder Consulting, a company that offers A Sixth Sense for Project Management®, a system for helping people work through change. The company clients include several Fortune 500 companies. Tres regularly presents at Project Management Institute meetings.

Dr. Robyn Odegaard is the president/owner of Champion Performance Development (*http://champperformance.com*). Robyn speaks nationally on team-building and leadership. She regularly consults with leaders to create and maintain high-performing teams in business and athletics.

Joann Perahia is a business systems facilitator specializing in the requirements analysis and data defining phases of application development. She has saved corporations millions of dollars in software development using her facilitating skills. Joann is currently the Vice-President of Sales and Marketing at Systemic Solutions, while managing her twins' acting careers.

Niloufer Tamboly, CPA, is a vice president of and project manager for Open Information Systems Security Group (*www.oissg.org*). She uncovers simple and profitable solutions for her clients and streamlines processes and workable solutions in business, finance, and technology areas of organizations.

Ron Taylor, PMP, is a project manager, lecturer, author, and consultant. He is the principal and founder of the Ron Taylor Group and past president of PMI's Washington D.C. chapter. During Ron's tenure as president, the chapter was named PMI Chapter of the Year, and Ron was named PMI's Leader of the Year. Ron is a contributing author with PMForum, Adjunct Professor of Management at George Mason University, and co–author of *77 Deadly Sins of Project Management* and author of *Nurturing Trust*. His latest book on leadership will be published in 2011. Ron has an MBA from the University of Kentucky.

Dr. Arthur P. Thomas, Assistant Professor of Practice and Professor of Record for the Project Management Curriculum, has taught in Syracuse University's School of Information Studies since 2001. Dr. Thomas's career has included IT positions from programmer to chief information officer (CIO) and corporate training positions from training specialist to chief learning officer (CLO). Art is also Chairman and CEO of Counterpoint Holdings LLC, a performance improvement consultancy.

About the Author

Bonnie Biafore began working at an engineering firm after graduating with a master of science in structural engineering. Her first assignment was to help select a computer-aided design system for the company and then implement it to help produce engineering drawings. Little did she know that this was her first crack at managing a project. That she had no idea what she was doing was no doubt obvious to everyone else involved.

As it turns out, with training and experience, Bonnie became pretty good at managing projects. In 2003, she received her Project Management Professional Certification (PMP) from the Project Management Institute (PMI).

When she isn't managing projects for clients, Bonnie writes about project management, personal finance, and investing. Her friendly writing style and irrepressible sense of humor help turn dry subjects that people have to read into something they want to read. Her *NAIC Stock Selection Handbook* won awards from both the Society of Technical Communication and APEX Awards for Publication Excellence. Project Certification Insider, her monthly column for the Microsoft Project Users Group, explains the ins and outs of topics on Microsoft Project's desktop certification exam.

When not chained to her computer, Bonnie hikes with her dogs, organizes gourmet meals, and works on a comedic novel about stupid criminals. You can learn more at her website, *www.bonniebiafore.com*, or email Bonnie at *bonnie.biafore@gmail.com*.

Contents

What do you think of this book? We want to hear from you!

Microsoft is interested in hearing your feedback so we can continually improve our
books and learning resources for you. To participate in a brief online survey, please visit:

microsoft.com/learning/booksurvey

What do you think of this book? We want to hear from you!

Microsoft is interested in hearing your feedback so we can continually improve our books and learning resources for you. To participate in a brief online survey, please visit:

microsoft.com/learning/booksurvey

Introduction

PROJECT MANAGEMENT has been around for centuries. After all, how do you think the Pyramids were built? Organizations have come to recognize that a lot of the work they do is project-oriented. And when they realize that good project management can save both time and money, that's about the time that people like you receive the call to be a project manager.

You aren't the only one. Membership in the Project Management Institute (PMI), a professional organization for project managers founded in 1969, reached 8,500 in 1990. Its membership topped 100,000 in 2003 and, by the end of 2010, was 330,000. More than 400,000 people have earned the Project Management Professional (PMP) credential.

If you have little or no formal education in project management, congratulations, you've become an accidental project manager. You probably earned the assignment because you're dependable and good at organizing your work. However, you may have only a vague idea of what you're supposed to do or what it takes to succeed. To compound the challenge, Microsoft Project can seem like a Japanese puzzle box—getting a handle on one feature leads to another feature that you don't understand.

Even if you know your way around a Gantt chart and can build a decent schedule in Project, chances are that nagging problems come up on the projects you manage. That's why project managers are so valuable. Nagging problems *always* come up on projects. By learning more about how to manage projects, you can prevent many problems and you can reduce the impact of many others. For example, scope creep is an all-too-common problem in which one small change to project scope after another sneaks into your plan until you have no chance of meeting your schedule or budget. Setting up a process for managing changes gives the project team the opportunity to say no to changes that aren't that important and to say yes to important changes even if they require a little more time or a little more money.

Although project management includes some techniques that are relatively straightforward, such as defining which task is the predecessor and which is the successor, most of what you do to manage projects is more touchy-feely. Communicating, negotiating, leading, and all other aspects of working with people can consume a lifetime of study, and you'd still have situations that make you stop and think.

The good news is that, as a project manager, you provide a highly valuable service to your organization, and your days will always bring something new and interesting. The bad news is that you're trying to learn new skills while you're overworked—you're trying to corral an untamed project, recover from mistakes you've made, and learn how to use Project as well. Training would help, but you don't have the time, and the training dollars in your organization are probably scarce.

Successful Project Management is here to help. This book tackles two broad topics that many project managers need:

- A practical education in project management

- Instructions for making the most of Project and other Microsoft Office applications to manage projects successfully

Successful Project Management isn't some ponderous textbook about project management. It's an easy-to-read guide to managing projects from start to finish. If you're managing projects for the first time, it acts as your mentor by providing practical advice for managing projects more successfully and avoiding the more common project management mistakes. If you're already managing projects, you can jump directly to a chapter to prepare for your next project management task or respond effectively to the latest project situation. The book uses plain English to explain project management tools, techniques, and terminology, so you can learn the lingo as you learn what to do.

Unlike many product-oriented books with chapter after chapter devoted to Project features, no matter how obscure, the primary focus of *Successful Project Management* is how to manage projects. However, you will find plenty of instructions for making the most of Microsoft products for project management. You'll learn how to choose the most appropriate feature for the situation you face. And you'll master Project features that are incredibly helpful but also incredibly confusing—until you know their secrets.

The organization of this book follows the PMI methodology and is broken into five parts that correspond to the PMI process groups: initiating, planning, executing, controlling, and closing.

- Part 1, "Getting a Project Started," corresponds to PMI's initiating process group and describes how to get a project off the ground. The first chapter is an introduction to projects and project management. The other chapter in this part of the book explains how to define what a project is supposed to accomplish, gain commitment to move forward, and work effectively with project stakeholders—people who have a vested interest in the successful outcome of the project.

- Part 2, "Planning a Project," describes how to define and prepare a plan for achieving project objectives. This part corresponds to PMI's planning process group. The first chapter is an introduction to project planning and explains all the components of a project plan and how they contribute to success. The other chapters in this part of the book explain in detail how to develop different parts of a project plan from the work breakdown structure (WBS) to a project schedule and budget. You'll also learn about some of the financial measures that executives use to evaluate projects. In this part of the book, you'll learn how to use Microsoft Word to author project plan documents, Project to build the project schedule, Microsoft Excel to develop a budget and analyze financial measures, and Microsoft Visio to construct project diagrams.

- Part 3, "Carrying Out a Project," corresponds to PMI's executing process group and describes what you do when you begin to implement the project plan you developed in Part 2. You'll learn how to evaluate project performance and manage the resources working on your project. Perhaps the most important chapter in the book, Chapter 11, "Communicating Information," not only describes how to build a communication plan for your project but also offers advice for communicating effectively in writing, in meetings, and via email. You can apply the techniques described in this chapter to every phase of your projects.

- Part 4, "Controlling Projects," covers the work you do almost immediately upon beginning to execute a project. This part corresponds to PMI's controlling process group and describes how you manage the changes that are an inevitable part of every project. You'll learn how to control change requests so they don't overwhelm your original schedule and budget. You'll also learn how to modify the project schedule in response to changes, balance the budget with other project performance measures to make good business decisions, and manage risks.

- Part 5, "Closing Projects," consists of three short chapters that correspond to PMI's closing process group. Although closing a project doesn't represent much of the time and effort in a project, the work you do is incredibly valuable to future projects. In this part of the book, you'll learn how to collect the lessons that people learned while working on a project, perform the tasks to tie up the loose ends at the end of a project, and store the results of a project for others to refer to in the future.

- Part 6, "Beyond Projects," describes how to select and prioritize the projects your organization undertakes when you don't have enough time, money, or resources to run them all. In this section, you also learn about additional methodologies for managing projects, including the critical chain approach and agile project management.

- The Glossary at the end of the book is a quick reference to the project management terms used in the book.

Chapters in the book describe what project managers do and how these activities help deliver projects successfully. You'll find practical advice about steps to take on large projects and steps that might be omitted for small projects. Many chapters include step-by-step instructions or recommended features for Project and other Office applications. In addition, this book includes several helpful features of its own:

- Sidebars provide in-depth discussion of project management techniques.

- Best Practices sidebars describe particularly effective practices used by many project managers to prevent problems or dramatically improve project performance.

- Tips highlight shortcuts and other simple but helpful techniques.

- Warnings represent minor problems and how to prevent them.

- Notes provide additional information about topics in the text.

- Project Files represent content that is available on the companion website.

Companion Content

All the project files discussed in this book can be found at the following address:

http://oreilly.com/catalog/0790145309419/

Please follow the directions.

Support for This Book

Every effort has been made to ensure the accuracy of this book and the companion content. Microsoft Press provides support for books and companion content at the following website:

http://www.microsoft.com/learning/support/books/

You can also look for updates and a list of errata at the following website:

http://oreilly.com/catalog/0790145309419/

Questions and Comments

If you have comments, questions, or ideas regarding the book or the companion content, or questions that are not answered by visiting the sites above, please send them to Microsoft Press via email to *mspinput@microsoft.com*.

1

Getting a Project Started

CHAPTER 1

Meet Project Management

IN THIS CHAPTER, YOU WILL:

- Learn what a project is and how it differs from other undertakings

- Gain an understanding of project management and the processes it represents

- Identify the benefits of managing projects

> *"All white-collar work is project work."*—Tom Peters

SO YOU'VE BEEN ASKED to manage a project. If you're new to project management, your first question is probably "What's a project?" No doubt it will be followed closely by "How do I manage one?" and finally "How will I know if I did it right?" In this chapter, you'll learn what a project is, the basics of managing one, and why project management is so important.

What Is a Project?

The good news is that you've probably already managed a project without realizing it. You stumble across projects every day—at work *and* at home. Besides the projects you work on at the office, some of the honey-dos taped to the refrigerator door at home are probably projects. The list on the following page shows some examples of both business and personal projects.

- Construct a suspension bridge

- Landscape the backyard

- Launch a new advertising campaign

- Move into a new house

- Discover a new drug and bring it to market

- Build a retirement portfolio

- Migrate corporate data to a new server farm

- Throw your spouse a surprise fortieth birthday party

- Produce a marketing brochure for new services

- Obtain financial aid for your child's college education

What is the common thread between these disparate endeavors? Here is one definition of a project:

A project is a unique job with a specific goal, clear-cut starting and ending dates, and—in most cases—a budget.

The following sections expand on each characteristic of a project so you'll know how to tell what is a project and what isn't.

A Unique Endeavor

The most significant characteristic of a project is *uniqueness*. Frank Lloyd Wright's design for the Fallingwater house was a one-of-a-kind vision, linked to the land on which the house was built and the water that flows past it. The design and construction of Fallingwater was unmistakably a project.

Although every project is different, the differences can be subtle. Building a neighborhood of tract houses, each with the same design and the same materials, might seem like the same work over and over. But different construction teams, a record-breaking rainstorm, or a flat lot versus a house built on a cliff transforms each identical house design into a unique undertaking: a project.

NOTE　Ongoing work that remains the same day after day is not a project. For example, building walls and rafters for manufactured homes that you ship to construction sites represents ongoing operations, which requires a very different type of management. Assembling the components of a manufactured home on site is a project.

A Specific Goal

Whether an organization launches a project to solve a problem, jump on an opportunity, or fulfill an unmet need, it commits its time, money, and human resources to the project to achieve a *specific goal*. This goal spawns the objectives the project must achieve and also helps determine the project *scope* (the boundaries of what work is and is not a part of the project).

Surprisingly, many projects aren't set up with clearly defined goals, which is akin to a herd of sheep without a Border collie. There's lots of activity and angst, but very little movement in the right (or even consistent) direction. That's why one of your first tasks in managing a project is determining what the project objectives are and making sure that everyone involved agrees on them.

SEE ALSO　Chapter 2, "Obtaining Approval for a Project," describes goals, objectives, and scope in detail.

Clear-Cut Start and Finish Dates

Although some projects seem like they never end, a project has a clear-cut *beginning* and a clear-cut *end*. The project goal helps delineate the start and finish of a project. When the overarching goal is clear and the lower-level objectives are well defined, it's much easier to tell when the project is complete.

SEE ALSO　Chapter 6, "Building a Project Schedule," describes the activities that go into scheduling start and finish dates, including estimating the work to be performed, assigning resources to tasks, and making a schedule realistic.

Within Budget

Projects aren't supposed to last forever. Nor should they consume every available resource like an organizational black hole. Every project has limited resources of some kind, such as a price tag set by the customer, a limited number of available resources, the number of work hours you can squeeze in between the start and finish dates, and so on. As project manager, you must do your best to deliver the project within the various limits you've been given. If you need more resources, you have to ask your management team or the customer for permission.

Something's Gotta Give

The main constraints on a project—time, cost, and quality—are inextricably linked. This set of constraints is so common that it's known by several names, such as the *project triangle*, the scope triangle, and the triple constraint. Figure 1-1 shows one interpretation of the project triangle.

FIGURE 1-1 For a given scope, you can choose the values for two of the three constraints (time, cost, and quality), which then determine the value of the third.

If you change any of these constraints, something else has to give. In other words, if you're building a house, you can build a good house quickly, but it'll cost you plenty. On the other hand, you could build a house quickly and cheaply, but it won't be very good.

In reality, project constraints are more than a triangle because you can juggle other factors, too. For example, if the customer won't budge on time, cost, or quality, you can look at changing the scope of the project, such as building a smaller house or one with fewer time-saving features. Resources are often a constraint. Although everyone might agree on scope, time, cost, and quality, a resource shortage could require a longer schedule or a higher price to bring on additional hands.

The good news is that you can balance project constraints in any number of ways. That's one of your tasks as a project manager, as you'll learn in the next section.

What Is Project Management?

Projects happen whether they're managed or not. Left unattended, projects seem endless, expend all available resources, and yet still don't deliver what they're supposed to. Some folks assigned to manage projects take great liberties with the guiding statement "Do whatever it takes." They get the project done, but they leave behind a path of destruction and dazed, exhausted workers. So, what is project management and how does it help achieve success?

Regardless of the shape and size of your project, project management boils down to answering the following questions:

■ **What problem are you solving?**   Dr. Joseph M. Juran, a project management consultant well known for his work on quality and quality management, defined a project as a problem scheduled for solution. One of the first steps in successful project management is correctly identifying the problem that the project is supposed to solve. As you learn in Chapter 2, most people jump straight to solutions instead of defining the problem. For example, "We need a deck in the backyard" is a solution for a landscaping project. Unless you know what the underlying problem is, you can't tell whether it's the *right* solution.

SEE ALSO	The section "Defining the Problem," on page 18, provides some tips on how to identify and document the problem to be solved.

NOTE	Sometimes, problems come in the form of opportunities of which you can take advantage. For example, you might undertake a project to solve a problem of high rates of product returns. Or you might launch a project to enhance a product to increase market share.

Behind even the simplest problem statement is a boatload of detail about the work to be done. What objectives must the project achieve? Are there specific requirements the customer has in mind? What work has to be done to achieve the objectives and satisfy the requirements? Depending on the details, the backyard landscaping work could be to install a deck; install a patio; or, if low-maintenance is the main objective, pave over the yard.

- **How are you going to solve it?**   You don't just let a team of carpenters loose in the backyard with lumber and nails and say, "Go build a deck." You have to develop a plan for getting the project done, including defining each task in detail, identifying the resources you need, determining how much they cost, and defining how long the work will take.

- **How will you know when you're done?**   If a project's objectives and requirements are well defined, it's easy to tell when you're done. If the objective of your project is to reduce product returns by 30 percent, you can count the number of returns and calculate the percentage improvement. With some projects, success isn't so clear-cut. Either way, you have to define success criteria up front in such a way that it's obvious whether or not you succeeded.

- **How well did it go?**   One sign that a project went well is when the customer signs off on the project and writes the final check for payment. You also have to evaluate how well the entire process went. Capturing lessons learned is an important but often ignored step at the end of a project. The project team meets to document what went well, what did not go well, the reasons for success or failure, and what could be done differently the next time a similar project comes up. With those insights, you can find ways to improve how you manage projects and achieve success more easily on future projects.

Project Management Processes

A project has a set of objectives, a start and end, and a budget. The purpose of project management is to achieve the project objectives on time and within budget. In reality, project management is an ongoing task of balancing the scope against time, cost, quality, and any other constraints placed on the project. According to the Project Management Institute's *Guide to the Project Management Body of Knowledge*, project management is divided into five process groups:

- **Initiating**   *Initiating* is officially committing to start a project. The anointed project manager unearths the real objectives of the project, identifies the potential project stakeholders, and works with the customer and other stakeholders to come up with an approach to achieve those objectives. In effect, the initiating phase answers the question, "What problem are you solving?" The project manager prepares a summary of the project and its business benefits. The initiating phase is complete when management gives approval to move to the planning phase.

- **Planning** *Planning* is working out the details of how you are going to solve the problem. During the planning phase, you identify all the work that must be done, who does it, when they do it, how long it takes, and how much it costs. With skill and some luck, the project achieves its objectives within the desired time frame and budget, producing results at the desired level of quality and without turning the assigned resources into burnt toast. Planning isn't complete without identifying the risks that could interfere with success and how to respond to them.

Planning up front pays off many times over during the execution of a project. You can either spend time planning early on or spend far more time putting out fires later.

SEE ALSO Part 2, "Planning a Project," explains how planning helps a project succeed and describes the components of a project plan.

TIP ✓ With the popularity of project management programs such as Microsoft Project, many people mistakenly consider scheduling a project to be the same as managing a project. They think of the schedule as the complete plan for the project. When you understand what project management really is, you can learn how to apply the features of Project to manage projects more effectively.

SEE ALSO Chapter 2 and Chapter 3, "Planning to Achieve Success" describe everything that goes into a project plan.

- **Executing** *Executing* a project is a project manager's ongoing work for the life of the project. The first step is launching the project. You get the project team on board and explain the rules. After that, you keep the project team focused on doing the right things at the right time—as outlined in the project plan.

SEE ALSO Part 3, "Carrying Out a Project," describes project management tasks during execution.

- **Controlling** *Controlling* a project is also ongoing work, but it focuses on monitoring and measuring project performance to see whether the project is on track with its plan. As the inevitable changes, issues, surprises, and occasional disasters arise, the project manager can determine the kind and magnitude of course correction that is required to get the project back on track.

> **SEE ALSO** Part 4, "Controlling Projects," covers how to control a project.

- **Closing** *Closing* includes officially accepting the project as complete, documenting the final performance and lessons learned, closing any contracts, and releasing the resources to work on other endeavors. Are the success criteria satisfied? Does everyone involved agree that the project is a success, and have they officially signed off on acceptance?

> **SEE ALSO** Part 5, "Closing Projects," discusses steps for closing a project.

BEST PRACTICES

At its best, project management is as much art as science. Getting to the true objectives and requirements can be tough enough. Then you must mix scope, time, cost, quality, resources, and other constraints in the right proportions to achieve those objectives. For example, if quality is the key to differentiating a product from the competition, a longer schedule and higher budget might be the preferred choice. If getting that same product to market before the competition is critical, reducing the product features (scope), increasing the size of your team, or accepting a slightly higher level of errors (reducing quality) might be better.

As project manager, you can't change constraints such as time, cost, or the resources assigned. However, you can control how you use them. If you can make your plan work without affecting anything or anyone outside of your project team, you can push on without having to ask for anyone's permission.

If you can't make your plan work, you can seek permission to change one or more of your project's constraints. For example, you can go to the management team with hat in hand, asking for more resources to shorten the schedule. As a last resort, you can appeal to the customer for more time, more money, or a reduction in scope.

Planning, scheduling, and controlling appear to be activities that you can perform in the privacy of your office. But in the real world, project management is about a lot of working with and communicating with people (see Chapter 11, "Communicating Information"). *Stakeholders* (all who have an interest in or are affected by the project) play a crucial role in the potential success or failure of the project, whether they have a vested interest in the success of the project, work on the project, or are affected by the project in some way. Stakeholders must agree on the problem to be solved, the strategy for the project, and what constitutes success. Moreover, stakeholders can be strong allies or dire enemies, so keeping them informed is one of the most important tasks project managers do.

Communicating with the rest of the project team is equally important. These people perform the work in a project. Team members must understand the work they must do and any work-related constraints. They must also flag problems that arise and collaborate to fix them. Project managers have to lead, sometimes coax, and occasionally cajole a team of workers to successfully complete a project.

The Benefits of Project Management

Delivering objectives on time and within budget—what more could customers want? These days, customers expect high-quality products and services delivered quickly, with a minimum of fuss, and always for the lowest cost. That's a tall order, but if your company can't fill it, the competition is ready to jump in.

More and more organizations turn to project management to meet these tough demands. With good project management, organizations can deliver what their customers want without burning out the people who make it happen. Contrary to the beliefs of some people, project management doesn't make projects take longer or transform organizations into inflexible behemoths. Planning ahead and managing to the plan, organizations can actually become *more* innovative, flexible, productive, and responsive.

SEE ALSO   See Chapter 20, "Other Project Management Approaches," to learn about project management methods that plan on change and embrace flexibility.

Bottom-Line Benefits

The business world cares about money, and that's one reason why project management is so popular. By managing projects well, organizations can see all kinds of improvements to their bottom lines:

- **Faster and better return on investment**   Delivering projects on schedule and without cost overruns means that customers achieve a better return on their initial investment and see that return more quickly.

- **Decreased time to market**   With on-schedule deliveries, the products or services that projects produce are ready to hit the market when the customer wants them.

- **Increased customer satisfaction**   Project planning identifies what the customer wants. And customers are happier when they get what they want or need.

- **Competitive advantage**   Delivering the right product or service at the right time is one of the best ways to whip the competition. Besides, project management relieves the project team from fighting fires, which means they have the time and energy to develop the best possible product or service.

- **Better support of strategic goals**   Project management keeps people focused on why a project is important and what it's trying to achieve. Without a project plan, people quickly lose sight of what they're trying to accomplish.

- **Flexibility**   A project plan is a road map of how the project is going to reach its goals. With a plan in place, teams can analyze the effect of changes that arise and develop an alternative more quickly.

- **Increased productivity**   Applying resources effectively and efficiently means that people get their work done more quickly, and when they finish one assignment, they're refreshed and ready to work on something else.

Benefits for the Project Team

Project management sounds like a lot of work—and it is. But the amount of work is nothing compared to what you and your team have to do if you *don't* manage a project. Consider the benefits that project management delivers to the project manager, the project team, and the project itself:

- **Choosing the right things to do**   If you don't know how big your television is, buying an entertainment center to hold it is tough. To succeed, you have to know what the requirements are. A project plan documents project requirements and helps the team deliver what the customer wants—the first time around.

- **Doing the right things**   It's easy to get sidetracked during a project. People come up with better solutions or additional problems to solve, which usually cost more, take longer, and can potentially kill the project with overruns. Re-arranging your pantry while preparing food for a dinner party could result in hungry guests.

- **Keeping calm and maintaining consistency**   Without a clear-cut plan, team members can get pulled in every direction. The marketing department wants to change the message. The sales team wants a different product to sell. And engineering declares the design unbuildable. Constant change makes it tough to stick to a schedule and budget, and makes team members cranky. Project management uncovers most of the needs and issues up front. If changes do occur during the project, the project plan makes it easier to adjust the course as well as understand the ramifications of the course adjustment. Agile project management, described on page 406, is a way to manage projects in which change is unavoidable.

- **Knowing where you stand**   Statements such as "It's going pretty well" or "It's not done yet" tend to make management nervous and often result in constant questioning and an unpleasantly close watch on the project. A project plan lays out where you're going and how you're going to get there. With a plan in place, you can measure how far you've gotten and satisfy anyone's curiosity about project status.

- **Maintaining good communication**   People are much happier when they know what's going on. Even bad news is easier to swallow if it's delivered early enough and with a plan for recovering.

- **Preventing problems and fire drills**   Project life is much more pleasant when you've identified potential problems up front and have found ways to prevent them or resolve them quickly should they occur.

- **Identifying manageable workloads**   Project management breaks down even the most monumental project into smaller, more manageable accomplishments. These pieces are less scary, easier to absorb, and easier to track. In addition, the people working on these pieces aren't frozen into inactivity by what seems like an impossible amount of work in an impossibly short period of time.

Summary

Good project management doesn't have to be costly, complicated, or cumbersome. In short, don't panic. You already know a lot about managing projects. If you've moved to a new home, hosted a family reunion, or remodeled a bathroom, you already know about achieving objectives, sticking to a schedule, working within a budget, and delivering quality. The rest of this book explains how to manage projects more efficiently and effectively, and how to use software tools to do so.

CHAPTER TWO

Obtaining Approval for a Project

"*If you don't know where you're going, you will probably end up somewhere else.*—LAURENCE J. PETER

YOUR BROTHER CALLS and asks to borrow your car and $10,000 for a project he has to do. He promises to return both when the project is done. You probably won't hand over the keys and the cash until you find out what his project is, why he is doing it, what he means by "done," and, if you're smart, what's in it for you. You should respond with the same misgivings and request for more information when a customer asks you to start a project without formal documentation of what you have to do. After all, if you don't know what you're trying to achieve, how can you figure out what to do, how long it will take, or when the work is done? Many a project is doomed to fail from the start because the goal of the project isn't clearly defined.

The initiating process is what gets a project off the ground. The goal is to get approval from the customer, management, and other stakeholders to begin planning. This chapter discusses the information you need about a project to get the go ahead to proceed. It shows how to use that information to build an overview of the project, perfect for presenting to the powers that be.

You begin by identifying problems and opportunities, so you can answer the question "What problem are you solving?" or "What opportunity are we trying to take advantage of?" With the problem or opportunity diagnosed and documented, you identify the objectives that the project is supposed to achieve. At that point, you can unleash your project team to find a solution. The project strategy is the approach you select to achieve your goal.

To successfully complete a project, you have to know what success looks like. You gather requirements to identify what you have to do and define the *scope* of the project: what the project's going to do and what it isn't. Then, you can document the project's success criteria; that is, quantifiable measures and deliverables that prove you have accomplished what you set out to do.

Because stakeholders are crucial participants in defining what a project has to accomplish, this chapter also describes different types of stakeholders, so you can tell what they expect from a project, and determine how to get them—and keep them—on board.

Summarizing a Project

Project customers, executives, and other stakeholders who approve projects typically have a lot going on. For that reason, a succinct and compelling overview of the project is the best way to get their approval to move forward. A project overview summarizes what the project is supposed to achieve, the business value it provides, the work it entails, and how you know when it's done. You can present this overview to the folks who have the authority to say yes. If all goes well, you can walk out with their signatures on the dotted line. That approval launches the planning process, which is described in the next chapter.

A brief overview is effective, because it doesn't require a ton of time to prepare or evaluate. Depending on the size of the project, the person who proposes the project may put the overview together. For larger projects, a small team of people knowledgeable in all aspects of the project may collaborate to construct the overview. If the project customers and management like the idea, they may say yes right away or ask for more information.

On the other hand, if they reject the idea, the project stops before you have spent too much money or time.

The project overview includes the following elements:

- **Problem or opportunity**   You describe the problem or opportunity that the project would address.

- **Project goal and objectives**   The project goal is the primary purpose of the project; that is, why you want to perform the project and what you are trying to achieve. However, that single goal may have several components, which are objectives. For example, the backyard remodel project may have the goal of providing entertainment opportunities for the entire family. However, the project may have additional objectives to keep maintenance low, limit light pollution, conserve water, and fit the family's budget.

- **Project strategy**   For some projects, you may have a strategy in mind at this stage. Sometimes, developing a strategy requires additional effort and resources. If you don't include the strategy at the proposal stage, you'll add it to your documentation when you start planning.

- **Deliverables and success criteria**   The deliverables for the project help define the boundaries of what is and is not included in the scope of the project. In addition, you need success criteria to specify how you know the project is complete and has successfully reached its goal.

- **Assumptions and risks**   Every project has risks or obstacles that could affect its success. Similarly, projects usually come with assumptions that need to be spelled out, so that the decision makers know what they are approving.

> **SEE ALSO**   The next several sections describe in detail the components of a project overview.

Approval isn't the only reason for a project overview. In many organizations, especially large corporations, the project manager may not get involved until after the initiating process. You may be assigned to plan and manage the project after it's been approved. Preparing a project overview can help you, the project manager, familiarize yourself with the project. In addition, if the initiation was performed by someone who isn't a project manager, you may not get the information you need to plan the project properly. The project overview is your way of filling in the blanks in the initiation documentation.

The project overview doesn't go into storage when you receive approval to proceed. It is also effective for helping team members understand what the project is all about, whether they are assigned from the start or join the team later on.

Defining the Problem

Organizations don't undertake projects for the fun of it. Usually, projects come about because an organization has a problem it wants to solve, a business objective to achieve, or an opportunity to cash in on. A project may also arise because of legislation or new customer requests.

The problem to solve or the opportunity drives all other aspects of a project, as shown in Figure 2-1. Without the right problem, you're not likely to select the right solution or strategy. And without the right solution, the best project plan and highest quality deliverables won't make stakeholders happy. If you've given an infant a bottle filled with water instead of formula, you know how disappointing the wrong deliverables can be.

FIGURE 2-1 The problem or opportunity drives all other aspects of the project.

Identifying the Problem

Identifying the problem that you're trying to solve may turn out to be harder than you'd think. In fact, there are almost always several obstacles to overcome to get to the heart of the problem:

- People *love* to solve problems—so much so that they sometimes come up with solutions to problems that aren't particularly troublesome. As they do with diseases, people often notice the symptoms first and only with analysis and diagnosis do they identify the underlying issue. Digging deeper to identify what a project is supposed to solve or achieve is crucial to success. As antibiotics won't help a person who has the flu, the best solution to the wrong problem will ultimately fail.

- Another obstacle is that people often don't know what they want and might have trouble describing what they want in words. Unfortunately, they're good at recognizing what they don't want, so the words you don't want to hear come all too easily.

- Furthermore, different stakeholders often want different results from a project, which sometimes conflict with one another. Like the blind men touching different parts of an elephant and describing the animal in turn as a wall, tree, fan, rope, snake, and spear, projects look different depending on people's perspectives. Spending time defining the problem synchronizes the different views to unmask the true project—what everyone involved recognizes as success.

To pinpoint problems, you're better off putting on your investigative reporter's hat. *Why* turns out to be one of the best questions for identifying a problem, opportunity, or business objective. If you ask someone to describe a problem, you're likely to get a solution instead. But if you ask stakeholders *why* the organization should perform the project, *why* something is a problem, or *why* a solution is needed, you're more likely to hear the problem (or some aspect of it.)

For example, consider a backyard remodel project. If you ask your family members for the problem, they might say the backyard needs a deck, a patio, a swimming pool, or a swing set. The question "Why do you want to make over the backyard?" might deliver an answer such as, "We can't do anything in the backyard because it's a big mud hole."

If people describe problems by providing solutions, you can sometimes reverse-engineer those solutions to find the real problem or business objective. Once again, the question *why* comes to your rescue. Simply ask your stakeholders why they need the solution they've suggested. Suppose your boss asks you to manage a project to create a centralized corporate database. If you ask why the company needs a centralized database, you might learn that groups can't obtain the data they need, the data contain duplicate or inconsistent records, the data aren't backed up properly, and so on. Those answers are all problems that a project can solve, but a centralized corporate database isn't the only—or necessarily the best way—to solve them.

Asking why a problem is a problem is also a powerful tool for unearthing business objectives. For example, why is poor access to data a problem? Perhaps support staff can't respond to customer requests. Why is that a problem? Well, the organization needs more support people, whose salaries increase costs, and frustrated customers take their business elsewhere. A few rounds of "Why is that a problem?" helps you discover that the business objective is to reduce costs and improve customer service.

Documenting the Problem

A problem statement documents the problem—not the symptoms or someone's premature hunch about a solution. You include the problem statement in the project overview, so stakeholders understand the problem that the project is supposed to solve.

PROJECT FILE | An example of a problem statement, Sample_Problem_Statement.docx, is available in the Chapter02 folder on the companion website.

ADDING CONSTRAINTS TO A PROBLEM STATEMENT

Solutions usually have no place in problem statements. But what if your organization has already made decisions that constrain the solutions you can use? You can include significant constraints in the problem statement (in addition to the assumptions section of the project plan) to ensure that the project strategy you choose takes those constraints into account. For example, if your organization is launching a project related to your corporate database, you can specify that the solution has to use existing hardware and software.

Although the symptoms and solutions that you gather from stakeholders usually don't appear in the problem statement, they're valuable components of your project plan. People's perceptions of the problem often end up as other project objectives, and these objectives help you decide which solution is best when you select a project strategy.

SEE ALSO   To learn more about types of objectives, see the next section, "Project Goal and Objectives." The section "Project Strategy," on page 24, describes how to develop a strategy for solving the problem.

Project Goal and Objectives

Think of the project goal as the guiding light for the project, the outcome that constitutes a successful solution to the problem. While the problem in the backyard is the mud hole, the goal is to have a backyard that the family can enjoy.

TIP   Because the goal helps obtain buy-in and guide the team, it should be easy to understand for anyone involved in the project. For that reason, you should be sure to avoid jargon or specialized terminology when you describe the project goal.

As you gather information about a project, you're bound to learn more about the expectations for the endeavor. Objectives flesh out the project goal and help define the scope of the project. Documenting and obtaining concurrence on objectives prevents misunderstandings and helps people focus on what's expected.

On time, within budget, and delivering the deliverables are the obvious contenders, but specific objectives for each project are unique. For example, a project to upgrade a financial institution's systems could include an objective of no interruption to market trading. The backyard remodel project might have an objective to keep as many of the existing trees as possible.

As you identify objectives, find out how important each objective is to the ultimate success of the project. If you must trim the list of objectives later to meet budget, schedule, or resource constraints, you can turn to the prioritized list to decide which objectives stay or go.

NOTE   The project plan represents a balance between scope, cost, schedule, and quality. As you develop the project plan, you might have to adjust your project objectives to maintain that balance given project constraints. If objectives change after the project plan is approved, be sure to revisit the entire project plan to rebalance its scope, cost, schedule, and quality.

Types of Objectives

Project objectives come in many flavors: business, financial, performance, technical, quality, and so on. For example, the components of the backyard remodel should be durable enough to withstand the abuse of three energetic children and two exuberant dogs, be easy to maintain, and cost no more than $5,000. Here are some of the types of objectives that projects must satisfy:

- *Business* objectives can cover a lot of ground, from tactical objectives like reducing the time that customers spend on hold or increasing membership renewals to strategic objectives like expanding into a new market or launching a product before the competition.

- *Financial* objectives deal with either budgets or the measures that organizations use to evaluate their performance. Some examples of financial objectives include achieving a specific return on investment (ROI), staying within budget, increasing revenue or profit, or cutting costs.

- *Performance* is another broad category of objectives. Meeting deadlines and sticking to the schedule, satisfying requirements, and conforming to specifications all fit in the performance bucket. For example, the backyard remodel project could have schedule objectives to not start excavation until the kids are back in school, but to complete the concrete work in October before temperatures drop below freezing.

- *Technical* objectives relate to technical issues, such as whether to use technology and which kind. For example, some projects might apply the newest technology, whereas others that must meet stringent uptime requirements might choose tried and true products. If the product that a project produces must work in less-developed areas, the project might include an objective to use readily available technology that is dependable or easy to repair without specialized tools.

- *Quality* objectives represent how good the results must be. For example, product returns should be less than a specific percentage, customer satisfaction ratings from surveys should increase to a specific level, or the number of service calls should decrease by a specific percentage.

NOTE Don't forget about objectives such as conforming to regulations or reducing the company's exposure to lawsuits.

UNDERSTANDING YOUR PROJECT'S BUSINESS VALUE

Management wants projects to deliver value to the organization, so many project managers think that the executives are responsible for making sure a project does deliver value. Tres Roeder of Roeder Consulting believes that project managers are more successful when they accept responsibility for the business results of the projects they manage.

To ensure business value, you must know more than the mechanics of managing projects. You must have a basic understanding of your organization's business, services, and products, and how the organization delivers value to its customers. That way, if your project begins to go astray, you can focus on how to deliver value and use the answer to bring the project back on track. For example, if your organization is known for high-quality products that last a lifetime, you know that you have to keep the project focused on delivering quality, even if the cost and duration increase.

Characteristics of Good Objectives

Good objectives make it easy for everyone to agree that the objectives have or haven't been met. Choosing objectives that are realistic helps keep the project on track, and the project team won't throw in the towel because the objectives are unattainable. Here are characteristics to consider as you define objectives:

- **Specific objectives**   These objectives clearly state what the project is supposed to achieve. If objectives are unclear or vague, team members won't know whether they are doing the right thing; or worse, customers tell you that the deliverables don't meet their expectations. Building a house is an objective, but building a three-bedroom, wheelchair-accessible ranch house is more specific.

- **Measurable or verifiable objectives**   These objectives are ideal because there's no question whether the project met them. Specifying that the program is easy to use turns out to be darned difficult to prove. Restate objectives with measurable or confirmable results, such as the program achieves 95 percent ratings for ease of use in user surveys.

- **Achievable objectives**   These objectives not only ensure that the project can succeed but they also maintain the morale of the project team. There's nothing wrong with setting challenging objectives to urge everyone to extend themselves. But unrealistic or downright impossible objectives simply sap people's desire to even try.

■ **Time-related objectives**   These objectives specify when the objective should be achieved. By adding interim objectives throughout your schedule, you can keep track of progress.

REACHING AGREEMENT ON OBJECTIVES

You can't please everyone all the time. Chances are good that the initial list of project objectives is more than the budget, timetable, and available resources can handle. Suppose you hire an architect to design your dream home. You happily ask for this and that until you get the construction bids from builders. And suddenly the separate his-and-hers master bathrooms go from a requirement to nice to have.

As you learn later in this chapter, stakeholders often have conflicting goals and expectations. A project manager has the unenviable job of helping stakeholders reach agreement on what the project will achieve. Stakeholders might pressure you to skip the time-consuming process of reaching agreement in order to get the work started. As project manager, you have to document all the goals, objectives, and expectations stakeholders have, and then negotiate with them to produce the final list of what the project should accomplish.

Project Strategy

High school seniors grouse about college SAT tests and don't realize that questions with only one correct answer are some of the easiest problems they'll deal with in real life. Projects almost always solve open-ended problems that have more than one correct answer. Fortunately for project managers and their teams, some answers are more appropriate than others. By evaluating alternatives in light of the project objectives, a project team can determine the best solution. Once you've selected a solution, the project strategy is where you document your choice in the project overview and plan.

Strategic planning for projects is similar to strategic planning in other areas of business. You must know where you want to go to make good decisions. A backyard that invites the family to spend quality time together leads to a much different design than one dedicated to winning the local gardening competition. You can't wait too long to strategize, or customers and stakeholders might have already made decisions that limit your options. If the kids found the brochure for the multistation slide/swing/sandbox, your hopes for a prize-winning iris garden could be dashed.

Identifying Alternatives

Once you know what the project is supposed to accomplish, a few brainstorming sessions with stakeholders can reveal more suitable solutions to consider. For example, consider the backyard remodeling project. The problem is a mud hole that prevents the family from enjoying the outdoors together. A family meeting to discuss the project could begin with each person's idea of a fun backyard: a garden, a grill, swings, and a tree house. But some family brainstorming might lead to a solution that incorporates a common area for the entire family along with backyard niches for each family member.

A QUICK GUIDE TO BRAINSTORMING

Brainstorming is one of the best ways to extract creative ideas from a group of people. Chaotic can be the descriptor of choice as people throw ideas out at random, but some rules increase the effectiveness of the technique.

- Clearly communicate the purpose of the brainstorming session.

- Set a time limit to focus brainstorming activity.

- Assign someone to facilitate the discussion. A facilitator welcomes all ideas and prevents criticism of others' ideas regardless of how wacky they seem at first, which in turn makes everyone more comfortable about participating. The facilitator also records all the suggestions on a flip chart or white board, so that participants can view them.

- When time is up, the group can categorize, merge, and refine the ideas into a list of options for further study.

Factors for Selecting a Project Strategy

The project strategy that stakeholders select must satisfy a gauntlet of conditions. The winning strategy must satisfy the primary business objectives and most of the other project objectives, but there are other tests to pass as well. Here are some factors to consider when evaluating project strategies:

- **Is the strategy feasible?** Feasibility is important if you're considering a solution that's unusual or untried. Feasibility studies determine whether the strategy will work before committing too many dollars and resources to a particular approach.

- **Does the strategy satisfy the project objectives?** Without an implementation plan, you don't have details about a strategy's deliverables, cost, schedule, or quality. Stakeholders must make educated guesses about how well a strategy satisfies the objectives.

- **Are the risks acceptable?** Every strategy has its risks. An informal risk analysis of all the possible strategies helps stakeholders eliminate precarious solutions.

- **Does the strategy fit the organization's culture?** If the organization has always written its own applications, a strategy that uses outside vendors is unlikely to succeed. Similarly, senior management that swears by technology might dismiss solutions that focus on process improvement. Cultural and psychological factors are not only tough to quantify but also tough to overcome. If stakeholders decide on a strategy that doesn't fit the organization's norms, success requires strong commitment from management, the project sponsor, and stakeholders.

Choosing the Project Strategy

Choosing a project strategy is a qualitative process. No one has enough information to make precise comparisons or judgments, and many criteria are subjective. A decision matrix, like the one shown in Figure 2-2, helps organize the objectives and other criteria, and can be as qualitative or as quantitative as you want.

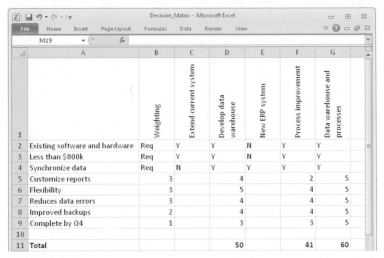

FIGURE 2-2 A decision matrix helps you evaluate solutions using project objectives and other criteria.

Here's one way to use a decision matrix to evaluate alternative project strategies:

1. Fill in the column headings with the strategies you've identified, such as New ERP System or Data Warehouse And Processes.

   Include one column for a weighting factor. If you use numbers such as 1, 2, and 3 for low, medium, and high importance, you can calculate weighted results to emphasize solutions that meet the most important criteria.

2. Add project objectives that are mandatory to the top rows of the matrix. If an alternative doesn't satisfy any of these make-or-break objectives, you can skip filling in the rest of that alternative's boxes.

3. Prioritize the other project objectives and criteria. If none of the strategies satisfies all the objectives, you can focus on the more important criteria.

4. Assign a value to rate how well an alternative satisfies each criterion. For example, in Figure 2-2, the answers are rated from 1 to 5, with 5 being the best. Table 2-1 demonstrates how to calculate the score for the Data Warehouse And Processes strategy.

TABLE 2-1 Calculate the Score for the Data Warehouse And Processes Strategy

CRITERIA	POINTS
Customize reports	$3 \times 5 = 15$
Flexibility	$3 \times 5 = 15$
Reduces data errors	$3 \times 5 = 15$
Improved backups	$2 \times 5 = 10$
Complete by 4th quarter	$1 \times 5 = 5$
Total	60

> **NOTE** Even with numbers and calculations to rate strategies, the results are merely approximate ratings. For example, results of 50 and 53 may be too close to call. Look instead for strategies whose ratings are significantly higher than the others, such as the "Develop data warehouse" and "Data warehouse and processes" strategies in Figure 2-2.

Gathering Requirements

Requirements are the nitty-gritty details that define the deliverables that the project must produce. Gathering requirements is challenging because it is part art, part science. Customers may or may not know what they need. Or they may tell you what they want in addition to what they need and leave it to you to differentiate the two. Because the requirements drive the project deliverables, scope, success criteria, and thus the rest of the project plan, you must strive to document the true requirements for your project. If you don't capture all the requirements, the customer won't be satisfied with the project results. If you gather requirements that aren't really necessary, the project will take longer and cost more than it should.

You can choose from many techniques for gathering requirements, each with pros and cons. Here are some of the more common approaches:

- **Reusing existing requirements** If you are working a project similar to one performed in the past, you can use existing requirements as a foundation for your current project. This approach reduces duplicated effort. In addition, you may be able to improve on the previous solution based on the customer's past feedback. Of course, you need documentation for your past projects to use this approach.

- **Build prototypes**   Prototypes stimulate creative ideas and help customers clarify what they need. Sometimes, prototyping can promote too much creativity, which leads to more requirements than necessary. Another danger with this approach is that the customer may mistake the prototype for a final solution.

- **Interview end users**   You can interview the end users for a product or service to identify the processes they use or the functions they require. A structured approach helps the people you interview provide the information you need. For example, prepare detailed questions for the first round of interviews. Then, after you document initial requirements, conduct a second round of interviews to review and refine the requirements.

> **TIP**   You can also obtain requirements for new products or services by observing the end users in their day-to-day activities. One risk with this approach is misinterpreting what the users are doing. To mitigate this risk, you can document requirements identified through observation and then review the draft requirements with the end users to clarify and refine them.

- **Conduct group requirement sessions**   If a project involves interaction among multiple groups, a group requirements gathering meeting is perfect for identifying the cross-functional processes.

- **Use methodologies such as business process modeling or use cases**   These methodologies are effective tools for identifying and describing processes and results. However, they work only as well as the people using them, so you may have to train resources and customers on the methodology before you can gather requirements.

> **SEE ALSO**   To learn about gathering requirements for software projects, see the book *Software Requirements*, by Karl Wiegers (Microsoft Press, 2003).

If you don't get requirements right in the beginning, you won't get the solution right at the end. Functional/specification workshops are still some of the best ways to obtain requirements for a business system, says Joanna Perahia, Vice President of Systemic Solutions, Inc.

Before you begin gathering requirements, develop a high-level view of the system and, from that, identify all the business departments involved. Then, hold requirements workshops and include everyone who has any connection to the function or process being revamped. The goal of the workshops is to obtain not only the requirements for the new endeavor but also the buy-in of all those departments.

To make sure the business people get their requirements out, use a meeting facilitator who is experienced on the business side. Consider holding separate sessions for managers and staff so everyone feels comfortable sharing their information. Otherwise, you won't obtain all the information you need. For IT projects, IT representatives attend the requirements sessions, but they don't participate in the discussion. The workshops are their chance to hear what the business side needs, not the time to hash out a solution.

As with any meeting, develop a specific agenda for each session. In addition, run the sessions as if they were outside seminars. If possible, conduct them away from the office and ask attendees to silence their mobile phones and pagers. Ms. Perahia also recommends conducting requirements sessions on Tuesdays, Wednesdays, or Thursdays. On Mondays and Fridays, people are distracted by the weekend past or coming up. Finally, before you complete the requirements sessions, get signoff from the stakeholders so you can move to the next phase.

Deliverables

Deliverables are the results the project has to deliver in order for the customer to say the project is complete. Deliverables aren't always as concrete as concrete foundations, but they have one thing in common: you can tell whether they've been delivered. If a deliverable is a tangible result, you can pick it up or look at it. A deliverable such as a new service isn't something you can touch. The true deliverable in this case is that the new service is available for customers to use.

Deliverables help define the scope of a project and identify all the work required to complete the project. As you include deliverables in a project plan, double-check that you have tasks and estimates for producing those results. For example, the effort required to produce documentation is sometimes overlooked. If the government is the client and 1,000-page reports are key deliverables, forgetting to schedule documentation work spells failure regardless of how successful you are with other project deliverables.

TIP   The purpose, scope, and deliverables for a project are often bundled into a document called a statement of work. This brief synopsis of a project is often included in legal contracts.

The first deliverables you identify correspond to the overall output of the project, whether it's a new service, a streamlined process, or a wireless GPS child collar that'll notify parents when kids wander from the yard. The final deliverable—that last milestone that triggers the big payment or celebration—is great for keeping the team focused on the ultimate project goal.

Projects can have other deliverables that must be obtained over the course of a project, such as a completed building inspection or signed certificate of occupancy. As you develop the work breakdown structure (WBS), you may identify intermediate deliverables because each work package and summary task contributes something to the final project. For instance, intermediate deliverables for a backyard remodel might include a design, blueprints, building permits, the delivery of construction materials, a poured foundation, a completed patio, and a signed building inspection certificate.

SEE ALSO   The section "Building a WBS from the Top Down," on page 72, describes breaking project work down from the highest-level summary tasks to the lowest-level work packages.

Interim deliverables aren't necessarily for the project customer. The construction blueprints, for example, are important for obtaining permits and bids, and for the contractor who builds the deck. But the homeowner might never see them. Furthermore, project management also generates interim deliverables, such as the project plan, status reports, and updated risk reviews.

Interim deliverables also give you a way to measure progress during the project. If you assign someone to analyze your product return business process, months could go by with no sign of completion. Many project managers try to define deliverables that occur at the same frequency as status reports, so they can judge the progress that's been made since the last report.

Here are some examples of deliverables for the backyard remodel project:

- Project requirements
- Initial design
- Final design and drawing set
- Construction permit
- Foundation complete
- Foundation inspection approved
- Framing complete
- Framing inspection approved
- Deck complete
- Final inspection approved
- Occupancy certificate

NOTE Projects for the government and some other organizations, such as foundations, include contractual requirements that can delay payments or trigger penalties. If your project includes contractual requirements, such as documentation or financial reports, be sure to include those items in your list of deliverables.

Success Criteria

Success criteria are the measurable results that the project must achieve in order for the customer to say the project is a *success*. For each deliverable and milestone in a project, you must define criteria that stakeholders use to determine whether the work to date has been completed successfully. Some success criteria are easy to identify. A tangible result, such as a patio ready for a party, tells you the project is done. A signed inspection certificate tells you that the county building department says the patio passed inspection, one form of success.

The best success criteria are those that are clear and quantifiable, such as higher revenues, increased profit, lower costs, or faster turnaround. For example, one success criterion could be increasing the profit margin to 10 percent. After the project is complete, you can generate a profit and loss report to determine whether the profit margin meets or exceeds that measure. Success criteria aren't always obvious. For example, customer satisfaction isn't tangible In this case, the success criterion may be an average rating of 8 or higher on a scale from 1 to 10, based on surveys you send to customers.

> **NOTE** It's easier to obtain approval for a project when success criteria mirror the measures the customer typically uses. For instance, success criteria based on financial results or business measures work well with executives. End users may be more comfortable comparing the results with the documented requirements and specifications.

The Scope Statement

The scope statement is a high-level view of what the project will do so the customer knows what to expect when the project is complete. The project scope states not only what *is* within the boundaries of the project, but also what *is not* so the customer and your team can tell whether work is within the boundaries of the project. Figure 2-3 provides an example of a simple scope statement for the backyard remodel. For example, the family has decided to take responsibility for the landscaping and the final finishes on the deck and patio to save some money. However, the included scope specifically includes grading the yard for the landscaping because the family doesn't own a grader.

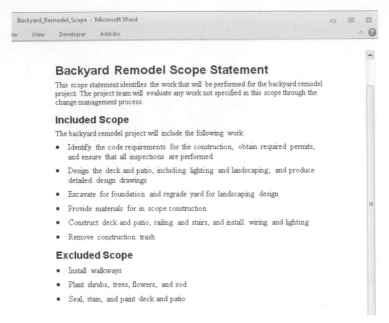

FIGURE 2-3 A sample scope statement for the backyard remodel project.

Documenting what is and isn't within scope helps eliminate unpleasant surprises for everyone. If you commission a sailboat designer in San Diego to build a custom sailboat, it's important to know whether the price and schedule include delivering the boat to your marina in Baltimore. If the designer asks when you're picking up the boat, and you thought it would be delivered, that phone call isn't fun for either one of you. You'll view the project as a failure, even though the sailboat is everything you wanted—except for the delivery snafu.

PROJECT FILE A sample scope statement, Backyard_Remodel_Scope.docx, is available in the Chapter02 folder on the companion website.

A clear scope statement makes it easy to spot changes that expand the project. For customers, a scope statement that contains inclusions and exclusions helps the customers decide whether the project is worth the price. For the project team, the scope statement makes it easier (although not pain-free) to discuss with customers the effects of additional requests on the project plan.

Preventing Scope Creep

If you thought the movie *The Blob* was scary, you already know why scope creep is the bane of project management. Without a clear scope statement, little bits of work and "Oh, would you add just this one thing" requests insidiously bloat the project scope until your budget, time, and resources are exhausted. Each request often sounds so simple that you don't see the harm in saying yes. But all the small changes can add up and doom the project, as illustrated in Figure 2-4.

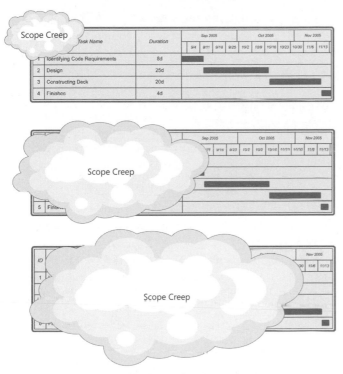

FIGURE 2-4 Scope creep is the bane of project management.

Fortunately, you *can* protect a project against scope creep and still give customers and stakeholders what they ask for. That's where the change management process comes in. If someone asks for a feature or a change that isn't in the project scope, funnel it to the change management process. If customers or stakeholders decide that the change is worth the additional time and cost, you can update your project plan to include it.

SEE ALSO   The section "An Overview of the Change Management Process," on page 300, describes how you use change management to document and manage change requests.

OTHER PROJECT CREEPS

Another type of creep is harder to prevent because your project team does the creeping—with the best of intentions. Engineers and other technical types are known for their perfectionism. Set the bar, and they'll try to raise it. Or programmers decide to add features because they're certain the customer would want them. The problem is that the project plan is based on the project objectives, but project team members are using up time and money to do more.

Sometimes, team members fall behind on their tasks. Yet, they report their tasks as on schedule because they think they will get back on track. They don't catch up and you discover that the tasks are late just when you expected them to be done.

Your best defenses against these creeps are clarity and vigilance. Begin by emphasizing what's in scope and the importance of meeting the project objectives. Then, if you notice that tasks are starting to run long, talk to team members to find out why. If team members talk directly to customers and stakeholders, be sure to ask if changes or additional requests are an issue. Gently remind team members that the objectives in the project plan should be their focus.

Assumptions and Risks

Assumptions can be dangerous because people don't realize they're making them. The customer just assumes that a task is part of the project, whereas the project team assumes just the opposite. As long as the assumptions go unspoken, trouble lies ahead. After you document assumptions, they lose their menace. Suppose you receive two bids from high-school kids for mowing your lawn; Kid A's bid is half the price of Kid B's bid. The difference is easy to understand when you know that Kid A assumes that you're providing the lawn mower, gas, and garbage bags.

■ **WARNING** Inspect the assumptions you gather for disguised risks. For example, if Kid A assumes that the weather will always be good on the weekends when she doesn't have school, there's a risk that the lawn will go unmowed during monsoon season.

Throughout the planning process, you must strive to uncover as yet unspoken assumptions. When you identify assumptions, add them to the project plan. In some cases, you can document assumptions about what will be done in the project scope or project objectives.

You can unearth conflicting assumptions by asking everyone involved to visualize project success. For example, ask the project customers, stakeholders, and members of the project team, "What results do you see when you think of this project as a success?" Write down everything they say. Don't be afraid to ask if there's anything else—more than once. The goal is to collect the assumptions that people haven't thought to voice. If the vision of success turns out to be much too large for the budget and resource pool, you can negotiate the project scope with the team instead of with lawyers.

Scan the definitions of success for conflicting views. Work with the team to resolve the differences. If the scope statement expands or contracts, evaluate whether you have to revise the rest of the project plan to support those changes.

SEE ALSO You must also analyze the risks that the project presents so that management can make an informed decision about whether to approve the project. You will perform a more thorough risk analysis during project planning. Chapter 15, "Managing Risk," describes the risk management process.

THE PROJECT MISSION STATEMENT

A problem statement identifies where you are, which is an important first step. The project mission statement states where you want to be—the purpose and the goals of the project. Like a game of tug-of-war, a project team won't get very far when people pull in different directions. The project mission statement conveys the vision of a project to the team, building commitment and aligning everyone to achieve the same goal.

Projects compete for money and resources, and not every project gets the okay to proceed. By communicating why the project is important, a project mission statement also reaffirms stakeholders' reasons for initiating the project.

"Would you tell me, please, which way I ought to walk from here?"

"That depends a good deal on where you want to get to," said the Cat.

"I don't much care where—" said Alice.

"Then it doesn't matter which way you walk," said the Cat.

"—so long as I get somewhere," Alice added as an explanation.

"Oh, you're sure to do that," said the Cat, "if you only walk long enough."

—Lewis Carroll, Alice's Adventures in Wonderland

As a project progresses, team members do work and make decisions. A project mission statement helps them decide whether what they are doing is moving the project in the right direction—preventing wrong turns or dead ends. And, should the going get tough, a mission statement helps boost morale by reminding everyone why the work they do is important.

NOTE Many organizations make the mistake of writing a project mission statement only to forget it in the throes of day-to-day activity. Keep the mission statement in people's minds by printing it on a certificate or laminated card that team members can pin to their cubicles or office walls. If the mission statement is brief, add it to the cover page of project documents.

Working with Project Stakeholders

Project stakeholders get their name because they have a stake in the outcome of the project. Stakeholders include the customers who receive and use the results of a project, departments or vendors that participate in the project, managers who are evaluated on its success, and the employees assigned to work on the project's tasks. As a project manager, you work with project stakeholders all the time, so it's worthwhile learning how to recognize them and work with them effectively.

Stakeholders influence a project throughout its life. During planning, they help define project objectives, requirements, and constraints; identify workable strategies; evaluate the project plan and schedule; and provide the funding for the project. After the project gets going, stakeholders do the work, help resolve issues that arise, decide whether changes are necessary, and control or increase the budget. Although the customers and the project sponsor are the most important to please, the sign of true success is a project that makes most, if not all, stakeholders happy.

Stakeholders don't wear "I'm a stakeholder" name tags. Some stakeholders who are incredibly important to the project might not realize they're stakeholders. For example, a marketing department could develop great plans for its new product launch website without inviting the web developers to participate in the requirements session to confirm that new features are feasible.

On the other hand, you're bound to get some folks who claim to be stakeholders but aren't—or who try to influence the project more than their stakeholder roles warrant. For instance, a group might see your project as a way to get its new website without having to foot the entire bill. The next thing you know, your project has a host of unnecessary requirements with no additional budget.

Identifying Stakeholders

Your first step in working with stakeholders is to find out who they are and make sure that you have the right ones on your team. The following sections explain the different types of stakeholders, how they contribute to a project, how you can identify them, and how to keep them happy. But if people are vying for stakeholdership and you don't think they should belong, don't be afraid to ask the project sponsor, the project customer, or other stakeholders to help you control who joins the stakeholder group.

Regardless of the role they play or the group to which they belong, stakeholders either contribute something to your project or want something from it. For example, the project sponsor gives you the authority to do your job as project manager and provides support when you ask for it. In return, the sponsor wants a positive outcome.

BEST PRACTICES

Conflicts arise in the project world, and some of the toughest to resolve are from stakeholders who *don't* support your project. Perhaps your project is the best solution for the overall objectives of the organization, but it hurts a few stakeholders' chances to meet their specific performance goals and thus their performance bonuses. Or, it requires one group to radically change the way it works to shorten the duration of a business process in which several groups participate.

When a project affects some groups more than others, stakeholders from those groups might push back. Stakeholders also might withhold their support if they don't get the benefits they hoped for from a project. Whether they try to discredit the utility of the selected solution, withhold resources that you need to complete the project, or doggedly drag the project down by raising false issues, these stakeholders do their best to achieve their objectives.

The first step to winning over reluctant stakeholders is to understand their concerns. If you don't know why they are fighting your project, you have little hope of convincing them to play nice. But by understanding their pain points and doubts, you might be able to redirect the project to make them a bit happier. For example, if a group has to change its workflow, you could reprioritize some of the development work to deliver that group's enhancements first.

Likewise, you can emphasize the benefits your project provides to the entire organization and hope that the stakeholders are magnanimous. Sometimes, you simply don't have any benefits to offer unhappy stakeholders. In that case, you can ask your project sponsor or supporting stakeholders to help you bring the stragglers on board. If performance goals are the issue, you might think that asking the executive team to change compensation plans would be the way to go. Unfortunately, executive teams, project sponsors, and other stakeholders won't always back you up. Compensation plans are complicated and hard to change. Truth be told, in the face of politics and the reality of working with people long after your project ends, executives often choose to maintain their other relationships at your expense.

As a project manager with unwilling and unmoving stakeholders, the best action you can take is to identify the risks that the situation presents, develop a workaround plan for those issues, and communicate the risks and options to your entire stakeholder group so it can make an informed decision about what to do. The solutions aren't as straightforward as accounting. There's no one right answer. The risks might never come to fruition. If the risks do arise, your workaround plan might resolve the situation successfully. Unfortunately, project management doesn't always deliver a happy ending. If an unwilling stakeholder damages your project, you might have nothing to do but hope that the team recognizes your best efforts.

SEE ALSO Chapter 15 describes techniques for identifying and assessing risks.

How Planning Tasks Help Identify Stakeholders

The good news is that the tasks you perform to prepare a project plan go a long way to identify many of the stakeholders. Here is a list of some project plan components and the stakeholders they help identify:

- Defining the problem statement helps identify the customer of the project. Who's having a problem that needs to be solved? What is the purpose of the project, and who benefits from the results?

- Project objectives and requirements can help identify additional customers and perhaps the project sponsor.

- Project strategy, scope, organization chart, and responsibility assignment matrix identify functional managers and team members. The responsibility matrix can be a great help for weeding out wanna-be customers. If people or groups aren't responsible for a part of the project, they aren't likely to be customers or stakeholders, either.

SEE ALSO The section "The Responsibility Matrix," on page 90, describes how you identify the roles that groups and people play within a project.

Project Customer

Project customers make three significant contributions:

- **Money**   The most important customer contribution is money because without funding, a project never gets off the ground.

  Surely, whoever pays the bills is your customer. Yes, the person or committee that has final authority over funding is a customer stakeholder. Even the most lavish budgets have their limits, and you need to know that limit. But the customer who controls the money usually has other goals besides staying within budget, such as a minimum ROI or positive comparison of benefit to cost.

  To keep a financial customer happy, you must stay on top of the financial performance of your project. At status reporting time, you must be able to explain negative financial results and how you plan to get those measures back on track. If runaway requirements are overwhelming your budget, the financial customer can be a powerful ally to help convince other stakeholders of the need for restraint.

SEE ALSO	The section "Understanding Financial Measures," on page 161, describes net present value, ROI, and other financial measures. Chapter 14, "Balancing the Budget and Other Project Variables," describes techniques for tracking financial performance.

TIP	In some cases, project sponsors play dual roles as project customers. For example, project sponsors often provide funding for projects that deliver products for external customers. This is also true for many projects that are launched to improve internal corporate processes or functions.

- **Influence**   Because customers pay for projects, customers usually have a lot of influence over what a project is supposed to accomplish: project objectives, deliverables, and specific requirements.

  Unfortunately, the customer who pays the bills often isn't the same one who defines the requirements. At a car dealer, your spouse, who is better at negotiating, might be holding the checkbook, but you're the one who decides whether the car satisfies your commuting requirements.

As you might expect, many people can play the role of the customer who identifies project objectives and requirements. In fact, the difficulty is knowing when to cut off the list of people who tender requirements. Your job is to find out who is authorized to make these kinds of decisions about the project. The project sponsor and the customer who pays the bills are a good place to start, but you'll also have to rely on your own judgment. In addition, the best and most knowledgeable customer representatives can clearly communicate what they want and can prioritize their requests.

TIP   For product-oriented projects, you can't include the ultimate customers: the people who buy the products. In these situations, you work with people or groups that represent the end users, such as a usability expert for a website or a marketing department with marketing research data.

- **Approval**   Customers approve deliverables as long as the objectives and requirements have been met.

There's nothing worse than getting to the end of a long project only to find out that the customer isn't satisfied. By working with the customers and other stakeholders to agree on objectives up front, specifying success criteria for a project, and having stakeholders sign off on scope and deliverables, you'll rarely encounter this kind of disappointment.

SEE ALSO   The section "Success Criteria," on page 33, describes what success criteria do and different ways to define them.

Project Sponsor

Projects present a tough organizational problem. They require cooperation between many departments, business units, and companies. But project managers almost never hold positions of authority high enough to oversee all the groups involved. Enter project sponsors—people who *do* have formal authority and are interested in seeing their projects succeed. Project sponsors don't always come from top levels of management.

What matters most is that they have enough authority to promote their projects and are willing and capable of taking action when needed.

Signing their names to project charters is only the first step in sponsoring projects. The best project sponsors play an active role in the projects they support from beginning to end. Although they appear to sponsor projects, what they *really* do is back the project manager and project team in their efforts. Here are some of the ways that sponsors help:

- *Lend authority* to a project manager by signing and distributing a project charter.

> **SEE ALSO**   The section "The Project Charter: Publicizing a Project," on page 51, describes how a project charter announces a project and informs everyone of the project manager's authority.

- *Provide guidance* to the project manager about the priority of objectives and performance measures.

- *Review the project plan* and suggest ways to build more support for the project.

- *Advise the project manager* on issues and politics that could harm the project.

- *Regularly review project status* and suggest ways to resolve problems and issues that arise.

- *Maintain the project's priority* and protect its resources within the organization's project portfolio.

- *Step in to resolve issues* when the project manager's authority doesn't do the job.

> **NOTE**   The project charter doesn't always work. Managers question authority, or entrenched bureaucracy makes working across department boundaries almost impossible. Intervention from a project sponsor can break the logjam and reiterate the importance of the project.

In return for all this help, the project sponsor wants to see the project succeed. You can win more points with your sponsors by keeping them informed. Good communication is a balancing act. Sponsors expect you to manage the project; they don't want you knocking on their doors every five minutes. However, when tough problems arise, they'd rather have you call them in early enough to help instead of finding out after it's too late to do anything.

SEE ALSO   Chapter 11, "Communicating Information," describes all kinds of techniques for communicating well.

TIP   If your project sponsors aren't as supportive as they could be, they might not know how they can help. Ask your sponsor for the support you want.

Functional Manager

Most companies use a functional organization: managers (called functional or line managers) oversee the performance of a business function, such as accounting, engineering, or marketing. These managers set policies for their domain, are accountable for achieving functional or departmental goals, and supervise the resources that perform the function. The resources for project teams come from these functional groups, so project managers must work with functional managers (with support from project sponsors if necessary) to get the resources they need when they need them.

With a work breakdown structure in hand, a project manager has a good idea of the skills and characteristics that resources should have. Obtaining those resources—and holding onto them—is one of the most common project management challenges.

SEE ALSO   Chapter 4, "Building a Work Breakdown Structure," explains how to define in detail the work that must be performed to complete a project including the skills that resources should have to perform that work.

Functional managers spend a lot of time overseeing their people's schedules—and listening to employees' complaints if they have too much work to do, not enough work to do, work that they aren't trained for, or work that they're overqualified for. They want their employees working on tasks to which they're suited and that are important to the organization's goals. A well-planned project schedule and clearly defined work are two ways to win over functional managers. If you demonstrate that your plan assigns the right kinds of resources to tasks and allocates those resources to work a reasonable number of hours each week, functional managers are more likely to fulfill your requests. Planning a project to keep resource workloads consistent is another way to gain functional managers' trust. You won't have to beg for resources to survive workload peaks or apologize for delays or downtime.

BUILDING RELATIONSHIPS WITH MANAGERS

Good relationships with functional managers pay off on project after project. Managing resources effectively is an important first step in building relationships with managers, but there are other ways to earn a manager's trust.

If you have more time than money, work with functional managers to give less-experienced resources a chance to develop their skills. You can pair these people with experts to get work done and help the organization cross-train its people.

After resources are assigned, functional managers respond much like customer stakeholders. The sooner they know about resource problems, the easier it is to solve them. Besides, they can offer solutions you might not think of on your own or find resources that you don't know about.

Communication is important for working with functional managers. Initially, they want to know what skills you need for your project and any resource constraints, such as cost, timing, or experience. For example, highly specialized resources are usually hard to come by. Tell managers when you need these resources and do whatever you can to maintain the dates for their assignments. If deadlines do slip, notify the managers as soon as possible so all of you can make alternative arrangements.

■ **WARNING** Assignments that leave people with little work to do for days on end are a sure way to lose resources to other projects. Another project manager might notice your resources' inactivity, or the resources might complain about having nothing to do. Then, when your project needs those resources, they're likely to be unavailable. In the worst case, idle employees could be laid off, not only raising issues for staffing current projects but also disrupting people's lives.

Team Member

The people who do the work for a project are stakeholders, too. They contribute their expertise and time to carrying out the tasks that make up a project. Team members are a diverse group. In reality, people who act as other types of stakeholders—customers, sponsors, and functional managers—are often team members as well. For example, customers participate in planning and requirements definition, which are project tasks as much as writing the copy for a new marketing brochure or ordering furniture for the new office are. Although team members might make other contributions to projects in other roles, their job as team members is to perform the work that they're assigned. What they expect in return is interesting work, communication, respect, and assignments that don't consume their every waking hour.

During project planning, you gradually develop a picture of the skills you need on your project team and work with functional managers to obtain those resources. As you bring team members on board, you must clearly communicate the work they're supposed to do. To gain their commitment, you must help them understand how their work fits into the big picture of the project.

As the project progresses, it's important to maintain this communication. Team members don't like surprises any more than executives do. Let team members know the work that's up next or notify them if work is delayed or changes have been made.

Project Manager

Identifying the project manager is easy. It's you. And this book is all about how you contribute to the success of your projects.

Documenting Project Stakeholders

"Who contributes to this project?" and "Who cares about the project's outcome?" are questions that help identify stakeholders, but to work with stakeholders effectively, you need to know more. When you add someone to your list of project stakeholders, make a point of learning the following information about that person:

- **Organization**   At the beginning of a project, you'll need some hints about who works for which company and in which department. Document the stakeholder's organization and department, although you'll eventually have this information memorized.

- **Advisers**   Find out who the stakeholder listens to. If you face delicate negotiations in the future, you can discuss options and fine-tune your approach with advisers before addressing the actual stakeholders.

- **Objectives**   Identify the stakeholder's objectives for the project and list the objectives in order of priority. This ensures that you involve the right people in discussions about a specific objective.

- **Contributions**   List what the stakeholder does for the project. These contributions help you identify who to go to for items such as funding, requirements, and approvals.

In the midst of project execution, you have a million details to remember. Don't count on keeping this information in your head. The form in Figure 2-5 provides one approach for documenting stakeholders.

PROJECT FILE The stakeholder analysis document shown in Figure 2-5, Stakeholder_Analysis.docx, is available in the Chapter02 folder on the companion website.

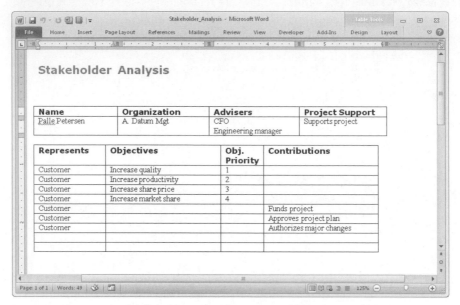

FIGURE 2-5 Keep track of stakeholders, what they want, and how they can help.

Obtaining and Maintaining Commitment

"The quality of a person's life is in direct proportion to their commitment to excellence, regardless of their chosen field of endeavor."
—Vincent T. Lombardi

Although a project needs commitment at all levels of an organization, a project sponsor is the executive who is the project's biggest fan, perhaps the person whose performance bonus depends most on the project's outcome. Management support is a boon to a project manager trying to resolve resource shortages, money issues, conflicting priorities, or differences of opinion on project direction.

But the commitment of the people who work on the project day after day is equally important. When team members appreciate the importance of the project, they work harder to meet expectations, stay on schedule, deliver higher quality, and think of creative solutions to problems that arise. In short, they devote themselves to delivering success.

Building commitment to a project doesn't require specialized project management skills. All it takes is good people skills. Of course, people skills are far more art than science and take time to master. This section introduces a few of the more effective ways to get people on board.

- **Know what stakeholders expect**   There are few things as delightful as receiving something that you didn't realize you needed, whether it is dual-control heated seats in your car or an easy-to-navigate web page. As project manager, the more you understand about what your stakeholders need—as well as what they want—the better equipped you are to meet and exceed their expectations.

  Keep in mind that understanding stakeholders' expectations doesn't mean delivering *everything* they ask for. You have to help stakeholders balance conflicting objectives like the list of requirements and the time and budget that are available. In some cases, your job is to explain to stakeholders why they won't get what they *want*—but they will get what they *need*.

- **Promote your project**   Face it. If you liked selling, you'd be a salesperson. The reality is that you have to do some promotion as a project manager. When you understand the importance of a project, you have to help other people understand its benefits as well. You must reassure the customers that the project delivers what they need. You must convince managers that their resources are vital to the project. And you must show the project team how the project benefits each member.

- **Make people feel important**   This chapter shows how every person involved in a project is important to its success. The best way to gain people's commitment is to help them see the importance of what they do. For example, testing has been an afterthought in many a software project. But the *test lead,* the job title of the person responsible for supervising and leading the testing of a software application, is one of the most influential people on a software project—the end users' advocate. The test lead makes sure that the software project requirements are measurable and realistic. The test plan documents what the software is supposed to do and how to measure success. And thorough testing finds defects that would otherwise frustrate end users and sap their productivity.

- **Keep people informed**   No one likes surprises. Tell people what they need to know, and when they need to know it. Remind team members about what's due now and what's coming up next week. Notify stakeholders if plans change or issues arise.

- **Be honest**   As a project manager, you should prefer to be honest than to be liked. Always saying yes makes you popular initially. Eventually, stakeholders catch on. Unfortunately, it's much harder to regain trust than it is to lose it.

TIP

Being honest doesn't mean being rude. If you must tell team members something they might not want to hear, give them a way to save face. For example, if a team member forgets an important aspect of his deliverable, say something like, "This requirement was at the end of the list, so you might have missed it. However, it's very important to the customer. Can you revise your work by tomorrow to include it?"

BEST PRACTICES

The authority conferred upon a project manager by the project sponsor is incredibly important, but you can't manufacture the clout that you need to manage a project. You have to earn it. This power or influence comes from several sources:

- **Expertise in managing projects**   This is necessary to do your job well. It also helps you convey confidence, which builds confidence and commitment in the rest of the team.

- **Technical or professional expertise related to the project**   This builds your credibility with the specialists working on the project. Without this expertise, team members might view you as a paper pusher—or worse, they might try to hoodwink you on project matters.

- **The ability to make good decisions**   This goes a long way to earn people's trust and respect. Although some people will disagree with your decisions, they're more likely to support you if they see that you solicit input, evaluate the input you receive, and then make decisions that do the most good.

- **Leadership**   This is a valuable skill, but it is especially important in project management, when you must influence a lot of people without built-in power.

Some of your stakeholders are powerful people, but you are the project manager and you know more about the project than anyone else. It's up to you to manage stakeholders' expectations and help them make the right decisions. If something doesn't make sense, raise a red flag. If objectives are unattainable or in conflict, point them out and help people agree on what's important. Ask for help if you need it, but also help stakeholders find solutions to problems. Most important, keep people informed and keep everyone moving toward the project goals.

The Project Charter: Publicizing a Project

Most managers in a hierarchical organization get their power from their position in the pyramid. If they change positions, they inherit the power of the new position. But project managers' authority is fleeting—it lasts only as long as the projects to which they are assigned. Formal acknowledgement of the project manager's authority is key. Otherwise, the project manager could run into resistance from functional managers who question their authority to request resources or spend money.

Before a project manager can delve into project planning in earnest, the project sponsor publishes a project charter to announce the project and, more importantly, to identify the authority and responsibilities of the project manager assigned to the project. Everyone involved in or affected by the project should receive a copy of the project charter. Publication doesn't have to be a formal affair. These days, the project charter is often delivered via email. (However, in some corporate cultures, a paper memo carries more weight.)

TIP

Keep a copy of the project charter close at hand. Hanging a framed copy on the wall isn't out of the question. As phone calls come in or people stop by your office with questions, referring them to the project charter is an effective way of communicating your authority.

Project charters come in several forms, from simple statements of the project manager's authority for a project to detailed documents that can pass as actual project plans. Here are the typical ingredients for a project charter:

- **Project name**   Brief descriptive names, such as Backyard Remodel Project, are fine.

- **Purpose of the project**   This can be the mission statement, a one-line summary of what the project is supposed to achieve, or a more thorough description of the business objectives for the project.

- **Project manager**   Include a sentence stating that the person named is the project manager for the project and will carry out the responsibilities identified in the charter.

- **Project manager's responsibilities**   Including a summary of the work the project manager does in the project helps the audience understand what the project manager needs as well as what project management entails.

- **Project manager's authority**   The project charter describes the extent of the project manager's authority and lists specific activities the project manager has authority to perform.

- **Formal announcement of the sponsor's or executive's support**   The charter begins the chain of commitment by putting in writing the sponsor's or customer's support for the project and the project manager. In effect, this announcement is like a power of attorney, stating that the project manager is empowered to perform specific tasks under the authority of the sponsor or customer.

> **PROJECT FILE**   See the file Project_Charter.docx in the Chapter02 folder on the companion website for one example of a project charter.

Although the project sponsor is the official author of the project charter and distributes it to stakeholders, in many cases, the project manager prepares the project charter for the sponsor's signature.

> **NOTE** The choice of the person who signs and distributes the project charter is important. The signature of the company president might look impressive, but that signature can backfire if she asks, "What project?" when someone asks her about your work. The project sponsor—the executive or manager who is ultimately responsible for the success of the project and actively supports it—or the project customer is an ideal choice to sign and send out the project charter.

Summary

The problem statement is the guiding light for a project. It tells the team what the project is supposed to achieve. The project objectives, requirements, scope statement, success criteria, and deliverables all help identify how you know the project is done.

Projects are collaborative efforts. Success is easier to achieve when all the stakeholders are committed to a project, from the customer who pays for the project to the people who do the work. The most effective way to gain commitment from this diverse group is with good people skills—tools that no project manager should be without.

A project overview is a synopsis of the project, which is just what you need to obtain approval to begin project planning. The customer and the management team follow your progress documenting the problem, objectives, and other aspects of the project. However, a meeting is the best way to review the project and obtain signatures to make approval official. Once the project is approved, the project charter is the official announcement that the project is about to begin in earnest. This document also conveys the project manager's responsibilities and authority.

2 Planning a Project

Planning to Achieve Success

- Learn the benefits of project planning
- Identify the components of a project implementation plan
- Learn at a high level what goes into an implementation plan

"You've got to be very careful if you don't know where you're going, because you might not get there."—YOGI BERRA

MAYBE ACTION MOVIES are to blame for making people want to jump in and *do* something instead of planning first. Competition and the overall fast pace of business makes the "Just keep driving and I'll get out the map" mentality quite common. Time, money, and resources are always in short supply while the list of project goals seems to grow longer. That combination is an almost irresistible goad to action.

Many project managers—and the executives who oversee them—look at the mountain of work and think they don't have time for planning. The truth is, the tighter the time and the tougher the constraints, the more important a plan becomes. Planning ahead is the only way you can do the right things *and* get them right the first time. This chapter introduces the components of a project implementation plan—what work will be done and when, and how much it will cost. You learn about each of these components in detail in later chapters.

What Is Project Planning?

No doubt you've heard the theory of putting enough monkeys in front of typewriters pounding the keys at random to eventually produce the works of Shakespeare. Take that theory another step and you might think that you don't need a plan because you'll eventually get the project right. Unfortunately, with limited resources, a project plan is essential if you want to complete your project successfully on the first try.

Project planning isn't all that different from other types of planning. The same questions that newspaper reporters ask to uncover a story—Who, What, When, Where, Why, and How—work equally well to plan a project.

GETTING STAKEHOLDER BUY-IN

Not soliciting input or feedback during the planning stage from the people who implement the plan is asking for trouble. Without buy-in, they're likely to say, "You want what done by when?" when they finally see the plan you've developed—sometimes, with good reason. People who don't perform the work often underestimate how long it will take or may forget work that must be done.

A project plan helps communicate the proposed approach to others and get everyone on board. Project managers don't have the authority to make every decision on a project, so they must rely on the support of management, key stakeholders, and executive sponsors to help them get the resources they need and to remove obstacles that get in the way of progress.

To give their support, stakeholders must feel comfortable that their needs are met and that the approach is feasible. An earnestly delivered "Trust me; it'll work" doesn't convince these folks. By documenting the plan to achieve the project goals, you give stakeholders the chance to evaluate the proposed project.

If the project begins to go awry, you may have to turn to stakeholders to approve more money, more time, scope changes, or other items to help get the project back on track. If you've earned stakeholders' trust with a good project plan, it's easier to keep their commitment when times are tough.

Team members who do the work during the execution phase have to be on board as well. Understanding the benefits of a project and their part in it helps team members take ownership, not only for their part but for the success of the project as a whole.

Pointing the Team in the Right Direction

Project teams are far more productive when they know what they're supposed to do and how they're supposed to do it. A project plan helps team members see where they're headed and stay focused on the destination.

Communicating the plan to team members does more than jump-start project success; it also helps them make good decisions during the course of their day-to-day work. And that's good news for the project manager who otherwise works nonstop answering team members' questions and making constant course corrections.

Tracking Progress

If you don't know where you're going, you can't tell how close you are to getting there. During project execution, a project plan tells you where you're supposed to be. By comparing your plan to where you really are, you can figure out whether the project is off course and how to get it back on track.

> **NOTE** Progress isn't progress if you're headed in the wrong direction, no matter how fast you're going. In *The 7 Habits of Highly Effective People*, Stephen Covey tells of a group hacking their way through the jungle. One member of the group climbs a tree and calls down to her teammates, "Hey! We're in the wrong part of the jungle." The reply shouted back is "Shut up! We're making good progress!" A project plan maps out your destination and how you're going to get there. Only then can you gauge how far you've gone and the true progress you've made.

BEST PRACTICES

Although it's tempting to circulate a project plan and request that stakeholders sign off on the plan, don't do it. The copies of the plan are likely to sit in stakeholders' inboxes only to be signed at the last minute without a thorough review. Later, you'll pay the price as people realize that the plan doesn't address their needs the way they expected.

A better approach is to schedule a sign-off meeting and distribute the project plan in advance. Ideally, stakeholders read the plan before coming to the meeting. However, as project manager, you should present the plan at the meeting, highlighting potential problems or conflicts.

Don't take head nodding as a sufficient sign that the plan is okay. Encourage questions—the harder, the better. To get the ball rolling, ask a few tough questions of your own.

Plans Change

Dwight D. Eisenhower once said that planning is everything, but plans are worthless. Huh? The reason Eisenhower considered plans worthless is because they change as soon as they are complete, if not sooner. Projects rarely unfold exactly the way you planned. Yet, project managers still plan because the act of planning uncovers so much valuable information.

So go ahead, plan, and document your results in a project plan. It doesn't have to stay the same. In fact, changes are a sign that a plan is being used.

An implementation plan for a project answers several questions:

- **What work do we have to do?** Breaks down the work into manageable pieces.

- **When will we start and when must we finish?** Sets the project schedule.

- **Who is going to do the work?** Identifies the project organization and resources.

- **How much is it going to cost?** or **How much do we have to spend?** Defines the project budget.

SEE ALSO Answering these questions takes some time and effort, which you learn in detail in Chapters 4 through 7. Chapter 4, "Building a Work Breakdown Structure," explains how to decompose work into assignable packages. Chapter 5, "Project Resources," talks about putting together the team that does the work. In Chapter 6, "Building a Project Schedule," you learn how to estimate effort, build a schedule, and assign resources to tasks. Chapter 7, "Working with a Budget," covers building a budget and setting up a schedule to track costs.

OBTAINING TIME TO PLAN

Regardless of how obvious the importance of planning is to project managers, management sometimes is adamant that work begin immediately. Giving in to management's demands may seem like the right career choice at the time, but it's only a temporary solution. When the project fails, as it's likely to do without a plan, your career is even more at risk.

Take the time to explain how planning helps ensure project success. Activities that your management wouldn't dream of performing without planning can be influential—for example, preparing the business plan for the next round of venture capital, planning for the acquisition of another company, or figuring out the best way to exercise executive stock options. If all else fails, negotiate a shorter amount of time for planning—it's better than nothing.

After you've fought for planning time, be sure to collect project performance measures and lessons learned when the project is complete. By demonstrating how your hard-won project planning led to project success, it will be easier to obtain planning time for the next project.

Project Planning Step by Step

Project planning is a series of steps that help determine how you are going to run the project to achieve its objectives. Figure 3-1 shows the steps to building an implementation plan for a project. This section introduces the parts of a project implementation plan, which are the results of these steps.

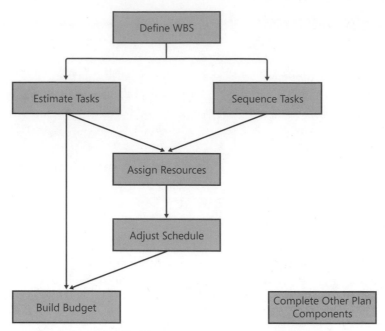

FIGURE 3-1 The steps of building a project implementation plan.

The Components of a Project Implementation Plan

Project planning includes a number of steps, but eventually the result is a tangible deliverable: the project plan. This section introduces the components of a project plan and explains why they're important.

Work Breakdown Structure

A work breakdown structure (WBS) is the key to a project plan. You must break down the project work into manageable chunks before you can build a project schedule, assign resources, or track performance. Chopping work up into smaller chunks helps team members understand the work to which they're assigned. These lowest-level subtasks are called *work packages*. After you start implementing your plan, you also track progress based on the completed tasks. Constructing a WBS isn't always easy because you can usually break down projects into subtasks in different ways, even if the work is the same.

SEE ALSO   Chapter 4 discusses techniques for developing a WBS.

Project Organization and Resources

Getting the right resources for a project makes a big difference. Working with fewer resources than you planned for or assigning people with less experience can delay the schedule. But people, equipment, and materials are almost always in short supply, so compromises are always a probability. The project plan doesn't just list resource names or generic skill sets. If you can delineate the skill sets you need, when, and for how long, it's easier to obtain resources or negotiate alternatives if the resources you want are unavailable.

SEE ALSO   Chapter 5 discusses project organization and resources.

The number of resources needed for different skill sets or the hours that resources are assigned each day is crucial for staffing decisions. Functional managers can evaluate resource requirements to determine whether the current staff can handle the project, some overtime will cover the gap, or hiring temporary or permanent staff is necessary.

Project Schedule

A project schedule is the timeline for a project. You first estimate the effort and duration for each work package in the WBS. Then you put the work packages in the sequence in which they must be performed to figure out when the project will finish

SEE ALSO   Chapter 6 describes how to transform a WBS into a schedule.

During project execution, project managers compare actual performance to the baseline project schedule to see whether work is on time or running late. Although finish dates for tasks indicate whether the tasks are on schedule, milestones in a schedule are another way to track progress. Milestones based on project deliverables are easy to evaluate; if the deliverable success criteria have been met, the milestone is complete. On the other hand, if the project is falling behind, you can make course corrections before the project becomes unmanageable.

Budget

Don't expect to hear that money is no object. Even if a project is launched to improve customer satisfaction, you can count on financial folks to calculate return on investment or the break-even date. Whether someone tells you how much money you have to work with or you have the luxury of calculating how much the project will cost, you do have to build a budget and then track performance against it.

> **SEE ALSO**   Chapter 7 explains what capital budgets are and shows how to set up a project schedule to track costs.

The level of detail that you include in a project budget depends on what stakeholders want to see. For example, a fixed-bid project might include only the fixed price for the entire project. However, behind the scenes, a detailed budget accounts for all the project costs, from labor to rental equipment to profit margin.

Risk Management Plan

Things do go wrong. Although some people enjoy putting out fires, you don't want them on your project team. The more sensible approach to managing project risk is to identify potential risks ahead of time and plan for how you'll handle them.

> **SEE ALSO**   To learn how to identify, track, and manage risks, see Chapter 15, "Managing Risk."

A risk management plan begins with what could go wrong—the concrete supplier might go out of business, the bonus that the homeowner hoped to use to pay for the project might be cut in half, or a buried power line might require a change in design. You estimate their impact and likelihood. For most projects, a risk management plan covers possible approaches for the risks with significant impact and reasonable likelihood.

But risk management doesn't stop with planning. Throughout the life of a project, you must monitor the risks you've identified and watch for new risks that may arise.

Communication Plan

Whenever people work together, communication is an essential ingredient for success. Truth be told, the lion's share of a project manager's job is communication. A communication plan describes how you're going to keep the people involved with a project informed. Communication strategies may be simple or sophisticated and can range from a weekly status report to a collaborative website. At their core, communication plans answer the following questions:

- Who needs to know?

- What do they need to know?

- When do they need to know it?

> **SEE ALSO**   Chapter 11, "Communicating Information," describes a communication plan and how to communicate effectively.

Quality Plan

Examples abound showing that it's easier, faster, and cheaper to do things right the first time than to do them over. A quality plan begins with the quality objectives for the project, whether they come from the organization's quality policies or customer requirements. The plan then describes the quality assurance and control strategies and activities used to achieve the quality objectives of the project.

Change Control Plan

Change is a given during the life of a project, whether it's a bonus you decide to contribute to your backyard budget or three weeks of rainy days that prevent the construction trucks from getting to your job site. With the rest of your project plan complete, you have a foundation for controlling change in a project. Project scope, deliverables, requirements, and pretty much the rest of your project plan set the baseline. After stakeholders approve the plan, you need change management to manage the changes to that baseline.

A change management plan describes the process for managing changes. The sophistication of change management depends on the size and complexity of the project. A small project might rely on a spreadsheet and email for change management. Mammoth projects might require change boards (committees of people who agree on changes) and different categories of changes. But change management boils down to a few steps:

- Recording change requests

- Evaluating cost, schedule, and quality impact for change requests

- Deciding the fate of change requests (accepting, rejecting, or requesting modifications)

- Accepting change requests and updating project documents to reflect the change

> **SEE ALSO**   Chapter 12, "Managing Project Changes," provides an overview of a change management process and describes how to track changes.

Summary

The amount of planning you need depends on the project you're managing. A few hours of planning are sufficient for a small dinner party for some friends, but the first moon landing required years of it.

Depending on the characteristics of your project, you might not need every project plan component presented in this chapter. As you're planning your project, consider each component and how it might help your project succeed. For small projects, a sentence or two might be enough to describe your communication plan or other sections. In the chapters that follow, you'll learn how to build each section of a project plan for projects large and small.

CHAPTER 4

Building a Work Breakdown Structure

"*The work was like peeling an onion. The outer skin came off with difficulty . . . but in no time you'd be down to its innards, tears streaming from your eyes as more and more beautiful reductions became possible.*"—EDWARD BLISHEN

THE DIVISION OF LABOR for dinner could be you microwaving a couple of frozen dinners while your spouse gets out the plates, forks, and napkins. But the surprise party for your parents' fortieth wedding anniversary is another story. You want the party to be amazing—like their marriage—so you don't want to forget anything. The best way to make sure that everything gets done is to break the project down into small, manageable pieces. You could divide the work into planning the party, buying the supplies, preparing the food, and decorating the backyard. Or you could keep track of the work that you've hired the caterer, bartender, florist, and tent wrangler to do.

Regardless of the way you break down the work, the important point is that smaller servings of work help the project manager (or party host, in this example) keep track of what's been done and what's on deck, and it also helps everyone working on the project perform their parts successfully. A *work breakdown structure (WBS)* is the tool that project managers use to divide a project into tasks called *work packages*. But a WBS helps everyone involved see the scope and organization of the work in one easy-to-read chart.

This chapter describes a WBS and how it helps you to plan and manage a project. You'll learn how to build one that effectively communicates the work to be done. This chapter also explains methods for decomposing work into properly-sized portions as well as techniques for getting your WBS into Microsoft Project so that you can begin building a project schedule.

> **SEE ALSO**   Chapter 6, "Building a Project Schedule," describes how to link tasks and assign resources to turn a WBS into a project schedule.

What's a Work Breakdown Structure?

A WBS is a simple though aptly named component of project planning. It shows the work in a project *broken down* into progressively smaller tasks. The tasks at the lowest level represent work you can assign to team members to perform.

A WBS is project management's answer to the proverbial question, "How do you eat an elephant?" The answer is "One bite at a time." In essence, a WBS details the bites—the list of tasks you must perform to complete a project. You use the work packages in the WBS to estimate the time and resources each deliverable takes, identify the types of resources you need, and link the work packages (tasks) to create the project schedule.

> **SEE ALSO**   The section "Estimating," on page 112, discusses several methods for estimating effort. Chapter 5, "Project Resources," describes the different types of resources you may use on your project and how to add them to your project. The section "Defining the Sequence of Work," on page 125, shows you how to create dependencies between tasks to put the tasks into sequence.

A WBS contains two kinds of tasks: summary tasks and work packages. As you can see in Figures 4-1 and 4-2, differentiating the two is easy:

- **Work packages** These are the lowest-level tasks that represent actual work that people perform, such as digging holes, pouring footings, and installing decking. Throughout this book, these tasks are called work packages or simply tasks.

- **Summary tasks** These comprise all higher-level tasks, which summarize several work packages or several lower-level summary tasks. For example, a summary task called Preparing Lumber, shown in the WBS in Figure 4-2, could include work packages of Cut Lumber, Treat Lumber, and Pre-Drill Holes in Lumber. But the Preparing Lumber summary task is also a part of a higher-level summary task called Constructing Deck.

> **NOTE** Some project managers refer to higher-level tasks as activities and bottom-level tasks as tasks, while others swap those definitions. Others use the terms activity and task interchangeably.

You can show a WBS either as a diagram or as an outline. A WBS diagram looks like an inverted tree, starting with the project summary task at the top and ending with the work packages at the bottom, as Figure 4-1 illustrates.

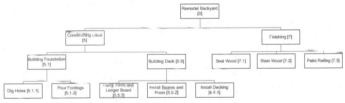

FIGURE 4-1 A WBS diagram shows the hierarchy of project tasks from the overall project at the top to work packages at the bottom.

> **SEE ALSO** The sidebar "Displaying a WBS as a Tree," on page 84, explains how to create a tree diagram in Project 2010.

A WBS in outline form shows the same information as a WBS diagram, but it takes up a lot less space. If you've built a list of tasks in the Task Sheet view in Project, the WBS outline shown in Figure 4-2 is an old friend. Each level in the outline is indented a bit more to the right. The first column in Figure 4-2 shows another component of a WBS: the *WBS code*. Following an outline-oriented numbering scheme, WBS codes show the level of the hierarchy to which tasks belong as well as which lower-level tasks belong to higher-level (parent) summary tasks.

	WBS	Task Name
0	0	⊟ **Remodel Backyard**
1	1	⊞ **Identifying Project Constraints**
19	2	Project Constraints Identified
20	3	⊞ **Designing Remodel**
50	4	Design Complete
51	5	⊟ **Constructing Deck**
52	5.1	⊟ **Building Foundation**
53	5.1.1	Dig Holes
54	5.1.2	Pour Footings
55	5.1.3	Inspect Footings
56	5.2	Footings Passed Inspection
57	5.3	Lumber Delivered
58	5.4	⊟ **Preparing Lumber**
59	5.4.1	Cut Lumber
60	5.4.2	Treat Lumber
61	5.4.3	Pre-drill Holes in Lumber
62	5.5	⊟ **Framing Deck**
63	5.5.1	Run Wiring
64	5.5.2	Install Beams and Posts
65	5.5.3	Hang Joists and Ledger board
66	5.5.4	Install Decking
67	5.5.5	Assemble and Install Railing
68	5.5.6	Assemble and Install Stairs
69	5.6	Deck Construction Complete

Backyard Remodel WBS

Task Sheet

FIGURE 4-2 A WBS outline indents tasks at each level of the hierarchy to show summary tasks and work packages in a compact space.

PROJECT FILE The Project file for the WBS that's shown in Figure 4-2 is Backyard Remodel WBS.mpp and is found in the Chapter04 folder on the companion website.

SEE ALSO   For more information about project files, see "Companion Content," on page xxiii.

The Benefits of a WBS

If you try to perform a project with only a vague direction, like "Remodel the backyard," chances are good that you'll forget to complete an important task, or the workers won't understand exactly what they're supposed to do. Part of the power of a WBS is that it presents project work in portions that people can handle. But more than that, a WBS does the following:

- **Helps the project planners identify the work to be done and determine the best way to decompose the work**   For example, as you identify summary tasks and work packages, you can evaluate different ways to summarize the work to find one that works best for the project and your organization.

- **Helps stakeholders visualize the scope of the project**   A WBS provides an overview of the project, which stakeholders can review at any level of detail they want.

- **Shows the work defined by the scope statement in more detail**   A scope statement is only a high-level view of the boundaries of a project. A WBS exposes the detailed tasks that comprise the overall project scope.

SEE ALSO   The section "The Scope Statement," on page 33, describes a scope statement and provides tips for creating one.

- **Helps people understand their work assignments**   Team members appreciate clear instructions about what they are supposed to deliver. A work package communicates the extent of an assignment. The relationship of the work package to the rest of the WBS increases workers' commitment by showing how their efforts contribute to success.

- **Exposes additional work to be done**   Project deliverables that don't have corresponding summary tasks or work packages in the WBS are a warning that you haven't yet identified all the work that the project requires.

- **Helps the planners develop more accurate estimates of a project schedule and costs**   With smaller tasks, team members can better estimate the level of effort and the materials and equipment needed.

- **Provides a foundation for measuring progress**   Once you begin executing the project, work packages and summary tasks are not yet started, in progress, or complete. By breaking work into smaller components, you have more points at which you can accurately measure progress.

Building a WBS

Constructing a WBS can be a challenge, because you can often break down projects in different ways, even if the work you ultimately perform is the same. You can tame WBS creation by applying the same divide-and-conquer technique that the WBS itself represents.

How to Build a WBS from the Top Down

You can create a WBS more easily and more accurately with a few simple steps. The procedure boils down to starting at the top and working your way down, and then fine-tuning and verifying the WBS by working your way back up to the top.

Step One: Identify High-Level Tasks Using Project Deliverables and the Scope Statement

Because project deliverables document the tangible results that a project is supposed to provide, you start your WBS by creating high-level tasks for every project deliverable you've identified. For example, if a deck in the backyard is one project deliverable, create a high-level task for constructing that deck.

> **SEE ALSO**   The sections "Deliverables," on page 30, and "Success Criteria," on page 33, describe project deliverables and success criteria and why they are important to managing a project successfully.

You break down high-level tasks by detailing intermediate deliverables. For example, a construction permit and blueprints aren't end results for the backyard project, but you need tasks in the WBS to produce them.

Don't worry about organizing tasks into top-level and lower-level tasks at this point. Later on you'll review your WBS to see if a different arrangement of summary tasks and work packages makes more sense.

A scope statement is a high-level view of what a project will do. Compare the scope statement to the tasks you've already added to the WBS. If an item in the scope statement isn't yet present in your WBS, add a task for it now. For example, the scope statement in Figure 2-3 includes "Design the deck and patio, including lighting and landscaping; and produce detailed design drawings." This one scope item identifies several project tasks:

- Summary task for the design phase of the project

- Task for designing the deck

- Task for designing the patio

- Task for designing lighting and landscaping

- Task to produce detailed design drawings

Figure 4-3 shows a high-level WBS created by reviewing deliverables and the scope statement for the backyard remodel project.

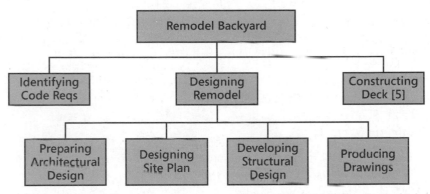

FIGURE 4-3 Project deliverables and the scope statement can provide ideas for the high-level tasks in a WBS.

Step Two: Fill In the Remaining Levels of Tasks That Make Up the Work in the Top-Level Tasks

For small projects, this step might be as simple as adding a few more tasks under each high-level task. The basic approach for identifying tasks at the next level is to ask what deliverables and tasks are needed to complete the summary task (sometimes called the parent task). Consider the top-level task Designing Remodel. What is involved in designing a new backyard? An architectural design, a site plan, engineering drawings for the structure, construction permits, and the approval of the client are all deliverables for the overall design. Add tasks to produce each of these deliverables.

> **TIP**
>
> If you're working on a large project and don't have a lot of time, the entire planning team can determine the top-level summary tasks for the WBS. Then, you can delegate decomposition of those top-level summary tasks to members of the planning team.

GOOD TASK NAMES

Task names that effectively communicate work are like poetry; they make their point in only a few well-chosen words. Every task name includes the desired result and the action that produces it. The deliverable is the noun in each task name, such as Site Plan. The action to produce the deliverable is the verb. For example, Identify Top 5 Risks clearly states the action and the desired result.

Weak task names reduce the effectiveness of a WBS. Task names without a verb leave the work to be performed in doubt. For example, a task name like Deck doesn't indicate whether the task is to design a deck, build it, or buy a new deck of cards for the Friday night poker game.

Vague verbs aren't much better. A task to analyze risks could go on forever, if you assign it to the worrywart on your team. Action verbs, such as identify or prioritize, communicate work more clearly.

Some project managers prefer to differentiate summary tasks from work packages by name. Because summary tasks represent ongoing activity, you can name summary tasks using the "ing" form of a verb (called a gerund if you want to impress your friends) and work packages with the present tense of the verb. For example, the design summary task might be Developing Structural Design, whereas one of the work packages is Select Components.

Consider the high-level task Designing Backyard Remodel. Here is the initial decomposition:

- **Preparing Architectural Design**   The design includes a deck, which means that the project needs an architectural design.

- **Designing Site Plan**   The project includes a design for landscaping the yard, although performing the landscaping is out of project scope.

- **Developing Structural Design**   Building a safe deck requires a structural design for the wood framing and foundation.

- **Preparing Final Drawing Set**   A set of drawings is required to show the client the design and to obtain a building permit.

- **Obtaining Building Permit**   The building permit is essential to begin construction.

Don't forget to include the project management tasks that you perform in the WBS. Although many project management tasks continue from project beginning to end, you need tasks to track the work you do.

BEST PRACTICES

Working initially in small teams is one of the best ways to build a WBS. If you have too many people involved at the beginning, you'll be herding cats: redefining work packages, changing approaches, and re-arranging summary tasks, yet rarely making visible progress.

Very large projects typically require a dozen or more levels to break down work into small enough pieces. In fact, the higher WBS levels often represent projects in their own right, each contributing major deliverables to the parent project—like the booster rockets, computers, communication system, and lunar module in the early space program. Put together a small group of people familiar with the entire project and knowledgeable in at least one of its aspects. This team can build the top two or three levels of the WBS. For instance, the managers from each department or company involved in the project can focus on the big picture tasks at the top.

When you reach the third or fourth level of the WBS, you'll need people with specific expertise to identify the work that is required. Delegate the further decomposition of these lower-level summary tasks to a smaller team, such as the structural engineering team that knows all the steps to preparing a structural design.

SEE ALSO   See the section "Creating the WBS in Project," on page 80, for tips on how to incorporate tasks from other teams into your project-wide WBS.

Step Three: Revise the Structure of the WBS

You can decompose most projects in more than one way. For example, one project manager might break a project into phases, such as planning, design, construction, and cleanup; whereas another might prefer to focus on completed products, such as houses, streets, and neighborhoods; or another likes to break work down by the department doing the work.

The groupings you use depend on your organization, the project objectives, and how you want to track progress. For example, breaking down work into construction phases makes it easy to track the work for different types of workers, such as carpenters, plumbers, painters, and landscapers. For massive construction projects such as building an airport, different companies are usually responsible for major deliverables. In situations such as these, you might break down the work into the subprojects that each vendor delivers: the terminal building, the runway, the baggage handling system, the parking garages, and final integration.

Revising the structure of the WBS provides a great opportunity to assemble the people who contributed to its construction. True, you'll have to play traffic cop to facilitate the meeting, but the interactions between experts and stakeholders can produce a more effective WBS and build more commitment to the project at the same time. In addition, the questions and discussions that people ask and talk about help identify missing work packages.

NOTE   Regardless of the structure you choose for higher levels of a WBS, the work packages remain the same.

Step Four: Verify the Structure of the WBS

The whole point of choosing a particular structure for a WBS is communication. The WBS is meant to help team members understand their assignments and help you to track progress. After you've revised the WBS, check that a summary task exists for each deliverable and that each summary task is important to at least one stakeholder. If not, you can safely move its work packages to another location in the WBS. For example, if a project includes a significant quantity of documentation, and the technical writing group manages documentation deliverables, a summary task called Producing Product Documentation makes sense. For a smaller project with one technical writer who works directly with the development team, you might include a work package for writing the users' guide within the summary task for developing the program.

TIP   In Project 2010, you can estimate from the top down using manually scheduled tasks, as described on page 123.

When to Stop Building a WBS

Work packages are like bowls of porridge in the fairy tale *Goldilocks and the Three Bears*. Work packages that are too big or too small are unacceptable—you want work packages that are just the right size. Large work packages make it difficult to get an accurate picture of progress. The team lead could reassure you that everything is on track for weeks only to ask for a two-month extension at the last minute. Work packages that are too small waste valuable time due to micromanagement. But how can you tell that a work package is just right?

Here are a few criteria for determining whether the WBS is at the right level of detail:

- **Progress and completion are measurable**   Work is broken down to a level so that status is easy to gauge at any point during the project.

- **Task duration is a reasonable length**   Break the work down to match your reporting periods (for instance, weekly or every other week). If you limit work packages to the length of your reporting period, work packages will be complete within two status-reporting periods. Many project managers like to break down work into packages that take between 8 and 80 hours (at least 1 day to no more than 2 work weeks).

- **Time and cost are easy to estimate**   Break work into portions that you can accurately estimate. For instance, you might have no idea how long it will take to build a house, but you do know that you'll need two days to tile the kitchen floor. After you've estimated the work packages, you can add up all your estimates to obtain totals for the whole project.

- **The work package has a clearly defined start and finish**   Decompose project work so that the start of each work package is triggered by another work package. In addition, a work package should have a clear indication of when it is complete, such as a deliverable or notifying a team member that a program is ready to test.

- **Work packages can continue without input from another task**   Once a work package starts, the work can proceed uninterrupted without the need for information or input from another work package.

- **The detail is at a level that you can manage**   Decompose project work only to the level of detail that you can and want to manage.

TIP	Most people can remember and work on up to five tasks without forgetting something. Even the most agile jugglers can rarely handle more than eight tasks, regardless of the help they get. To maintain focus on the work, limit your WBS to no more than eight levels. If the size of the project requires more than eight levels to reach the right amount of detail or duration, consider breaking the project into subprojects. The top-level project can have five to eight levels in its WBS, and each subproject can have its own multilevel WBS.

WHEN TINY TASKS ARE OKAY

Although tracking tasks that take less than a day would overwhelm most projects with excessive supervision and near-paralysis from nonstop status reporting, short tasks have their purposes. Consider a television nightly news show. In 30 minutes, the show hands off the limelight from the anchor to reporters in the field, the weatherperson, the sportscaster, and several commercial interruptions. Complex projects that must finish within very short time frames require a detailed execution plan, and work packages of very short duration are the answer. For example, installing software programs in a production environment with limited downtime is one example where short duration tasks are necessary. Besides identifying the intricacies of teamwork, short duration work packages quickly highlight delays.

Of course, a lot of planning goes into a television news show, and that planning isn't broken into minute-long segments. For projects with some complexity, only a small number of tasks will be short in duration.

Building a WBS from the Bottom Up

With small projects, you can identify project work from the bottom up. You assemble your team for a rousing session of brainstorming. If the project is small enough, the entire team can collaborate to identify work packages and assemble them into a WBS. For example, the team on the backyard remodel project identifies work package tasks, such as digging holes, pouring footings, cutting lumber, and so on. Then, you can then add summary tasks to group the work packages to make them easier to plan and manage.

An alternative approach is to work as a team to identify top-level summary tasks. Then, the team breaks up into smaller groups to identify the work for each top-level summary task. When the subteams are done, the entire team gets together to review the WBS, and add missing tasks, or remove redundant ones.

■ **WARNING** Building a WBS from the bottom up has a few disadvantages. When you start at the bottom, you might define work at too high or too low a level of detail. In addition, it's easier to forget some of the work when you don't use an organized approach to identifying tasks.

Recording a WBS

You can choose from several techniques for assembling the summary tasks and work packages for a WBS, depending on your work environment, the size of your team, and the programs that you prefer to use. Low-tech methods such as sticky notes on a whiteboard to high-tech methods such as using an LCD projector to show tasks as you build them in a Microsoft Office application can work equally well. Here are some methods to consider for your WBS deconstruction sessions:

- **Sticky notes**   Although sticky notes are low-tech, they're great for capturing tasks as your team shouts them out in rapid-fire fashion. Sticky notes are easy to move around as you search for the ideal structure for your project. Every team member can have a pad of sticky notes, so no one person is stranded as stenographer.

   You can use sticky flip chart pages to act as summary tasks. When you assign a work package to a particular summary task, place the small sticky note on the big sticky page containing that summary task.

■ **WARNING** Adhesive is the primary downside to the sticky note approach—specifically, its tendency to grow less sticky with time. Ideally, you should transfer the results of a sticky note session to Project or another program before you leave the meeting room. If you must transport your large sticky pages, fold and carry them very carefully so the WBS doesn't get rearranged during the journey back to your office.

■ **Microsoft Project**   If you plan a project on your own, you can build the WBS directly in Project, which saves you the step of transferring the WBS from another program when it's time to build the project schedule.

In Project, the Task Sheet pane on the left side of the Gantt Chart view is perfect for building an outline of your tasks. (On the Task tab, in the View group, click Gantt Chart to display the Gantt Chart view.) In the Task Sheet pane, you indent and outdent tasks to represent summary tasks and work packages. And you can move individual tasks or groups of tasks around as you rearrange the WBS structure.

> **SEE ALSO**   The next section, "Creating the WBS in Project," describes the steps you use to create a WBS in Project.

■ **Microsoft Word or Microsoft Outlook**   Because many team members don't have Project, they can use Word or Outlook to build task lists. Most team members are familiar with these programs. Team members can easily indent, outdent, insert, move, or delete tasks. In Project 2010, you can readily copy tasks from a Word document or Outlook email message and paste them into Project.

> **SEE ALSO**   The section "Pasting Tasks into Project," on page 83, explains how to copy tasks from another program into Project.

> **TIP**   As an alternative, you can use mind-mapping software, such as XMind or MindManager, during brainstorming sessions to capture the tasks identified by the team.

Creating the WBS in Project

Regardless of the method you choose to capture work packages and summary tasks, ultimately, you want your WBS in Project so you can turn it into a schedule. But before you can use Project task dependencies to link tasks to build a schedule, you need those tasks in Project at the correct level of the WBS. If you capture work on a white board or with sticky notes, you can type the tasks directly into Project.

SEE ALSO The section "Defining the Sequence of Work," on page 125, explains how to link tasks to put them into the correct sequence.

For all but the smallest projects, transferring handwritten tasks into Project represents a marathon of typing names and indenting tasks. In Project 2010, you can easily insert, rearrange, promote or demote, and delete tasks in the WBS as you go. Here are several techniques you can use to build your WBS in Project:

Summary

- **Insert a new summary task for subtasks you select.** To create a summary task that comprises several existing tasks, select the subtasks, as shown in Figure 4-4. On the Task tab, in the Insert group, click Insert Summary Task. (The icon label is "Summary" and the icon looks like a summary taskbar with a yellow asterisk.) Project inserts a summary task at the level of the selected tasks, indents the selected tasks to the next lower level, fills in the new task's Task Name cell with the text "<New Summary Task>", and selects the text so you can type the name of the new summary task.

- **Insert a new subtask.** In the row below an existing subtask, click the Task Name cell and press Insert. The new task is at the same outline level as the task you clicked.

- **Insert a new stand-alone summary task.** Click the Task Name cell in the row below the new summary task and then press Insert. Fill in the task name and press Enter. Select the task you just created, and then on the Task tab, in the Schedule group, click Outdent Task (a green left arrow) until the task is at the level you want.

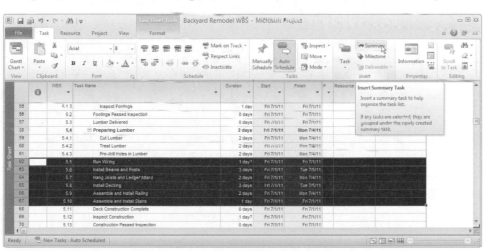

FIGURE 4-4 To insert a summary task for several existing tasks, select the tasks, and then use the Insert Summary Task command.

- **Change a summary task into a subtask.** Select the first subtask for the summary task. On the Task tab, in the Schedule group, click Outdent Task (the green left arrow).

- **Demote a subtask to the next lower level.** Select the task, and then on the Task tab, in the Schedule group, click Indent Task (the green right arrow). The task moves to the next lower level. The task above it changes into a summary task.

- **Promote a subtask to the next higher level.** Select the task, and then on the Task tab in the Schedule group, click Outdent Task (the green left arrow).

- **Move a subtask to another summary task.** Click the ID cell, which is the first column in the table, for the task that you want to move. When the pointer changes to a four-headed arrow, drag the task to its new location below the summary task that you want.

> **TIP**
>
> To indent, outdent, move, or delete several tasks at once, select all the tasks you want to work on simultaneously. (To select adjacent tasks in the outline, drag across the tasks; to select individual tasks, press and hold Ctrl, and then click each task.) Then use the methods in this section to modify the tasks.

- **Delete a subtask.** Click the ID number for the task to select the entire task row and then press Delete.

> **NOTE**
>
> If you select the Task Name cell and press Delete, Project deletes the text in the cell. However, if you click the Smart Tag with an X that appears to the left of the Task Name cell, choose the "Delete the entire task" option.

- **Delete a summary task.** To delete a summary task and all its subtasks, select the summary task, and then press Delete. Or right-click the summary task and choose Delete Task from the shortcut menu.

Pasting Tasks into Project

Pasting tasks is a real time-saver when team members build portions of the WBS in Word or Outlook. When you paste tasks from a Word 2010 document or an Outlook 2010 email message into a Project 2010 file, either program inserts the tasks and indents them based on the indenting in the Word document or email message.

1. To paste tasks into Project, open the Word document or Outlook email and select the tasks that you want to paste into Project (see Figure 4-5).

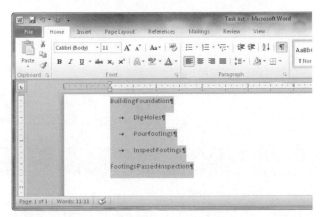

FIGURE 4-5 Select the tasks that you want to paste into Project 2010 in a Word 2010 document or an Outlook 2010 email message.

2. Press Ctrl+C to copy the tasks to the Windows Clipboard.

3. In Project 2010, click the blank Name cell in the table where you want to paste the tasks, and then press Ctrl+V.

    Projects inserts the task names into the Task Name cells and indents the tasks to the same level they were in the Word document or Outlook email (see Figure 4-6).

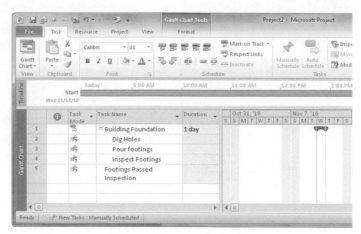

FIGURE 4-6 Project uses the indenting from the Word document or Outlook email message to determine the WBS level in the task list.

DISPLAYING A WBS AS A TREE

If you build a WBS in Project, you can transform it into a tree diagram using a Microsoft Visio–based Visual Report (if you use Project 2007 or later and also have Visio installed on your computer). The built-in Task Status Visual Report template gets you started, but you have to tweak the report to show the WBS levels you want to see:

> **SEE ALSO** For more information about generating and customizing visual reports, see the section "Working with Visual Reports," on page 233.

1. With the Project file open, on the Project tab, in the Reports group, click Visual Reports.

2. In the Visual Reports - Create Report dialog box, click Task Status Report, and then click View.

3. Select all the top-level tasks in the Visio diagram.

4. To expand the top-level tasks to show the next lower level in the WBS, in the Visio PivotDiagram task pane, in the Add Category section, click Tasks:Tasks (see Figure 4-7).

5. Repeat step 4 until you see all the WBS levels you want.

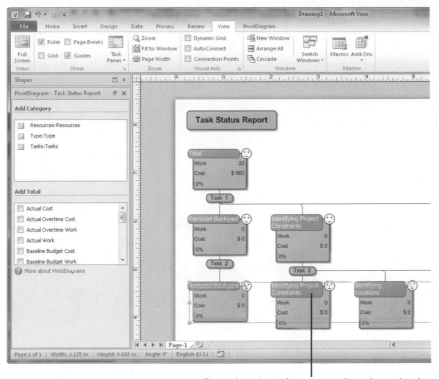

First select the tasks to expand to a lower level

FIGURE 4-7 Click the Tasks:Tasks category to shows another level of tasks in the WBS.

PROJECT FILE	The Chapter04 folder on the companion website contains a Visio visual report, WBS.vsd, which displays the WBS for the backyard remodel project.

Detailing Work Packages

If you ask your teenage son to clean his room, the results might not be what you had in mind. You can improve the chances that your son will meet your expectations by specifying that cleaning a room includes hanging up clothes, making the bed, vacuuming the carpet, dusting the furniture, and neatening the papers on his desk. Similarly, a brief name for a work package in a WBS isn't enough to tell team members about the project work they're supposed to perform. Documents that describe work packages in more detail help the team members assigned to the tasks do their work correctly and completely.

A work package document identifies the work to perform, how to tell that the task is complete, and how to tell if it was done correctly. If the details of work are documented elsewhere, a work package can be quite simple. For example, blueprints describe exactly how to frame a building or where to run wires. The work package can briefly describe the extent of the work, such as Frame First Floor Walls, but reference the blueprints or specifications for details.

Sometimes, work packages do require more detail. If work isn't described elsewhere, or the person assigned to the task is new, you should make the work package more specific. Creating a checklist of the subtasks that comprise a work package can guide junior team members through the work, but checklists also help more experienced workers to remember all the steps. For example, the work package for installing a new server in Figure 4-8 includes a checklist of tasks to perform, a completion state, and reference documents that the assigned resource could turn to should questions arise.

FIGURE 4-8 Work package documents provide the detail that team members need to complete their tasks successfully.

FAST ACCESS TO WORK PACKAGES

As the project manager, you can keep work package documents close at hand by adding a hyperlink from the task in the Project file to the work package document. To create a hyperlink in a Project task, do the following:

1. In Project, right-click the task that you want to link to a work package document, and then choose Hyperlink on the shortcut menu.

2. In the Insert Hyperlink dialog box, in the Link To pane, verify that Existing File Or Web Page is selected.

3. Navigate to the folder that holds the work package document and double-click the name of the work package file.

After you create a hyperlink, in the Indicators cell of the Task Sheet, you'll see a hyperlink icon, which looks like the earth with one link of chain. (If the Indicators column isn't visible, right-click the heading row of the table and choose Insert Column on the shortcut menu. In the drop-down list, choose Indicators.)

PROJECT FILE   In the Chapter04 folder on the companion website, you'll find a Microsoft Word template for a work package, which is called Work Package.dotx.

Summary

A WBS is an organized list of tasks required to complete a project, broken down from the highest-level summary tasks to the specific work packages that the project team must perform. It is the foundation for estimating work, choosing resources, building a project schedule, and eventually tracking progress. Small teams of people can tackle different areas of a WBS. A management team might work on the high-level WBS, whereas teams of experts might flesh out the lower levels and work packages. Regardless of how you develop a WBS, you can choose from several methods for getting the WBS into Project so it's ready for the next planning steps.

Project Resources

"Leadership is the art of getting someone else to do something you want done because he wants to do it."—DWIGHT EISENHOWER

PROJECTS ARE a lot like stage plays. People have their roles to play, and if someone forgets the lines, an awkward silence descends over the entire production. What's more, unless improvised conversations are part of the entertainment, the playwright, director, and producer might be unhappy about actors making up dialogue as they go. As a project manager, you must set the stage for your project, ensuring that team members know the parts they play and who is responsible for what.

In this chapter, you'll learn about the responsibility matrix and project organization chart—two documents that line up the participants for your project. The first identifies the groups that participate and the level of responsibility that they carry. The second shows the reporting structure for team members within the project team as well as to the organizations beyond the boundaries of the project.

But you won't get very far until you actually put together teams of people who do the project work. This chapter also discusses approaches for building a team of resources to perform tasks and then describes how to add those resources to a Microsoft Project file so you can assign them to tasks.

The Responsibility Matrix

The purpose of the *responsibility matrix* (sometimes called the *responsibility assignment matrix*) is to state, with no room for misunderstanding, who is responsible for different parts of a project and who has authority to make or approve decisions. Projects can suffer when *no one* accepts responsibility for activities. But they can also suffer when too many groups consider an activity as their responsibility, such as when subordinate or ancillary groups try to add their requirements to an already overburdened project. The responsibility matrix dramatically improves project communication, not only by identifying who's in charge and who's doing the work, but also by identifying groups that need to be consulted and those who merely need to know what's been decided.

The responsibility matrix *isn't* a detailed document of every person assigned to a project. It identifies the groups involved in a project and their level of responsibility for major portions of tasks and deliverables. That means you can put it together early in your project planning process, long before you identify the specific resources for your team, all the tasks in the project, or allocate resources to tasks. Here are a few of the benefits that the responsibility matrix provides:

- **Resolve conflicts over who's responsible**   Reviewing the responsibility matrix with stakeholders during project planning can identify areas of the project that have multiple groups who think they're in charge. By working through disagreements at the beginning of a project, before tensions rise and people have delineated their turf, you can resolve those conflicts *before* someone has to make an important decision.

- **Identify orphaned areas of the project**   If you hear someone say "I thought *you* were going to do that," who knows how many tasks represent work that groups consider someone else's responsibility? If the responsibility matrix shows that no one is responsible for doing the laundry, the project environment could get ugly—and smelly.

- **Clarify interaction between stakeholder groups**   Projects often require complex interactions between groups, each of which contributes to deliver the solution. The responsibility matrix outlines the interactions between groups, which is especially helpful in today's business world, with outsourcing, partnering, subcontracting, and other arrangements between organizations.

    For example, the telephone menu systems that you can talk to rely on a telephone network, voice recognition software, a software application for the menus of commands and the behavior they initiate, business systems that provide rules about situations like returns, and database servers that contain customer records. It's easy to end up with confusion about who does what when calls from customers who want to talk to customer service consistently get cut off. The responsibility matrix might show that the technical support group is responsible for troubleshooting problems and consulting other technical groups if necessary to resolve the issue.

Responsibility Levels

The responsibility matrix shows four levels of responsibility, from those who need to be notified when something happens to those who have the final say. However, the four levels are usually abbreviated to the acronym *RICA*:

- **R** indicates that a group is *responsible* for completing the work in a section of the project. For example, a high school junior who's applying to colleges is responsible for filling out the college application forms (regardless of how much he wishes his friends who write well would author his college essays).

- **I** stands for *inform*, which means that the group merely needs information about the task, such as the postal service, which needs to know where the student's mail gets forwarded when he's at college.

- **C** indicates that the group is *consulted* about decisions in a section of the project. The group participates in discussions about a decision or direction but isn't ultimately accountable. For example, a guidance counselor or relatives who attended the colleges in question can help the student decide whether the schools are a good fit, but beyond that, they don't have any authority in the decision.

- **A** stands for *accountable*. A group that is accountable can make decisions about the section of the project, approve deliverables or other group's decisions, and delegate groups to do the work. For example, the parents are accountable for their contribution to the cost of college. They can set the amount of money they can provide to pay for college, and if funds are limited, they might also be accountable for choosing a school that they can afford. Each college is accountable for deciding whether the student passes its entrance criteria.

> **NOTE** If your organization doesn't follow these types of responsibilities, you can still use this model to build your own version of a responsibility matrix using other responsibility levels.

Creating a Responsibility Matrix

The aptly named *responsibility matrix* is a two-dimensional matrix that links stakeholder groups in the columns with major sections of the project in rows, as shown in the example in Figure 5-1. In the cell at the intersection of a stakeholder group and a section of the project, you add the levels of responsibility that the group has over that part of the project.

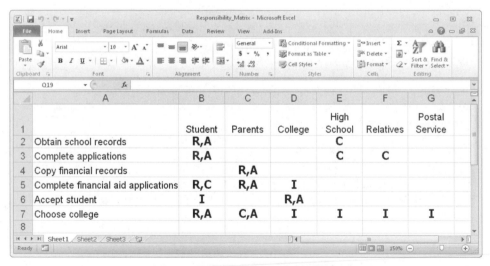

	A	B	C	D	E	F	G
1		Student	Parents	College	High School	Relatives	Postal Service
2	Obtain school records	R,A			C		
3	Complete applications	R,A			C	C	
4	Copy financial records		R,A				
5	Complete financial aid applications	R,C	R,A	I			
6	Accept student	I		R,A			
7	Choose college	R,A	C,A	I	I	I	I
8							

FIGURE 5-1 Because a responsibility matrix is like a spreadsheet with stakeholders in columns and project sections in rows, Microsoft Excel is a great tool for building one.

Here are some guidelines for choosing the stakeholders and project sections that you add as column headers and row labels:

- **Major sections or activities**   In the cells in the first column of the matrix, list the major sections of the project. The responsibility matrix is not where you identify who is responsible for each task in a project. For example, the items that you list in the project scope statement often correspond to the sections of the project that appear in the responsibility matrix.

- **Stakeholder groups**   In the cells in the first row of the spreadsheet, list the key stakeholder groups for the project. You don't add individual names, in part because you might not know them yet, and more important, because those assignments are made later when you build the project schedule. The only time you might add someone's name to the responsibility matrix is when that person alone completes a significant part of the project or is the only person who makes a decision.

TIP   Determining the groups for the responsibility matrix can be a challenge, particularly if you are managing a project in a large multinational corporation or one with complex politics. In these situations, you can turn to the project customer and project sponsor for help identifying the groups.

With the stakeholders and project sections identified, you can start filling in the cells in the middle. Stakeholders can play more than one role, so a cell shows every responsibility that a stakeholder group has for that section of the project. For example, a college is responsible for evaluating the student's application and has the final authority to decide whether to accept the student.

The Project Organization Chart

In addition to identifying the groups that are involved with the project, project team members also need to know the chain of command for the project. If a question arises or a decision is needed, who do team members go to? And if someone wants to escalate a problem that is taking too long to resolve, who should be called next? Most organizations use organization charts to document who reports to whom; similarly, projects rely on project organization charts to show the reporting structure for people involved with a project.

Project organization charts often show additional relationships besides the chain of command within the project. If you're managing a project that delivers a product to an external customer, the project organization chart shows some of the reporting structure within the customer's organization. For example, if the Director of Accounting who sponsored the project must report progress and performance to the Chief Financial Officer, who, in turn, reports to the Board of Directors, the project organization chart shows those reporting lines as well. Similarly, in organizations that use functional departments, people report not only to someone on the project but also to their functional managers.

Project organization charts are almost identical to regular organization charts, so you can use the organization chart template in Microsoft Visio to document the project chain of command. In Visio, on the File tab, click New. In the Template Categories section, click Business. To create a new organization chart, double-click Organization Chart. Visio creates a blank drawing and displays the Organization Chart stencil. You can drag and drop shapes onto the drawing to create the chart, as shown in the sample organization chart in Figure 5-2.

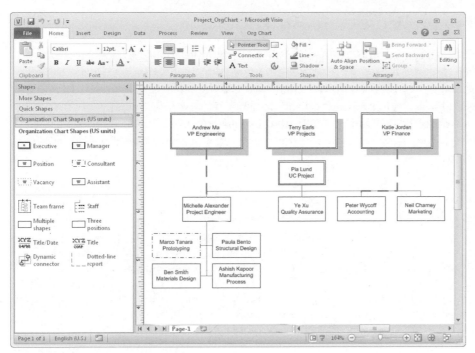

FIGURE 5-2 The Organization Chart template and stencil provide everything you need to build a project organization chart, including dashed connectors to indicate reporting outside the project.

PROJECT FILE   The project organization chart Visio drawing, Project_OrgChart.vsd, shown in Figure 5-2, is available in the Chapter05 folder on the companion website.

If you have information about the project organization in another program such as Excel, Microsoft Access, or a Microsoft Exchange Server directory, you can import names and titles from those programs into your Visio diagram. On the Visio 2010 Org Chart tab, in the Organization Data group, click Import and follow the steps in the wizard.   Import

Putting a Project Team Together

Early on in a project, a small team of people work together to define and plan the project. Once you have the work breakdown structure (WBS) defined, you're ready to line up the rest of the resources you need to do the work. As you identify the work that must be performed to complete project tasks and document it in work packages, you can identify the skills needed by the resources who do that work. Initially, it makes sense to identify resources by their skills: backhoe operator, copy editor, or senior Java programmer with financial background.

> **SEE ALSO** Chapter 4, "Building a Work Breakdown Structure," describes the work breakdown structure and provides instructions for creating one. To learn about specifying detailed instructions about the work to be performed, see the section "Detailing Work Packages," on page 85.

The members of the initial planning team typically remain involved with the project from start to finish, although they aren't necessarily dedicated full time to it. Here are some examples of people who help plan the project:

- **Project manager**   You are in charge of the project, so you focus on the plan that's being developed. You will be responsible for the scope, schedule, quality, budget, and other components defined during planning.

- **Facilitator**   Project planning meetings can become unruly, particularly if the project is political or affects multiple groups. A facilitator keeps the meeting under control and makes sure that the attendees remain focused on the agenda. The facilitator should be unbiased about the project and should understand the goal of the meetings. A project manager who is not connected to the project is a great candidate.

- **Customer**   The project customer (or a representative of the customer) might consider planning as your responsibility and not want to attend. You must convince the customer to attend or send a representative to the planning sessions to build buy-in to the plan, resolve problems, and address changes.

- **Project sponsor**   This person helps sell the project to the executive team and has the authority to drive the project from start to finish. The sponsor helps resolve issues and ensures that the plan being developed satisfies the project objectives.

- **Core team**   If you have a core group of people knowledgeable about the project and assigned to work on it, they are instrumental in estimating effort and identifying the types of resources required.

- **Functional managers and process owners**   Include the managers from the functional groups that are affected by the project. Functional managers have to buy in to what the project is going to do and the project deliverables. If a project affects processes, invite the process owners to the planning sessions so they can help develop a plan that integrates effectively with the existing processes.

- **Resource managers**   By inviting the resource managers who have the resources your project requires, you can get an initial commitment for the skill sets or other resources you need.

> **SEE ALSO**   The section "Working with Project Stakeholders," on page 39, describes the different types of stakeholders and their roles in a project. The section "Running Meetings Well," on page 285, describes the role of a facilitator in detail.

Obtaining resources that have the right skills or characteristics is usually a challenge. Some resources are simply scarce, such as a consultant who is an expert in physical and computer security issues and who is also fluent in German, Italian, and Japanese. Other resources might be more plentiful but still hard to obtain because every project uses them, such as a backhoe operator for construction projects.

As temporary endeavors, projects don't have resources of their own. Most of the time, you obtain the people who perform project work from functional managers in your organization, the project customer if you are performing a project for another organization, or through vendors and partners. Although it's tempting to ask for people you know are right for the job or you've worked with before, the better approach is to provide resource managers with work packages and assignment information. With the work package, the time frame, and any constraints such as cost, the managers can determine the best people for the assignments. And the side benefit is that you build relationships with those managers as someone who lets them do their jobs, not a prima donna who shows up demanding this and insisting on that.

GETTING RESOURCE ESTIMATES RIGHT

When you first build your project schedule, you won't know how many resources you need. As you craft work packages into a sequence of tasks, you estimate the number of resources you want to assign to those tasks. The trick is to assign enough resources to keep task durations shorter than centuries, but not so many that teamwork looks like a bumper car ride. From these generic skill-based assignments, you develop a preliminary plan of how many resources you need with different types of skills.

However, if the schedule is too long or too costly, you have to revise it. To shorten the schedule, you might add resources to some of the tasks. To reduce costs, you might replace resources with less expensive ones. The reality is that putting your project team together is an iterative process that begins with your initial schedule and continues until the project finishes.

After you successfully acquire resources for a project, the next challenge is keeping those resources assigned to your tasks. Assigning people to work 12-hour days and weekends not only increases overtime costs but also leads to burnout, errors, rework, and employee turnover—none of which is a characteristic of a successful project. Conversely, assignments that leave people idle for days on end are open invitations to lose those resources to other projects. Then, when you need those people, they might still be working on their other assignments, or in the worst case, laid off.

Assigning resources effectively is the antidote to all these problems. As you'll learn in Chapter 6, "Building a Project Schedule," estimating work accurately and assigning the resources you need based on their true availability produces a more realistic schedule. Fine-tuning the schedule to maintain more consistent workloads helps keep resources available and simplifies managing who should be doing what.

Optimizing resource allocation provides additional benefits that simplify project management in the long run. Functional managers will be more likely to assign their best resources when they have good information about assignments and confidence that the schedule is realistic. Team members are more likely to willingly accept assignments on projects that won't consume their every waking hour.

Creating Resources in Project

Before you can assign resources to tasks in Project, you must tell Project about those resources. You can start by specifying a few key fields, such as the resource name, the type of resource, and rate or cost. But Project includes many additional fields that you can use to fine-tune resource assignments, such as work resources' availability and codes that indicate the skills they possess. Unsurprisingly, Project provides several methods for entering information about resources. This section describes the different types of resources you can define in Project, how to add resource information to a Project file, and the information you can store about resources.

Types of Resources

Although people perform project work, you may need other types of resources depending on the type of project. For example, a conference requires meeting spaces, tables, chairs, meals, and handouts. A construction project requires equipment, such as backhoes, cranes, and saws; as well as materials, such as concrete, lumber, and hardware. Project 2010 uses work, material, and cost resource types to represent the different types of resources you need to complete projects:

- **Work resources**   People and equipment both count as work resources, because you schedule their time. For that reason, work resources directly affect your project schedule. Whether you need a giant construction crane or someone to jockey it around, the tasks in your project are affected by when those resources are available and how much of their time you can get. In most cases, the cost for work resources is based on how much of the resource's time you use, such as paying someone by the hour or renting a crane by the day.

- **Material resources**   Materials consumed during a project, such as concrete, steel, paper, and food, don't affect the schedule unless they don't arrive when they're needed. However, materials cost money. Unlike work resources, material costs are measured by quantity. In Project, you assign the quantity of materials you need, so the program can calculate the cost.

- **Cost resources**   Projects may incur other expenses, such as travel, training, meeting room rentals, fees, and so on. Project 2007 introduced the cost resource type to track costs that aren't related to hours worked or quantities consumed. You set up cost resources for the different types of expenses you want to track. Then, you can assign each cost resource you use for a task and specify its cost for that task. You can look at the total cost for a cost resource to see how much you spent on that expense.

SEE ALSO   Project also has budget resources, which help you compare your project costs to your budget. To learn how to use budget resources in this way, see Chapter 7, "Working with a Budget."

PROJECT MANAGEMENT TECHNIQUE

The human resources you need for a project typically start out as skill sets rather than specific names. Generic resources are like placeholders you can use to rough out a schedule and determine how many resources you need with different sets of skills. You assign generic resources representing skill sets to tasks in Project to estimate task durations and resource requirements. If the schedule takes too long or costs too much, you can modify resource assignments, such as adding resources to shorten duration, or using less expensive resources to reduce cost.

When the schedule, costs, and resource requirements look good, you can go to your management team to get specific resources. When you identify your flesh-and-blood team, you add them to Project as well. You can replace the generic resources with specific resources.

SEE ALSO   To learn how to replace generic resources with specific people, see the section "Assigning Resources to Tasks," on page 137.

Adding Resources to Project

For projects with only a few resources, the Resource Sheet view in Project displays a table with the most commonly used fields for resources. (To display the Resource Sheet, click the View tab, and then, in the Resource views group, click Resource Sheet.) However, if you work with dozens or hundreds of resources and store the information you need in another program, it's much easier to import data into Project.

Depending on the type of resource (work, material, or cost), fields in the Resource Sheet may contain different types of information. For example, material resources are priced per unit, such as gallon, cubic yard, or carton. For a material resource, the Material Label field is where you name the measurement unit and the Standard rate field shows the cost per unit. A work resource doesn't have a Material label, and the Standard rate field fills in initially as dollars per hour. As you can see in Figure 5-3, cost resources don't get a cost until you assign them to tasks, so the Standard rate field doesn't contain a value.

		Resource Name	Type	Material	Initials	Group	Max.	Std. Rate	Ovt. Rate	Cost/Use	Accrue	Base
12		Architect	Work		A		100%	$60.00/hr	$0.00/hr	$0.00	Prorated	Standard
9		Backhoe	Work		BH		100%	$300.00/day	$0.00/hr	$0.00	Prorated	Standard
15		Building Permit	Cost		BP						Start	
4		Carpenter1	Work		C1		100%	$50.00/hr	$0.00/hr	$0.00	Prorated	Standard
7		Carpenter2	Work		C2		100%	$50.00/hr	$0.00/hr	$0.00	Prorated	Standard
11		Client	Work		Cl		100%	$0.00/hr	$0.00/hr	$0.00	Prorated	Standard
13		Concrete	Material	Cubic Yard	Conc			$50.00		$0.00	Prorated	
5	◆	Crew Member1	Work		CW1		100%	$30.00/hr	$0.00/hr	$0.00	Prorated	Standard
6		Crew Member2	Work		CW2		100%	$30.00/hr	$0.00/hr	$0.00	Prorated	Standard
3		Drafter	Work		Dft		100%	$50.00/hr	$0.00/hr	$0.00	Prorated	Standard
10		Dumpster	Material		Dmp			$0.00		$450.00	Prorated	
2	◆	Engineer	Work		Eng		100%	$50.00/hr	$0.00/hr	$0.00	Prorated	Standard
8		Foreman	Work		F		100%	$50.00/hr	$0.00/hr	$0.00	Prorated	Standard
16		Inspection	Cost		Insp						End	
14		Lumber	Material	Linear feet	Lbr			$5.00		$0.00	Prorated	
1		Project Manager	Work		PM		100%	$50.00/hr	$0.00/hr	$0.00	Prorated	Standard
17		Travel	Cost		T						Prorated	

FIGURE 5-3 Some fields in the Resource Sheet apply to specific types of resources, such as the Overtime Rate for work resources and Material Label field for material resources.

Importing Resources

As you might expect, you can import resource information into Project as you can task information. Project accepts data from Access databases, Excel workbooks, XML files, and delimited text files. But you can also import resources directly from an Address Book or Active Directory.

Add
Resources ▾

For example, to import resources from an Address Book, on the Resource tab, in the Insert group, click the arrow to the right of Add Resources, and then click Address Book. (If your organization uses Active Directory to store information, click Active Directory to import resources from that repository.) In the Select Resources dialog box, you can choose the address book you want, such as your Outlook address book.

Excel provides the Microsoft Project Plan Import Export Template, which includes the Resource_Table worksheet with columns that map directly to Project resource fields. Here are the steps for creating and importing an Excel workbook of resource information:

1. In Excel, on the File tab, choose New.

2. Under Available Templates, click Sample Templates.

3. Click Microsoft Project Plan Import Export Template, and then click Create, as shown in Figure 5-4.

   Excel creates a new workbook with columns that correspond to the most commonly used Project resource fields.

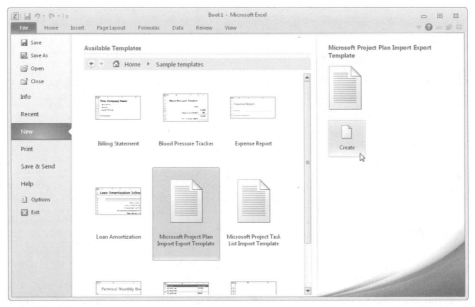

FIGURE 5-4 When Excel and Project are both installed on your computer, Excel offers the Microsoft Project Plan Import Export template and the Microsoft Project Task List Import Template.

4. At the bottom of the Excel window, click the Resource_Table tab.

5. Enter resource information into the appropriate cells, as shown in Figure 5-5, and then save the file when you're done.

FIGURE 5-5 Fill in the cells for the type of resource you are creating, such as Material Label for a material resource.

6. To import the resources from the Excel workbook, in Project, open your Project file.

7. On the File tab, choose Open and navigate to the folder that contains the Excel workbook with your resource information.

8. Below the folder list, click the Microsoft Project Files button, and then choose Excel Workbook, as shown in Figure 5-6.

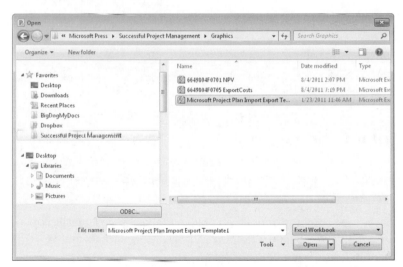

FIGURE 5-6 When you choose Excel Workbook, the dialog box displays all the Excel files in the folder.

9. Double-click the file name for the Excel workbook. The Import Wizard appears.

10. On the Welcome To The Project Import Wizard page, click Next. On the next page, select Project Excel Template, and then click Next.

11. On the Import Wizard – Import Mode page, select Append The Data To The Active Project, as shown in Figure 5-7, and then click Finish.

    Project imports the resources to your Resource Sheet.

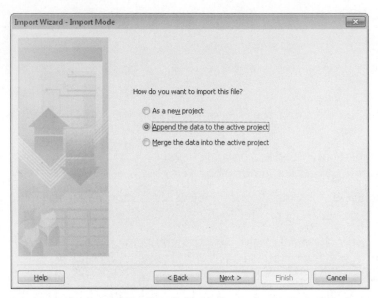

FIGURE 5-7 The Append The Data To The Active Project option tells Project to add the resources to blank rows in the Resource Sheet.

Resource Information

If you want to get the most out of Project, you can put a variety of resource fields to work. This section describes the most popular resource fields you can use and what they do.

Resource
Sheet

You can manually add resources to your Project file in the Resource Sheet. To open the Resource Sheet, on the View tab, in the Resource Views group, click Resource Sheet. The Resource Sheet (refer to Figure 5-3) appears.

If you don't see a resource field that you want to fill in, double-click a resource row in the Resource Sheet view to open the Resource Information dialog box, shown in Figure 5-8. You can also insert a column for a resource field in the Resource Sheet by right-clicking the table header, and then clicking Insert Column on the pop-up menu.

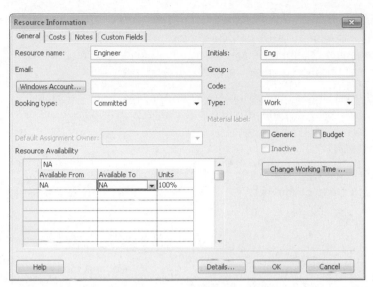

FIGURE 5-8 The Resource Information dialog box includes all resource fields, not just the ones visible in the Resource Sheet.

Basic Information

The two most important resource fields are Resource Name and Type, but other fields come in handy. Here are some guidelines for filling them in:

- **Resource Name**   If you are adding a resource that represents a job or skill set, fill in Resource Name with the job name, such as Carpenter. To add a real person, fill in the field using the format "Last Name, First Name." Project then displays people sorted by their last names, which makes it easier to find the people you want.

- **Type**   Project includes work, material, and cost resources. Work resources are those that contribute time to a project, such as people and equipment that you rent by the hour or day. When you create a work resource, Project automatically adds "/hr" to the value you type in the Std. Rate field. Material resources are physical resources that a project consumes, such as gasoline or lumber. When you set the Type field to Material, the value in the Std. Rate field is simply a dollar value. Cost resources represent other costs that don't fall into the work or material category, such as travel or fees.

- **Material Label**   For material resources, enter the units that the material comes in. For example, for gasoline, the Material Label might be Gallon.

- **Initials**   If you display the resources assigned to tasks in Gantt Chart view, full resource names take up a lot of space, particularly for tasks with several assigned resources. By typing initials or abbreviations in the Initials field, you can display compact resource identification on taskbars.

- **Max. Units (Maximum Units)**   For a work resource, the Max. Units field specifies the percentage of a workday that the resource is available, such as 50 percent to indicate that the resource works half-time.

> **SEE ALSO**   The section "Building Reality into a Schedule," on page 143, explains how to use Max. Units in more detail.

Cost Information

If you track project costs, you can define the pay rates or costs for work and material resources. Here is a summary of cost fields you can specify:

- **Std. Rate**   This is the pay rate for a work resource or the cost per unit for a material resource. For example, a work resource's pay rate of $50 per hour appears as $50.00/hr. For a material resource, type the price per unit, such as $2.85 for a gallon of gasoline, and then in the Material Label cell, type the unit of measure, such as Gallon.

- **Ovt. Rate**   This is the pay rate when a resource works longer than the standard workday. Some companies pay the same rate for overtime. Salaried employees don't get paid extra for additional hours they work. In either case, you don't have to use the overtime feature in Project and you can skip this field. Fill in this field only when someone is paid extra for overtime hours and you use Project's overtime feature to track them.

> **SEE ALSO**   The section "Calculating Costs in a Project Schedule," on page 168, provides step-by-step instructions for adding costs to resources.

- **Cost/Use**   This represents a fee that you pay each time you use a resource. For example, if you pay $400 each time you have to bring a crane on site, add that cost in the Cost/Use field.

- **Accrue At**   Tells Project when the project incurs a cost. Start represents a cost that occurs at the start of a task, such as the lumber that you pay for when it's delivered. End represents a cost that occurs at the end of a task, such as a consultant's fee that you pay only after the consultant's work is complete. Prorated shows the cost spread out over the duration of the task, which is typical for the labor costs associated with the people who work on tasks.

> **SEE ALSO**   The Resource Information dialog box has fields for five different rates for a resource, which is helpful for resources whose costs differ depending on the type of work or to reflect increases in wages that will take effect at some point in a project's schedule. See the section "Specifying Rates for Work Resources in Project," on page 171, for more information.

Resource Availability

Project provides two ways to specify when resources are available. In the Resource Sheet, you can choose a resource calendar in the Base Calendar field to specify working and nonworking time. For example, the Standard calendar as initially defined in Project shows working time from 8:00 A.M. to 12:00 P.M. and from 1:00 P.M. to 5:00 P.M. Mondays through Fridays. If resources work a different schedule, such as the night shift, you can assign another calendar, either a built-in calendar like Night Shift or one that you customize; for instance, with Monday through Saturday as working days.

In the Resource Information dialog box, on the General tab, click Change Working Time tab to specify working and nonworking time for only the current resource. On the General tab, the Resource Availability section enables you to specify the percentage of time that a resource is available over time. For example, if your construction workers are available 50 percent of the time between April 1 and April 30, 100 percent of the time between May 1 and October 31, and unavailable from November 1 through March 31, you can fill in rows of the Resource Availability table, as illustrated in Figure 5-9.

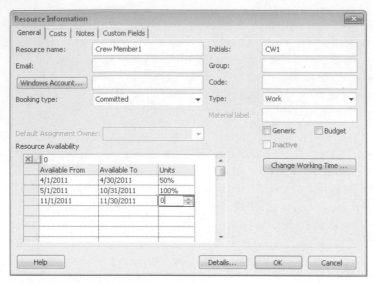

FIGURE 5-9 In the Resource Availability table, you can set the percentage of availability for a time period.

Categorizing Resources

Project offers two fields for categorizing resources. The Group field, which is visible in the Resource Sheet view, is useful if you want to sort, group, or filter tasks based on the department to which resources belong.

On the other hand, Outline Code fields (Project includes Outline Code1 through Outline Code10) enable you to build a hierarchy; for instance, to reflect the organizational structure of your company or the skill sets of the resources. For example, you could set up Outline Code1 to represent the reporting structure within your organization, such as Pres.Eng.Struct to represent the structural engineering department. To use an outline code to represent skills, you might set up Outline Code2 with one value, such as IT-Sys-UNIX to represent UNIX system administrators.

Custom
Fields

To set up outline codes for resources, on the Project tab, in the Properties group, click Custom Fields. In the Customize Fields dialog box, in the Type drop-down list, click Outline Code to view and configure the outline codes you can define. In addition to specifying whether the outline levels include letters or numbers, you can specify how many characters or digits each level can contain and the separators between the levels. You can also specify valid entries at each level to limit codes to the ones that you define.

You can apply a custom outline code to a resource in the Resource Information dialog box. Click the Custom Fields tab (refer to Figure 5-9). Resource outline codes that you've set up will appear on the screen. In the Value cell, type the code for the resource.

Summary

During project planning, you create the responsibility matrix to identify which groups are involved in different parts of the project, the level to which each group is involved, and, most important, who has the final say for that part. Then, when you begin building your project schedule, you'll also begin to identify the resources you need to perform the work. The project organization chart is like a regular organization chart, except that it shows who people report to both within the project environment and in their respective companies.

But to finalize a schedule in Project, you must assign resources to tasks, which means you must add resources to Project. You can specify resources in Project in several ways, depending on whether you have existing resource information and where you store it. You can also fill in only the basic information or specify resources in great detail.

CHAPTER 6

Building a Project Schedule

"Time flies. It's up to you to be the navigator."
—ROBERT ORBEN

WHEN YOU BUILD a work breakdown structure (WBS), you define the work the project team must do. After you've put your project team together, you know who you have to work on project tasks. To build a project schedule, you need a few more pieces of information: how much time each task is likely to take, the order in which the work must occur, exactly who does the work, and any constraints on the schedule, such as deadlines you must meet.

Time estimates for how long tasks should take can make or break a project. Underestimating and overestimating are both dangerous, but no one can predict the future with complete confidence or accuracy. In this chapter, you learn several ways to estimate project tasks. You also learn about estimation pitfalls to avoid and ways to improve your predictions.

Putting project tasks in the right order can be surprisingly easy or maddeningly difficult. For example, unless you're working in unusual gravitational conditions, building a foundation has to finish before you can start building anything on top of it. This chapter also describes the options you can choose for building a sequence of tasks and when to use each one. You also learn a few tips for building wiggle room into your schedule.

Until you assign resources to tasks, you don't know when tasks might start or end. You can define task duration first and then assign the resources you need to complete the work in that time frame. Or you can assign the resources that are available to determine how long tasks will take. Either way, those resource assignments complete your initial schedule.

This chapter shows you how to assign resources in Microsoft Project, regardless of whether you start with durations or hours of effort. It also identifies common misconceptions about resource assignments that can lead to unrealistic schedules—and how you can apply Project features to bring your schedule back to reality. In addition, you'll learn to use Microsoft Project features to build a schedule that's easy to maintain.

After you assign resources and balance their workloads, chances are stakeholders will tell you that the project has to be finished faster, for less money, or a combination of the two. You'll learn a few techniques for adjusting project schedules and how to do so using Microsoft programs.

> **SEE ALSO** Chapter 4, "Building a Work Breakdown Structure," describes several ways to break down the work that a project requires. Chapter 5, "Project Resources," explains the different types of resources that projects use and how to document them in Project.

Estimating

Estimating how long a project will take and how much it will cost is challenging for several reasons. Eternal optimists overestimate how much work can be done in a given amount of time. Other people are pessimistic and deliver high estimates to ensure that they cover all the bases. Unless you know who is who, you don't know which type of estimate you're getting. Another issue is whether the work you're estimating is familiar. For example, construction projects have a long history to back up estimates for new buildings. However, estimating how long it will take to build a rocket ship to take people to the next galaxy amounts to guessing because no one has done that before.

BEST PRACTICES

Decisions about which projects to run depend on good estimates, so you have to estimate project performance as best as you can. Low estimates and high estimates both can raise issues.

You might be tempted to give stakeholders the numbers you think they want to hear, but low estimates are a setup for bad business decisions. Low estimates undermine financial analysis. The first casualty is *return on investment* or *ROI*, which is the percentage return that a project delivers on the money invested in it. Lower work estimates equate to lower estimated costs, and thus, a more attractive ROI. For example, suppose your company requires an ROI of at least 15 percent. A low estimate might make a project appear to meet the required 15 percent ROI, but when the project is over, the ROI ends up at 8 percent. The company didn't earn the profit it expected from its investment in the project. Even worse, the investment could have been put to better use on a different project with a better and more likely ROI.

Optimistic estimates can make project teams miserable. Team members work hard to meet targets that, in reality, are unattainable, which damages morale and the will to succeed. As the project manager, you spend time trying to get projects back on track—when it was the estimates that were off track. And status meetings with stakeholders aren't much fun when projects are behind schedule and over budget, even if an unrealistic estimate is to blame.

Excessively conservative estimates are no better than optimistic ones. First of all, high estimates have a nasty habit of coming true. Whether team members take more time to increase quality, work at a more leisurely pace, or stakeholders ask for more features, projects often consume whatever time and budget they receive. An overestimated project might achieve its objectives, but it might not deliver as attractive an ROI as it could have with a more accurate estimate. High estimates depress project ROI, potentially below the minimum required. Or a drawn-out schedule delivers a product too late, so the company decides to cancel the entire endeavor.

Another insidious problem with overestimating is that *other* worthy projects get passed by. Most organizations use estimates to determine how many projects they can run in a year based on the resources they have and the project money that's available. A bloated schedule keeps resources tied up and squeezes other projects off this year's project roster. In turn, the organization won't earn the profit that those additional projects could have provided.

SEE ALSO   Choosing the projects that make the most sense financially depend on cost estimates and the resulting financial measures. Forecasted project costs are based on estimates of time and effort. Chapter 19, "Selecting and Prioritizing Projects," explains how to use project costs and financial measures to pick the right projects. You can learn more about these measures in the section "Understanding Financial Measures," on page 161.

Duration or Effort?

Before you start estimating project tasks, you have to make sure that everyone estimates the same thing. Duration and effort (that is, work hours) are not interchangeable, even though they are both measured in units of time.

Effort is simply the work time needed to perform the work. If you estimate that it takes 8 hours for a carpenter to construct the supports for a deck, the effort is 8 hours.

Duration is the working time between the start and finish of a task; in other words, the working hours the assigned resources work on the task, not including weekends or other nonworking time. Resources aren't 100 percent productive every work hour of every work day. Email, phone calls, meetings, breaks, and other interruptions can chew up 25 to 50 percent of a person's work day. For example, if the carpenter you assign to construct the deck supports works uninterrupted, the task duration is 8 hours, the same as the effort. Suppose other crew members ask the carpenter for help, which takes 4 hours. The duration for the deck supports changes to 12 hours, or 1.5 work days.

SEE ALSO   The section "Building Reality into a Schedule," on page 143, describes ways to modify resource assignments in Project to reflect productivity.

Duration is also affected by how many resources are assigned to the task and how much time those resources are available to work. For example, if you assign two carpenters full time to the task, the duration shortens to 4 hours. However, if you assign one carpenter who is available only 50 percent of the work day, the task duration lengthens to 16 hours, or 2 work days.

Adding resources shortens duration only up to a point. When you reach that point (called the crash point), the duration begins to go back up. In addition, the decrease in duration isn't linear as you add resources. Resources take time to come up to speed on the project and their assignments. In addition, each time you add a resource, the task involves more coordination and communication, so the total task effort increases. For example, a team of carpenters discusses how to construct the supports, talks about who does what, and trips over each others' lunch boxes.

TIP Some tasks can't be assigned to more than one resource. For example, as much as a pregnant woman would like to shorten her pregnancy, only one woman can carry a baby and the duration is nine months, give or take a few days.

Sensible Estimating Practices

The best way to get your estimates approved *and* see them become reality is by delivering realistic numbers and backing them up with data and analysis. The snag, of course, is how you get those realistic estimates in the first place. Estimating is both an art and a science, and mastering this skill takes time. This section introduces a few techniques that can help you reduce the inherent uncertainty of estimates and satisfy your stakeholders' desire for accuracy.

Get the Right People to Estimate

Good estimates start with experience. Someone who's never built a patio doesn't know the work involved or how long it takes. The people who estimate work have to understand the work that's being done. The best estimates come from the people who will do the work because they take into account their capabilities or limitations. For example, one programmer needs a week to get up to speed on a brand new assignment, whereas another needs only two days.

TIP   Commitment is another reason to obtain estimates from the people who do the work. Team members are more likely to try to meet the targets that they set themselves. However, it's impossible to include every team member in estimating large projects. Choosing knowledgeable people for estimating is the next best option. As long as team members consider estimates realistic, they work to meet them. But they're likely to give up if they're given unrealistic estimates that someone else prepared.

GET THE RIGHT NUMBERS

Asking several people to provide estimates is a good way to double-check your numbers. If one person estimates that developing a brochure takes 80 hours, and another tells you 40 hours, you can investigate to identify the discrepancy. For example, the 80-hour estimate includes the time for the writer, copy editor, and graphic artist; whereas the 40-hour estimate represents only the writer's time. The different values could also arise from assumptions about the resources' skill levels or productivity.

It doesn't matter whether you pick the estimated number of work hours (or days) or estimated duration and the number of resources for that time. However, if you have a preference, ask each estimator to provide you with the same kinds of estimates.

Estimating Methods

You can choose from different methods of estimating depending on the type of project and your organization's experience. The right method is the one that is likely to produce the most accurate estimate for the project at hand. Learning to identify the best method is a matter of experience. This section describes a few of the more common estimating approaches used:

- **Existing information**   Existing information can provide more accurate estimates based on the effort required for similar work performed in the past. It comes in several forms. If your organization keeps track of performance on previous projects, you can use actual data for similar work to estimate work on your new project. If you don't have an historical record of project data, you can estimate work based on what people remember from earlier projects. On the other hand, your organization may not have experience with a particular type of project, but others may. In that case, you can turn to experienced third-party vendors, consultants, or other experts to help you build your estimates.

- **Parametric models**   These models use factors to calculate the work and cost for a project, such as when contractors use square footage, and the time or cost per square foot to estimate a construction job. Because construction is well documented, the industry has many estimating programs and databases of typical construction costs to help builders with their estimates.

- **Program Evaluation and Review Technique (PERT)**   This is a method of estimating that looks at best, worst, and most likely results. It comes in handy when there are too many unknowns to estimate tasks with certainty. You can create schedules based on three different durations for each task to show project stakeholders the shortest, longest, and most likely durations for a project. By asking for best, worst, and most probable estimates, estimators think about the work more and take into account what could go wrong (or right). For example, you expect the task for pouring the foundation to take 5 days and the task for constructing the deck supports to take 2 days. However, if work goes incredibly well, the foundation might be completed in 3 days and the supports in 1 day. On the other hand, if the weather doesn't cooperate or other problems arise, the foundation might take 8 days and the supports 3 days.

- **The Delphi technique**   This technique uses the collective intelligence of a group of people to produce an estimate. With this approach, you ask five or six experts to produce estimates independently of one another. You share the anonymous results with the group and then ask each person to produce a second estimate. Repeat this step one or more times to further refine the estimates. Use the average of the last round of estimates as the final estimated value.

> **SEE ALSO**   Learn more about the Delphi method and variations of the basic approach at *http://en.wikipedia.org/wiki/Delphi_method*.

Estimating with Microsoft Excel

If you don't have an industry-specific tool to help you estimate project costs, Excel can calculate estimates based on parameters and formulas. For example, you can calculate the hours of effort by multiplying the square footage of a project by a factor.

Excel also comes in handy for estimating the most likely values when you use the PERT technique. As shown in Figure 6-1, you can fill in the worst duration, most likely duration, and best duration for each work package in a project. Then, you can either choose one of the values, for example, to use the pessimistic value for a task that almost always runs into trouble, or you can calculate a weighted average of the three values.

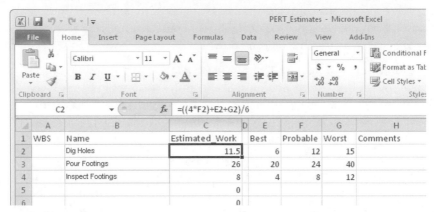

FIGURE 6-1 An Excel file can calculate the average of the three PERT values.

> **NOTE**   Project 2010 doesn't include the PERT add-in that was available in previous versions. You can use Excel to calculate more accurate estimates based on three values. If you want to harness the statistical power of PERT, you can use a third-party program that integrates with Project, such as @Risk for Project (*www.palisade.com*) or Risk+ (*www.deltek.net/products/riskplus/default.asp*).

PERT calculations typically apply a weighting of 4 to the expected duration and a weighting of 1 to each of the optimistic and pessimistic durations. You can change these weightings. For example, if you want more weight on the bad news, change the weighting to 4 for the pessimistic duration and 1 for both optimistic and expected.

> **PROJECT FILE**   A sample Excel file with PERT duration calculations, PERT_Estimates.xlsx, is available in the Chapter06 folder on the companion website.

Improve Estimates as You Go

Estimates are almost always a trade-off of accuracy versus time and money. If you want to estimate how long it'll take to get to your aunt's house for Sunday dinner, a quick review of the mileage and road conditions is enough to get you there with 20 minutes to spare either way. But if you're estimating the time you need to make your flight for a much-needed vacation, you might consider the mileage, road conditions, time of day, line at the ticket counter, line at security, terminal your flight leaves from, and whether you have to stop for gas. You can't afford the increase in ticket price for the next flight, and you don't want to think about missing your cruise ship.

Organizations balance these trade-offs all the time. They don't need absolute accuracy for early go/no-go decisions. But they're willing to pay for that accuracy when a fixed-price bid is in the offing. Here are typical levels of estimate accuracy and when you're likely to use them:

- **Go/no-go decisions**   These decisions require the least amount of accuracy. For large projects, feasibility studies often determine if a project moves forward; and whether the issue is cost, timing, or technology. Organizations spend some time and money up front so they don't waste lots more later on a dead-end project. Without feasibility studies, order-of-magnitude estimates are sufficient for early go/no-go decisions. For example, your client wants to build an office building that'll cost no more than $6 million and take no longer than a year. You can roughly estimate the usual cost and time per square foot for office construction to determine whether the time and budget is achievable.

- **Project selection**   This level requires more accurate estimates. To calculate potential finish dates and performance measures, you need to know something about the project scope and objectives, but not necessarily the entire project plan. For example, the scope is a 20,000-square-foot office building, but you don't know whether it will be a single-story or multistory building. At this point, you can estimate the schedule within a few months and a few million dollars.

- **More stringent project selection**   This level requires even more accurate estimates, often produced after organizations fund projects through initial planning. For example, with a list of project objectives and scope on which all the stakeholders agree, you can develop a WBS and estimate the work required with reasonable certainty. After you know that the building has four stories, you can refine your estimate.

- **Project milestones**   Milestones such as the completion of a phase, are good times to reevaluate estimates. When you have the final drawings for the building and construction bids in hand, you can estimate every construction task to tell your client that the building is going to take nine months and $5 million. When the steel framing is complete—a few weeks late—you can adjust your estimate if you can't make up that time on finish work.

BEST PRACTICES

Perhaps the most important aspect of estimating is setting realistic stakeholder expectations, which wouldn't be difficult if everyone waited patiently until you finished your analysis and deemed your estimate complete. The problem is that stakeholders, executives, and managers seem to ask for estimates before you know enough to prepare them.

Suppose you're riding the elevator to your office on Monday morning, looking forward to your first cup of coffee and semiconsciousness, when the project sponsor steps on, smiles, and casually asks, "How's the project schedule shaping up? Any idea when you expect the project to finish?" You hesitate, knowing that the answer you give will either help or haunt you to the last day of the project.

Ballpark estimates are almost always too soon (for the finish date) and too low (for resources and costs). Without your planning documents, you can easily forget a few big tasks or hundreds of small details that make up a complete project. Unfortunately, stakeholders tend to remember the estimates that you provide under friendly pressure.

Instead of providing a ballpark estimate, say something like "We haven't finished our analysis yet, but I should be able to answer your question in [fill in the amount of time]." What the questioners won't admit is that they're just fishing. They don't expect you to give them an answer, but if you do, they're happy to hold you to it. If you feel as if you must give a ballpark estimate, give yourself contingency funds to account for the risk you're taking. Similar to the premium pricing that businesses request to offer a fixed-price bid, a ballpark estimate should be your most conservative estimate multiplied by a safety factor.

The Problem with Padded Estimates

If you assume that project delivery dates and costs follow the typical bell curve, you have a 50-50 chance of staying within the bounds of the budget and schedule—not very comforting odds. And because tasks always seem to take longer and cost more, bringing a project in on time and within budget looks difficult, indeed. Some people try to gain an advantage by padding their estimates—adding extra time to their tasks so they can recover from unexpected problems. True, padding increases individuals' chances of delivering to their estimates, but if each level of management adds its own padding, the resulting estimates look like sumo wrestlers by the time the project sponsors see them. Padding games usually end badly. One of the most common padding practices is when managers cut every number they receive, assuming they're padded. Team members remember that their last estimates were cut so they thicken the padding the next time around. The final numbers end up the same, but the cycle of padding and cutting grows longer and trust drops lower.

BEST PRACTICES

Padding that's public is a different story. Savvy stakeholders, executives, and project managers work together to reserve some money to act as a margin of safety for schedule and budget. Instead of every person or group having personal padding, the project shares a smaller pool and distributes the padding only to those who need it.

Project contingency funds are like the contingency funds a bank requires when you build a house, which is money reserved to resolve issues that might arise, such as price increases. Contingency time on a project works the same way. You set some time aside before the ultimate due date in case delays occur. Contingency funds and time are intended to handle known risks. You know they can happen. What you don't know is how bad they'll be if and when they do.

Management reserve is a safety margin for unknown risks—potential problems that aren't in your risk-management plan. Management reserve time and money doesn't appear in a project plan, but management can dole it out at its discretion—without having to ask sponsors or customers for more.

SEE ALSO   Chapter 15, "Managing Risk," discusses how to use contingency planning and management reserve as part of a risk-management strategy. Another approach is to add buffers to summary tasks so that all the subtasks can take advantage of the same pool of padding. Page 123 describes how to use manually scheduled tasks to add buffers to a project schedule.

Bottom-up Estimating

Bottom-up estimating starts at the bottom—the work packages for a project. You estimate the effort and cost for every work package and roll up the estimates at each level of the WBS until you have an estimate for the entire project. Project makes it easy to generate bottom-up estimates because summary tasks automatically roll up the cost, work, and duration of their subordinate tasks into totals.

If you estimate a project from the bottom up by figuring the time needed for each work package, it's easy to forget about the additional time you need for communication and distributed collaboration. The time that tasks take increases exponentially with project size and complexity. As you add people to a project, you have to factor in more time for communication and collaboration. Geographically distributed teams increase complexity and time. Despite email, instant messaging, and collaboration websites, working with people in other places or time zones introduces delays. For instance, team members might have to wait for colleagues on the other side of the world to start their work day to resolve an issue. Even walking to meetings on a sprawling campus can eat up project time.

If your project is complex in some way, it's a good idea to increase your estimates to handle that complexity. Unfortunately, there's no handy guideline for choosing a complexity multiplier other than your experience or historical data. Because Project doesn't have a feature to incorporate complexity, increase your estimates for complexity *before* you enter any values in Project.

Top-Down Estimating

Top-down estimating involves breaking up a project into pieces and gradually allocating time and cost to smaller and smaller components. Top-down estimates are accurate only if you start with reasonably accurate top-level estimates, so this method is best if your organization has performed similar projects in the past. For example, if your company has remodeled dozens of backyards in the past, you can use past projects to estimate that this remodel will take 3 months and about $30,000. From those high-level numbers, you can allocate time and dollars to the lower-level components, such as 3 weeks and $6,000 for building the deck.

> **SEE ALSO** The next section, "Top-Down Planning," describes how you can use manually scheduled summary tasks in Project 2010 to compare your top-level estimates to more detailed estimates for work packages.

Top-Down Planning

Sometimes, the project customer or the management team may tell you how long they want your project to take. You estimate the work to see whether it can be done in that timeframe. One approach to this type of top-down planning is to create summary tasks using the estimates that you get from management and create work package tasks using estimates you get from your team. Then, you compare the duration of the sequence of work packages to the summary task duration. If a summary task has a longer duration than its work packages, you're all set. If the work packages take longer, you either figure out a way to shorten them or go back to management to request more time.

In Project 2010, you can use manually scheduled summary tasks for this type of top-down planning. Manually scheduled summary tasks are also helpful when you want to build buffers between phases or major components of your schedule. Follow these steps to use summary tasks in either of these ways:

1. To change an existing summary task to manually scheduled, display the Entry, Summary, or Schedule table. In the Task Mode cell for the summary task, click the down arrow and choose Manually Scheduled.

Summary

To create new summary tasks as manually scheduled, first click New Tasks in the status bar at the bottom of the Project window, shown in Figure 6-2, and then click Manually Scheduled. All new tasks are created as manually scheduled until you change this setting. To create a new summary task, on the Task tab, in the Insert group, click Insert Summary Task.

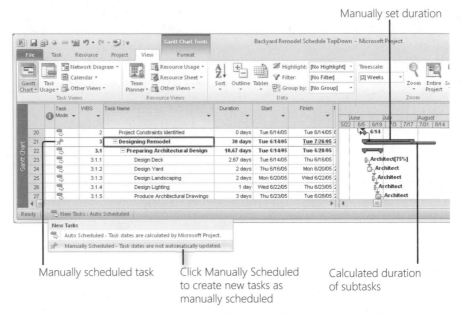

Manually set duration

Manually scheduled task

Click Manually Scheduled to create new tasks as manually scheduled

Calculated duration of subtasks

FIGURE 6-2 A pushpin icon appears in the Task Mode cell for manually scheduled tasks.

2. Type the duration in the summary task's Duration cell, such as the duration that the management team gave you.

The summary task bar changes to match the duration you entered. The second narrow task bar immediately below the summary task bar, shown in Figure 6-2, represents the rolled-up duration of all the subtasks. If the subtask duration is shorter than the summary task duration, the rolled-up task bar is blue. If the subtask duration is longer than the summary task duration, the rolled-up task bar is red to indicate that the summary task isn't long enough. If a subtask finishes later than the summary task finish date, the subtask task bar is bordered with a dashed line, and red squiggles appear under the summary and subtask finish dates to indicate a scheduling problem.

> **NOTE** If you want to add a safety buffer to a manually scheduled summary task, first find the duration for the subtasks. Total the subtask duration and the buffer you want, and type the new duration in the summary task Duration cell.

Defining the Sequence of Work

Now that you know the work you must do and how long it should take, a project schedule also requires the order in which the work must be done. As tempting as it might be, college students can't take four years of courses in one semester and party the remaining seven semesters. Partial differential equations won't make much sense without calculus as a foundation. Furthermore, there aren't enough hours in the day to attend all those classes and do all that homework.

The ideal schedule in Project is one that mirrors real life and adjusts automatically as you change task values. If one task experiences a delay, all the tasks that follow it are delayed as well. To achieve this ideal, every dependency that exists between tasks in real life must exist in the Project schedule as well. The next section describes the different options for linking related tasks in a schedule.

Types of Task Dependencies

Although tasks connected by dependencies are called successors and predecessors, a *dependency* is really about control not chronology. A dependency between two tasks specifies how one task controls the scheduling of the other, not which one comes first. The independent task (called the *predecessor*) determines the scheduling of the dependent task (the *successor*); and the predecessor can occur before, at the same time, or after its successor. You can choose from four types of dependencies:

- **Finish to start**   This is the most common type of dependency. It's also the easiest to understand, because control and timing follow the same order. When the predecessor task finishes, the successor task begins. For example, when a construction crew finishes setting up the forms for a concrete foundation, the crew starts pouring the concrete into the forms.

- **Start to start**　In this dependency, the start of one task triggers the start of the second. Start-to-start dependencies often come with a delay (called a *lag*) between the tasks. For example, a road crew starts placing traffic cones to close a lane on the highway. Ten minutes after the crew begins, the line painting machine starts painting lines in the closed lane.

- **Finish to finish**　In this dependency, one task continues only as long as another task is in progress. For example, traffic flaggers stop directing traffic when construction work is complete.

- **Start to finish**　This dependency is confusing, but it isn't needed very often. With start-to-finish dependencies, the start of the predecessor controls the finish of the successor. The confusion arises because, in most cases, the predecessor occurs *after* the successor. For example, if you start evaluating requests for proposal (RFPs) on December 1, that date controls when vendors stop working on their RFPs. They deliver their documents in whatever state they're in and hope for the best.

Identifying the Correct Dependency Type

You've probably heard the adage about everything looking like a nail when you're holding a hammer. Don't fall into the trap of thinking that the start of every task is triggered by the finish of another. Although the majority of task dependencies are finish to start, many tasks connect to others with the other three dependency types. You can identify the best type of dependency for less common situations by asking a series of simple questions. If you typically think about timing when choosing dependencies, ask the following questions about control to identify the correct dependency type:

- **What does this task need before it can start?**　Identifying predecessors is usually easier than finding successors. Ask this question to find the tasks that act as predecessors for the task you're evaluating. With the predecessor and successor identified, you know which two tasks to link.

- **Does the start or finish of the predecessor control the successor?**　The answer to this question determines the first half of the task dependency type. For example, if the finish of the predecessor controls the successor, the dependency type must be either finish to start or finish to finish.

- **Does the predecessor control the start or finish of the successor?**　This question finalizes the type of dependency. For example, if the answer to question 2 is "finish" and the answer to this question is "start," the dependency type is finish to start.

LAG AND LEAD

In real life, tasks don't always follow each other immediately. Sometimes, there's a lag between tasks, and at other times, they overlap (called *lead*). In Project, you can further qualify the dependency between two tasks with a lag. For example, if you can't begin to paint until the primer has dried, the finish to start includes a 4-hour lag. To define an overlap between two tasks, you use a negative value for lag.

Adding lag time to task dependencies is perfect for showing waiting time (like concrete curing) or overlaps. In Project, you can define lag with either duration or a percentage of the duration of the predecessor task.

Creating Task Dependencies

If you've ever calculated start dates, finish dates, and slack by hand, you already know the value of task dependencies in Project. When you create a dependency between two tasks, Project uses that relationship to recalculate the schedule whenever durations, start dates, or finish dates change. Building a schedule is simply adding all the dependencies between tasks, and they appear in the proper order. When you're done, the top-level project summary task shows the overall duration of the project (which is known as the *critical path method*, or *CPM*).

Because task dependencies are the foundation of scheduling in Project, it's no surprise that you can choose to create task dependencies in several ways. Here are the most common techniques and when they come in handy:

- **Using a Microsoft Project task form** This technique is the most flexible way to create dependencies. You can choose any type of dependency or add lag to the links. On the View tab, in the Split View group, choose More Views. In the More Views dialog box, click Task Form or Task Details Form, and then click Apply. As demonstrated in Figure 6-3, the start of the footing inspection lags 5 days after the footings have been poured.

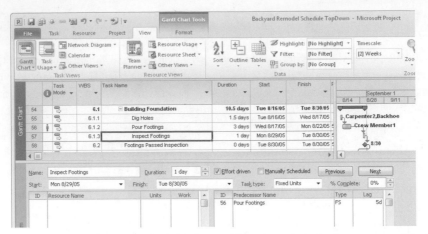

FIGURE 6-3 A task form includes fields for specifying the task dependency type and the lag between the two linked tasks.

- **The Link command**   This is the easiest way to create a finish-to-start dependency, which is the dependency you're likely to apply most often. Select the predecessor task, then select the successor task, and finally, on the Task tab, in the Schedule group, click the Link icon. Using the Link command is also helpful when you can't see both bars in the Gantt Chart at the same time.

- **Dragging between two tasks**   If you can see the bars for both tasks in the Gantt Chart (refer to the Dig Holes task in Figure 6-3 to see an example of a Gantt Chart bar), dragging from the predecessor to the successor gives you a visual cue that you're creating the dependency correctly. You see a link from the predecessor to a link of chain on the successor, and a box pops up showing you the finish-to-start dependency you'll create when you release the mouse button.

> **SEE ALSO**   The drawback to dragging between task bars is that you can create date constraints by mistake. The section "Keeping Dependencies Flexible," on page 129, describes how you can end up with unintended date constraints and how to get rid of them.

AUTOMATED DEPENDENCIES

Project can adjust dependencies for you as you modify tasks—which can be a help or a hindrance. When you create a new project schedule in Project, the program automatically selects the Autolink Inserted Or Moved Tasks check box in the Project Options dialog box.

These automated dependencies can be a great timesaver. You can insert, remove, and rearrange tasks and let Project add or modify the dependencies for you. With this option selected, when you insert a new task between two tasks, Project automatically removes the dependency between the two original tasks and creates finish-to-start dependencies to link the original predecessor to the new task and the new task to the successor.

If you want to control the dependencies between tasks, clear this option's check box. For example, you might want to reposition a task under a different summary task while maintaining all its current task dependencies.

To turn off automated dependencies, do the following:

1. On the File tab, choose Options.
2. In the Project Options dialog box, click Schedule.
3. Under the heading Scheduling Options For This Project, clear the Autolink Inserted Or Moved Tasks check box.
4. Click OK to close the Project Options dialog box.

Keeping Dependencies Flexible

When project execution begins, your project takes on a life of its own. The schedule that you carefully crafted during planning becomes obsolete almost immediately. To keep up with changes regardless of how many or how quickly they arrive, you need a flexible schedule in Project.

However, if you're new to Project, you might set specific start and finish dates to tasks or apply date constraints, such as the date when a task must finish; these constraints throw flexibility out the window. Even more frustrating, some scheduling shortcuts add date constraints that you don't realize you're creating. This section describes how date constraints can ruin your scheduling flexibility and how to use them properly along with other Project features to keep your schedule responsive to change.

The Right and Wrong Way to Use Date Constraints

People new to managing projects may start by setting the start dates for tasks instead of linking them to predecessors and successors. By doing so, they will have to change the start dates manually if the predecessors take longer than planned. Another pitfall is using the Finish No Later Than constraint in Project to represent a deadline. Unfortunately, this date constraint does not ensure an on-time delivery.

However, date constraints do have their place in a schedule. When you have restrictions on when tasks can occur, date constraints are exactly what you need. For example, suppose someone is on vacation until September 22. You can assign a Start No Earlier Than date constraint set to 9/22/2011 for tasks that resource works on. Project will ensure that those tasks start on or after 9/22/2011.

The Task Details Form contains the fields for setting date constraints. On the View tab, in the Split View group, choose More Views. In the More Views dialog box, click Task Details Form in the Details drop-down list, and then click Apply. As demonstrated in Figure 6-4, the start of the footing inspection is set to start no earlier than 9/7/2011.

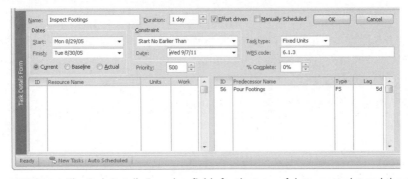

FIGURE 6-4 The Task Details Form has fields for the type of date constraint and the constraint date.

Setting Specific Start and Finish Dates

Sometimes, tasks must occur on specific dates, such as a conference, training class, or meeting with a very popular consultant. A date constraint can fix either the start date or finish date, but not both. With Project 2010 manually scheduled tasks, you can set the start date, finish date, or both, to the specific dates you want.

Although you can set an option to specify the scheduling mode you want to use by default, you can change the scheduling mode for tasks any time you want:

1. On the View tab, in the Data group, click the down arrow to the right of the Tables icon, and then click Entry, Schedule, or Summary.

   By default, the Entry, Schedule, and Summary tables include a column labeled Task Mode. To include the Task Mode field in another table, right-click a column heading and then choose Insert Column. In the drop-down list, choose Task Mode.

2. Click the Task Mode cell for the task you want to change, click the down arrow that appears, and then click Auto Scheduled or Manually Scheduled.

   If you set a task to manually scheduled, the Task Mode cell displays an icon that looks like a pushpin, as shown in Figure 6-5. The Auto Scheduled icon looks like a task bar with a right arrow. The task bar style in the timescale changes to show whether the task is manually or auto scheduled, also shown in Figure 6-5.

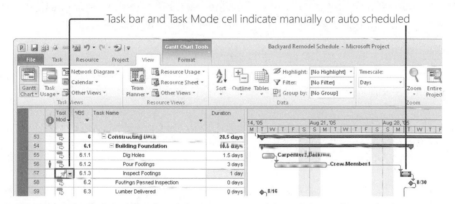

FIGURE 6-5 The Task Mode cell and the appearance of the task bar indicate whether a task is manually or auto scheduled.

> **NOTE** The scheduling mode is available only in Project files saved in the Project 2010 file format. If you open a file created with an earlier version, you can see but can't change the value in the Task Mode cell. If you save a Project file to an earlier file format, manually scheduled tasks revert to automatically scheduled.

Setting Deadlines

Deadlines are dates that you don't want to miss, but some deadlines are harder than others. For example, tax returns are due on April 15, but you can file for an extension with the Internal Revenue Service if your return isn't ready. However, if your company faces a $5 million penalty for delaying the opening of a new airport, you'll do everything you can to meet the deadline date. In Project, date constraints don't ensure that your schedule successfully meets required dates, so the deadline feature is a better way to keep track of crucial dates. Project calculates the schedule based on the task dependencies you've set, and highlights missed deadlines with an indicator.

To add a deadline to a task, do the following:

1. Open the Task Information dialog box by double-clicking the task for which you want to add a deadline.

2. Click the Advanced tab.

3. In the Deadline text box, type the deadline date. You can also click the down arrow to display a calendar and then click the date.

4. Click OK.

When you add a deadline to a task, Project displays an outlined arrow at the task's deadline date in the Gantt Chart view, as demonstrated in the Assemble and Install Stairs task in Figure 6-6. If the Gantt bar for the task ends before the outlined arrow, it meets the deadline. But the task is late if its bar ends to the right of the green arrow. Project displays a red diamond with an exclamation point inside it in the Indicators column to make missed deadlines obvious.

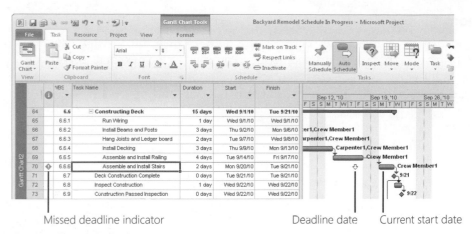

Missed deadline indicator   Deadline date   Current start date

FIGURE 6-6 Project displays an arrow to show a task deadline and displays a warning indicator if the task is scheduled to miss its deadline.

Adding Schedule Milestones

Milestones highlight important project events whether they are hard deadlines or flexible dates. In the days of yore, a milestone was literally a stone that marked one mile from the last stone. For people working on projects, milestones don't measure distance, but mark progress, events, or achievements, such as the completion of a phase, a delivery of materials, or a payment for work performed.

In Project, the distinctive black-diamond shape for milestones provides easy-to-see cues for all kinds of events. You can use milestones to draw attention to significant events without worrying about delaying your project. In Project, milestones are tasks that have zero duration, so you can add as many milestones as you want without affecting finish dates one second.

Types of Milestones

The last task in almost every project schedule is a milestone because it clearly shows the finish date: early, late, or right on time. However, milestones work equally well for many types of events. The following sections describe several uses for milestones.

Decisions

Moving forward on a project often depends on a decision. Many organizations commit to projects one phase at a time and decide to proceed to the next phase only if the results from the previous phase are acceptable. A milestone can act as the gatekeeper for these crucial decision points in a project, as Figure 6-7 illustrates.

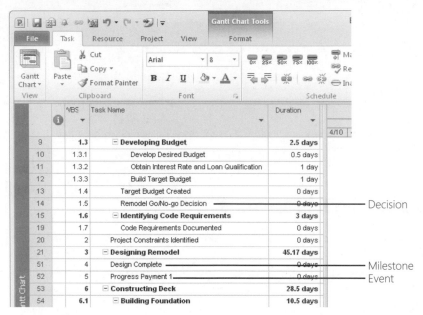

FIGURE 6-7 Milestones can represent decisions, events, or progress in a project.

- **Decision**   For many projects, particularly those with high risk and significant cost, estimates or feasibility studies might determine whether a project receives funding to continue. The estimating or feasibility study tasks link to a milestone, which represents the go/no-go decision. If the project is canceled, the milestone represents the end of the project. If it receives approval to continue, the successors to the milestone begin.

  Some choices aren't as final as go/no-go decisions, but they affect a project so significantly that work can't continue until the choice is made. For example, construction on a house can't begin until the homeowner chooses the builder. A milestone for this type of decision makes it easy to delay the work that follows if the decision takes more time than you expect.

TIP An approval is a special case of a decision milestone. Often, additional work can't begin until previous work has been approved, such as when a county building inspector must approve the electrical wiring before the drywall crew starts finishing walls. Approvals can act like go/no-go decisions or as starting milestones for additional work.

■ **Project start**   Starting a project with a milestone makes it easy to reschedule the entire project should the kickoff date change. For example, if the board of directors doesn't approve your project during its May meeting, you can move the entire schedule simply by changing the date for the starting milestone to the date of its August meeting.

Progress

The true progress for a project is hidden within its work packages, but you can view overall progress with milestones at key achievements throughout the life of a project. Just as a milestone is helpful at the beginning of a project, it's handy at the end of a project as well, particularly if the finish date is crucial to success.

SEE ALSO See the section "Setting Deadlines," on page 132, to learn how to track deadlines in a project.

Typically, you want to see progress long before you reach the end of a project. Keeping a project on schedule is much easier if you have checkpoints regularly spaced between the start and end dates. If you reach an interim milestone only to find that you're behind schedule, you can take corrective action while there's still time to recover. For example, if you're building a new superhighway, you could create milestones for every mile of road, so you aren't surprised by a multiyear schedule overrun.

TIP Milestones are also handy for highlighting handoffs between teams. Although handoffs usually occur at existing project milestones, such as the end of a phase, a milestone indicating whenever a handoff occurs notifies the new owners of their responsibilities.

Events

You can use milestones to show brief events that occur during a project. For example, if you hold an ice cream social for your team once each quarter, you can add a milestone on that date. As long as the event is short in duration, you don't have to bother setting its duration or assigning resources to it.

> **SEE ALSO** See the section "Setting Specific Start and Finish Dates," on page 130, to learn how to tie an event to a fixed date.

Deliveries

Many projects have external dependencies that are just as important as the work done by the project team. If you don't manage the work and simply expect deliveries on specific dates, milestones are the answer. For example, you don't manage the people at the building supply company who assemble the lumber order for the backyard remodel—but you want the lumber on site in time to begin construction. You can use milestones for any kind of external dependency: deliveries of raw materials, preassembled components, equipment, or the rockets for the next space shuttle launch.

Creating Milestones

 Milestone

Creating milestones is easier than creating work tasks. On the Tasks tab, in the Insert group, click Milestone. Project 2010 inserts a new task with the name <New Milestone> and sets the Duration to 0 Days. The task shape in the Gantt Chart changes from a bar to a black diamond. And because the duration is zero, you don't have to assign any resources to the milestone—unless you want the milestone to appear in reports or views filtered by resource.

> **NOTE** To change an existing task to a milestone, click the task's Duration cell and set its duration to 0 Days.

NAMING MILESTONES AND DELIVERABLES

When you add milestones to your schedule, the diamond shapes only help distinguish milestones when you view the Gantt Chart. Using different naming conventions for milestones, work tasks, and summary tasks makes it easy to tell tasks apart wherever you see them.

Milestones often relate to project deliverables. For example, design drawings are a deliverable, but the approval of those drawings might be a milestone that triggers a progress payment. To name milestones, begin with the deliverable name and add an adjective, such as Design Drawings Approved.

Assigning Resources to Tasks

You can choose from several ways to assign resources. The method you choose depends partly on the details you want to specify for the assignment and partly on preference. The following sections describe several ways to assign resources.

SEE ALSO To learn how to modify resource assignments, see Chapter 13, "Modifying the Project Schedule."

Assigning Resources in the Task Sheet

If you want to add only one person to a task and assign that person with her maximum units, the Task Sheet is the easiest place to do so. All you have to do is choose the resource name in the task's Resource Names cell. Project automatically assigns the resource to the task with the resource's maximum units from the Resource Sheet.

SEE ALSO To learn what maximum units represent, see the section "Creating Resources in Project," on page 99.

Here are the steps for assigning a resource in the Task Sheet:

1. If the Gantt Chart view is not visible, on the Task tab, in the View group, click Gantt Chart.

2. If the Resource Names column is not visible in the table, on the View tab, in the Data group, click the down arrow to the right of the Tables button, and on the submenu, choose Entry.

3. In the table, click the Resource Names cell for the task to which you want to assign a resource, and then click the down arrow that appears on the right end of the cell.

4. In the list, select the check box for the resource you want to add, as shown in Figure 6-8.

   If you want to add additional resources, select their check boxes.

5. Press Enter. Project assigns the resource to the task. If the resource's maximum units are 100 percent, all you see in the cell is the name of the resource. However, for any other value of units, Project displays the percentage in the cell after the resource name, such as Carpenter [50 percent].

TIP When you assign resources in the Task Sheet, you can copy resources from one task to another. For example, if several consecutive tasks use the same resources, position the pointer over the lower-right corner of the first task's Resource Names cell. When the pointer changes to a plus symbol, drag over the rows that use the same resources.

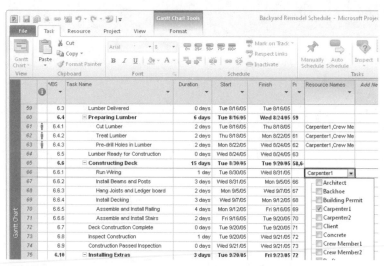

FIGURE 6-8 You can assign one or more resources directly in the table by selecting the check boxes for the resources in the drop-down list in a task's Resource Names cell.

Assigning Resources in the Task Form

If you want to assign one or more resources with different units, a task form (Task Form, Task Details Form, or Task Entry) is easier to use than the Task Sheet. You can add several resources, each with its own units and work.

How you assign resources to tasks depends on whether you created those tasks in Project by specifying task duration or the estimated work for the task. For example, if you create tasks using estimated work, the task duration is the length of time the task will take with one resource working on it. If you assign more than one resource, you want the duration to decrease to reflect the additional people working. On the other hand, if you estimate task duration, you also estimate how many resources you planned to assign. In this case, you want the task duration to remain the same as you add the number of resources you planned.

If the Task Form isn't visible, on the View tab, in the Split View group, select the Details check box. In the Details drop-down list, click Task Form.

TIP You can switch views between one pane and two. If only one pane is visible, double-click the rectangular box immediately below the vertical scroll bar to display the bottom pane in the view. To switch to a single pane, double-click the horizontal divider between the two panes.

Here are the steps for adding resources when you want the task duration to remain the same:

1. In the table, select the task to which you want to assign resources. The task information appears in the Task Form in the bottom pane.

2. In the Task Form, click the first blank Resource Name cell, and then, in the Resource Name list, choose the name of the first resource you want to assign.

3. If you want to assign a resource at a specific unit percentage, click the Units cell in the same row and type the percentage, such as 50 percent for Carpenter1 in Figure 6-9.

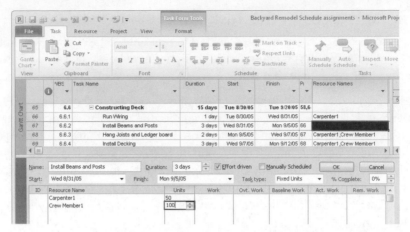

FIGURE 6-9 You can specify resources' units or the number of hours they work.

TIP

If you want to assign the amount of time that the resource spends on the task, click the Work cell and type the number of hours, days, or other periods. If you specify both the units and the work, Project recalculates the task duration automatically.

4. To add another resource, click the next blank Resource Name cell. Repeat steps 2 and 3 to assign the next resource.

5. After you assign all the resources, click OK.

    The task duration doesn't change. If you didn't specify values in the Work cells, Project calculates the work for each assignment based on the units for each resource and the task duration, as shown in Figure 6-10.

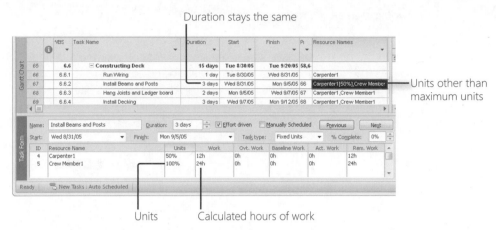

FIGURE 6-10 Project calculates the work for each assignment, while keeping the task duration the same.

If you created your tasks with duration equal to the estimated effort, you want the task duration to decrease as you add resources to the task. When you use effort-driven scheduling, Project keeps the total amount of work constant as you add or remove resources. Here is how you take advantage of this behavior to adjust the task duration as you add resources:

1. In the table, select the task to which you want to assign resources. The task information appears in the Task Form in the bottom pane.

2. In the Task Form, select the Effort Driven check box, if it isn't already selected.

3. In the Task Form, click the first blank Resource Name cell, and then, in the Resource Name list, choose the name of the first resource you want to assign.

4. Click OK to save the task.

   Project calculates the total work based on the task duration and the resource's units. For example, if you assign one resource to a 3-day task, the total work is 24 hours.

5. To add another resource, click the next blank Resource Name cell and choose the second resource. If you want to assign the resource with different units, click the Units cell and type the percentage.

6. Repeat step 5 for each additional resource you want to assign.

7. After you assign all the resources, click OK.

Project keeps the total work for the task the same, but recalculates the task duration based on the resources assigned and their units. For example, as shown in Figure 6-11, the total work of 24 hours is reallocated so each of the 3 assigned resources works 8 hours and the task duration decreases to 1 day.

FIGURE 6-11 Project keeps the total work the same and adjusts the task duration when you add or remove resources.

Assign
Resources

Using the Assign Resources Dialog Box

The Assign Resources dialog box, shown in Figure 6-12, has all kinds of helpful features for assigning resources. To open this dialog box, on the Resource tab, in the Assignments group, click Assign Resources. In the Assign Resources dialog box, you can choose resources by clicking the cells to the left of their names. But you can do a lot more:

■ Click the plus symbol to the left of Resource List Options to filter the list of resources you see. For example, you can locate resources who have enough time available to perform the task. When you click the plus symbol, it changes to a minus symbol, as shown in Figure 6-12.

■ Click Replace to replace the selected resource with a different one, for instance, when your carpenter goes to the hospital after an accident.

■ Click Graph to see how much work the resource has or the time that the resource is available.

> **TIP**
>
> ✓ Unlike many of Project's other dialog boxes, which don't let you work in other parts of Project until you close them, the Assign Resources dialog box is especially useful because you can leave it open while you work in the Gantt Chart or other windows.

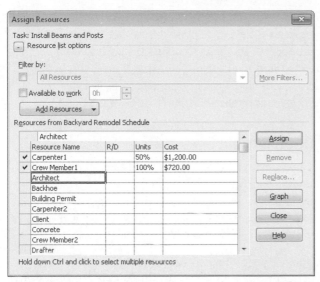

FIGURE 6-12 The Assign Resources dialog box is the most powerful tool for assigning resources.

> **NOTE** The Team Planner view is new in Project 2010 Professional. Team Planner shows each resource in the project in a separate row with the tasks to which they're assigned in a timescale. Unassigned tasks are grouped at the bottom of the view. You can drag an unassigned task to the resource's row to assign it to that resource. Drag a task from one resource to another to reassign the task. If you're manually scheduling a project, the Team Planner view is a handy way to assign or reassign resources to tasks.

Building Reality into a Schedule

The initial schedule you build based on estimated effort is an ideal rarely achieved in real life. Your initial work package estimates don't tell the whole story. You have to consider whether factors such as project complexity or remote project teams warrant increasing estimates before you enter tasks into Project. To make matters worse, team members' productivity may be reduced when they attend training, take vacations, or work on several assignments at once. In addition, people simply aren't 100 percent productive every working hour.

To deliver on time, you must take resource issues into account when you build a project schedule. For example, if the blasting crew is having a "blast" elsewhere and you don't trust the carpenter to remove some bedrock, you have to adjust the schedule for when the blasting crew is available. Understanding the factors that expand project schedules is only the first step to building a realistic schedule. Project offers features you can use to model these alternate realities and this section tells you how to apply each one.

Accounting for Nonproject Time

One of the most dangerous project scheduling assumptions is that team members who work a 40-hour week actually spend 40 hours on their assigned project tasks. Attending staff meetings, filling out time sheets and insurance forms, and picking up snacks for the team uses up work time—sometimes reducing productive time by 25 percent or more of each day.

Work environments can affect productivity, too. Project teams that are scattered on several floors of a high-rise building might spend time riding different elevator banks to meetings. Or a cube next to a loud and persistent sales rep could dramatically reduce someone's output.

If you schedule your project as if resources are always productive, your schedule is doomed to come in late. But good morale is another advantage to scheduling based on actual productivity. If you assign resources at 100 percent, most people have to work a 10-hour day to keep up. When you assign resources with the time they really have available, the team members know that you're doing the right thing and that, in itself, can boost productivity.

In Project, you can model productivity in a couple of ways. The easiest approach is to redefine the standard 8-hour work day to 6 hours, but that hides the problem with productivity. The more effective approach, which keeps the productivity level in view, is setting the units that resources work when assigned to a task. For example, to schedule team members for 6 hours of project work in each 8-hour work day, in the Task Form, set a resource's Units field to 75 percent. As you can see in Figure 6-13, reducing resource units from 100 percent to 75 percent increases a 2-day duration to 2.67 days.

TIP   Instead of specifying lower units for every assignment, you can reduce your resources' maximum units in the Resource Sheet. That way, Project 2010 automatically fills in the reduced maximum units when you assign a resource to a task.

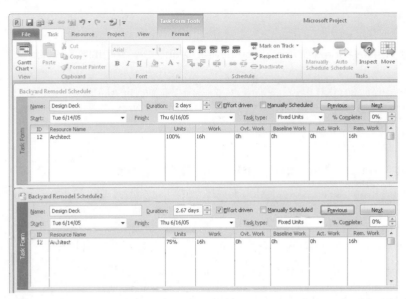

FIGURE 6-13 Setting units for task assignments changes the duration of tasks while showing the level of productive time.

TIP If your company work day is 9 hours, you can change the default calendar to show 9-hour work days. Don't forget to change the default setting for the hours in a day. On the File tab, click Options. In the Project Options dialog box, click Schedule and type a new value in the Hours Per Day text box. You can also change the default hours per week or the number of working days in a month.

If you change the units you use for resource assignments, explain the apparent shrinkage of the work day to stakeholders or the functional managers who might wonder why you aren't using their people full time.

Adjusting Tasks for Resource Productivity

The resources you obtain can affect the task durations you estimate. If you're lucky enough to get the fastest carpenter, the 80 hours of work you estimated might take only 60. If you have to make do with a less-experienced resource, the hours of work and task duration have to increase to reflect that the novice doesn't get as much done.

When you replace the assigned resource, adjust either the task duration or the value in the resource's Work cell to your new estimate. Add a note to the task explaining the reason for the change. (Right-click the task and click Notes in the shortcut menu.)

■ **WARNING** Sometimes, physical constraints limit the scheduling you can do. For instance, if you have only three hammers, assigning more than three carpenters to the same task ends up with someone standing around. Add notes to your project tasks about these limitations, so you don't ignore them when you're trying to shorten project duration.

Managing Part-Time Workers and Multitaskers

People who work part-time make tasks take longer because they don't work 8-hour days to begin with. For example, working half-time doubles task duration. If someone works part-time, you must modify his maximum units in Project. For example, the maximum units for someone who works half-time is 50 percent.

Here are the steps for setting a resource's maximum units:

Resource
Sheet

1.   On the View tab, in the Resource Views group, click Resource Sheet.

2.   In the Resource Sheet window, in the Maximum Units cell for the resource, type the percentage that the person usually works, such as 50 percent for half-time.

People who work on several tasks at once spend only a portion of their time on each task. You might think assigning them to tasks is simply a matter of making sure that the units assigned add up to no more than their maximum units. But pulling people in too many directions comes with a hidden penalty. Each time they switch tasks, they have to reorient themselves and those small delays add up.

The best way to prevent this productivity drain is to limit the number of tasks that someone works on simultaneously to no more than three or four. To look for times when a resource is overcommitted, run the Who Does What When report. Generate this report by doing the following:

1. On the Project tab, in the Reports group, choose Reports.

2. In the Reports dialog box, click Assignments, and then click Select.

3. In the Assignment Reports dialog box, click Who Does What When and then click Select. When the report appears, look for weeks in which the resource has hours assigned to several tasks.

Scheduling Around Nonworking Time

One of the serious drawbacks of team members is that they don't work 5 days a week every week of the year. Even if you reduce resource units to account for training, company-wide meetings, and paperwork, you still have holidays, personal days, sick days, and vacations to consider. In Project, you use *calendars* to set the working days and nonworking days that the program uses to schedule work. Project doesn't schedule work to occur on days you define as nonworking time.

You can apply calendars with working and nonworking days to your entire organization, to specific resources, or to specific tasks:

- *The Standard calendar* that comes with Project applies to every project and task you create and every resource you assign. You can modify the Standard calendar to reflect your organization's holidays and time off that applies to everyone, such as a two-week closure at a manufacturing plant, shown in Figure 6-14.

  To modify the Standard calendar, on the Project tab, in the Properties group, click Change Working Time. In the For Calendar list, select Standard (Project Calendar). (If a task-oriented view, such as the Gantt Chart, is visible, Project automatically selects the Standard calendar in the Change Working Time dialog box.) Modify the dates and click OK to close the dialog box.

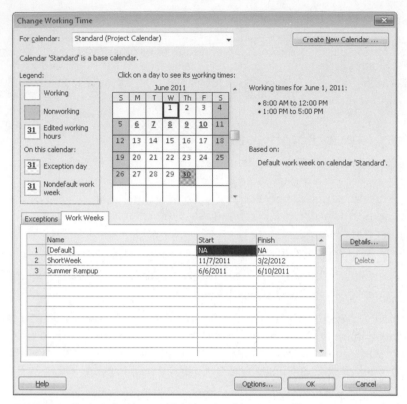

FIGURE 6-14 Project displays working days in white; nonworking days are gray and underlined; and nonstandard working days are shaded and underlined.

■ *Resource calendars* apply to specific resources that you use. If you schedule tasks around people's vacations, you can create a resource calendar for each person and change the vacation days to nonworking days.

To modify a resource calendar, on the Project tab, in the Properties group, click Change Working Time. In the Change Working Time dialog box, in the For Calendar list, choose the resource whose calendar you want to change. Modify the dates and click OK to close the dialog box.

TIP   Unless you want to spend your days updating resource calendars in Project, you're better off using reduced resource units in task assignments to account for sick days and personal days.

- *Task calendars* are ideal for tasks that run during standard nonworking time. For example, if you run computer backups over the weekend, a calendar specifically created for the backup task won't affect resources or other tasks.

    Setting a task calendar works differently from the Standard and resource calendars. Before you can apply a calendar to a task, you must create the calendar in the Change Working Time dialog box. Click New, name the calendar (for instance, Backups) and specify the working and nonworking time. For example, the Backups calendar might show every weekend as working time and every weekday as nonworking time. Click OK to close the dialog box.

    To assign the calendar to a task, in the Gantt Chart, double-click the task to open the Task Information dialog box. Click the Advanced tab. In the Calendar list, choose the calendar for the task and click OK.

Identifying Nonworking Time with Workweeks and Exceptions

Work weeks in a Project calendar identify which days of the week are working and nonworking days, as well as the work hours for each working day. You can define as many work schedules as you want for the same Project calendar, like a shorter summer work week and the standard work week for the rest of the year. Defining a work week is perfect if a work schedule spans several weeks or months. You create the work week and specify the dates when the work week is in force. You define work weeks on the Work Weeks tab, in the Change Working Time dialog box, and then click Details to modify the work hours.

> **NOTE** A work week applies to one contiguous date range. If you want to use the same work schedule in the summer of 2011 and again during the summer of 2012, you have to define two different work weeks.

Exceptions are another calendar feature. They're great for nonworking time, such as holidays, but they also work for some alternate work schedules. For example, you can define exceptions for half-days before holidays. You can also create recurring exceptions, for example, to schedule a one-week plant closure the last week of every calendar year. You have to name each exception you create and specify the date range to which it applies.

Shortening a Project Schedule

Most of the time, the schedule you build finishes later than stakeholders had hoped. Before you start looking at paying people overtime or working the weekends, there are a couple of alternatives that can shorten schedules.

Regardless of which method you use to shorten the schedule, the tasks on the critical path are the first place to look. The critical path is the longest sequence of tasks in a project, which means the finish date for the critical path determines the finish date for the project. The critical path has no slack, which is the amount of time a task and its predecessors can slip without affecting the finish date of the project. The critical path gets its name because the project will be delayed if a delay occurs on the critical path. However, any decrease in the duration of the critical path means the project finishes sooner.

TIP The tasks that belong to the critical path can change if some tasks take longer or shorter than planned. For example, if a one-week task that isn't critical turns into a four-week task, that delay could make the task critical.

The Fast-Track to an Early Finish

You *fast-track* a project by scheduling tasks to run concurrently that were originally scheduled one after the other. Although they don't know it, the people you see driving to work while simultaneously drinking coffee, shaving, and reading the newspaper are fast-tracking their commute. And much like those harrowing trips, fast-tracking comes with its share of risks. However, fast-tracking can shorten a schedule without increasing cost.

Projects usually have tasks that you can overlap with few issues. For example, if you're painting a room, one person can finish painting the walls while a second person starts painting the trim around the windows. The problems arise when decisions made in overlapping tasks affect work that's already been completed; for example, in a construction project that pours the concrete foundations while the architects complete the final design. If a part of the design requires concrete in a different location, some rework is in order. The other problem with fast-tracking is that the overlaps between tasks leave less time to recover when something goes wrong. You might have no choice but to slip the schedule, reduce the quality, change the scope, or increase the budget.

Choosing Tasks to Fast-Track

The most effective way to fast-track a project is to overlap tasks on the critical path. To get the most from fast-tracking, check the longest tasks on the critical path for fast-tracking, as shown in Figure 6-15. They provide the largest potential decrease in duration with the fewest number of risks to manage and the fewest number of changes to the schedule.

Project makes it easy to find your attractive fast-track candidates. To find the longest critical tasks in Project, do the following:

1. To display all the tasks on the critical path, on the View tab, in the Data group, click the down arrow to the right of the Filter box; and then, in the Filter list, choose Critical. Project displays critical path tasks as solid red bars.

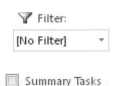

2. Hide summary tasks so you see only the critical work tasks that determine the duration of the project. On the Format tab, in the Show/Hide group, clear the Summary Tasks check box.

3. To sort the critical path tasks by duration, click the down arrow to the right of the Duration heading, and then click Sort Largest to Smallest.

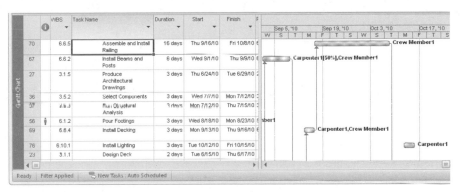

FIGURE 6-15 Looking at the longest critical path tasks shows you the best tasks to overlap.

4. After you identify critical tasks with long durations, remove the Critical filter (choose the All Tasks filter) and re-sort your schedule by a field such as WBS or ID.

Partial Overlaps

Most of the time, you fast-track a project by starting the next task before its predecessor is complete. For instance, you might tell the crew to start installing decking before all the supports are in place. In Project, these partial overlaps are easy to add—all you have to do is apply a negative lag to the dependency between the two tasks.

You can edit a dependency by double-clicking the link line in the Gantt Chart view. If your schedule link lines look like spaghetti, an alternative is to double-click the name of the successor task in the Task Sheet. In the Task Information dialog box, click the Predecessors tab to see the predecessor tasks. To overlap the two tasks, in the Lag cell, type a negative number of hours, days, or other periods, as shown in Figure 6-16. Click OK to save your changes. You can see the resulting overlap in the background in Figure 6-16.

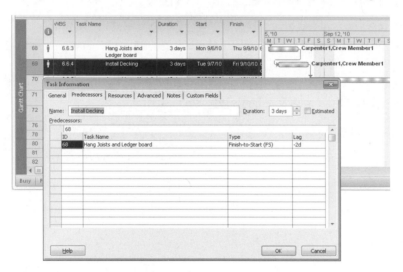

FIGURE 6-16 A negative value for lag between tasks results in an overlap.

Running Tasks in Parallel

Another way to fast-track a project is to schedule tasks concurrently—as long as they use different resources and the risks are acceptable. In Project, this approach requires adding and removing links rather than editing the dependencies that are already there. To run two tasks simultaneously, delete the dependency between them. In the Gantt Chart view, double-click the task dependency link line and, in the Task Dependency dialog box, click Delete.

The problem with this technique is that the successor task often disappears as soon as you delete its dependency. Without the predecessor, the successor doesn't know where it belongs, like mountain climbers without a sherpa. To prevent this disappearing act, link the successor to its new predecessor first and *then* delete the original dependency, as described in the following steps:

1. If the Task Form isn't visible, on the View tab, in the Split View group, select the Details check box. In the Details drop-down list, click Task Form.

2. Right-click the Task Form, and then click Predecessors & Successors.

3. In the Task Sheet, select the successor task you want to run in parallel.

4. To add a link to a new predecessor, click the first blank Predecessor Name cell in the Task Form. Click the down arrow that appears, and then choose the name of the new predecessor, as shown in Figure 6-17.

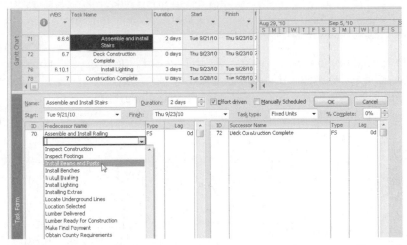

FIGURE 6-17 Display predecessors and successors in the Task Form to simplify working with task dependencies.

5. To delete the dependency between the old predecessor and the successor task, click the Predecessor Name cell for the old predecessor task, and then press Delete.

6. To ensure that the old predecessor still drives at least one project deliverable, se-lect the old predecessor in the Task Sheet. If the successor list is empty in the Task Form, click the first blank Successor Name cell, click the down arrow that appears, and then choose a project deliverable.

> **SEE ALSO** The section "Creating Task Dependencies," on page 127, describes other methods for working with links between tasks.

A Crash Course on Project Crashing

Adding more resources to a project to shorten its duration is called *crashing*, perhaps because of the traffic jams that occur when hordes of new team members try to pry their way into tasks that people are already working on. To nonproject managers, crashing seems like the most obvious thing to do—if Sam needs 4 weeks to develop a marketing plan, surely Sam and Rachel can produce it in only 2 weeks.

If stakeholders offer more resources to shorten the project schedule, you're better off recommending other strategies, such as fast-tracking, first. Or you can spend some time optimizing your schedule in other ways like reducing lag times between tasks or elimi-nating nonessential items in the project scope.

> **SEE ALSO** The previous sections in this chapter describe several methods for short-ening a project schedule.

The Danger in Crashing Projects

You can't add more resources to a pregnancy to deliver a baby in 5 months instead of 9. In practice, at some point, adding resources begins to increase duration instead of short-ening it. New resources aren't familiar with the tasks at hand and are less productive than current team members. And who guides the new members up the learning curve? Usu-ally the experienced, most productive members of the project team do, and they should be working instead to finish tasks.

As well, the extra help that you receive is often less-than-qualified for the work. You might need HTML programmers, but management gives you COBOL programmers instead. Even if the new resources have the right skills, they might have less experience than the people you already use. And, despite these risks, crashing typically costs more, as you'll see in the next section.

Time Versus Money

When you crash a project, you hope to trade off more money for less time. This strategy can make economic sense in the long run, for example, to bring products to market before they become low-margin commodities. Because stakeholders rarely want to spend more money than necessary, you'll probably be asked to show the trade-offs and recommend the best tasks to crash.

As you do with fast-tracking, you inspect the critical path for ways to shorten a schedule. Reducing duration on tasks that aren't on the critical path won't shorten the overall project duration one bit. But crashing a project isn't simply locating all the tasks on the critical path and assigning more resources to them. Some tasks cost more per week to crash than others. And the more you crash a project, the more expensive it becomes. Why spend $100,000 to shorten the schedule by 12 weeks, when 8 weeks and $50,000 will do?

By crashing the most cost-effective tasks first, you shorten the schedule to the duration you need for the lowest possible cost. *Crash tables* calculate the relative costs of shortening the critical path by crashing different tasks. For example, as the crash table in Figure 6-18 demonstrates, crashing one task might cost $1,000 for each week you eliminate, whereas another task costs $4,000 per week.

To analyze crash options, start with the longest tasks on the critical path. You'll need their duration and current cost. Of course, you have to determine how much you can decrease the task durations and how much that will cost. When you have that data, an Excel worksheet can help you calculate the crash cost per week for each task. Sorting the tasks by the crash cost per week quickly shows you the least costly tasks for crashing.

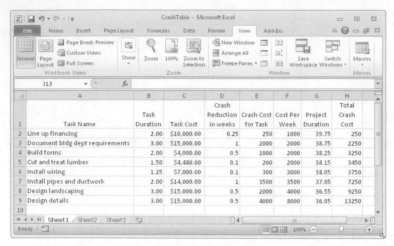

FIGURE 6-18 By sorting critical path tasks using the crash cost per week, you can identify the most cost-effective tasks to crash to obtain the schedule duration you need.

TIP   For tasks with the same crash cost per week, crash the longer tasks first. You'll crash the fewest tasks to reach your goal.

In the worksheet in Figure 6-18, the Line Up Financing task costs $10,000. You can shorten the duration by 0.25 weeks for a total crash cost of $250. If you need to reduce the duration some more, you can crash either the Document Bldg Dept Requirements task or the Build Forms task. They both cost $2,000 per week to crash. However, the Document Bldg Dept Requirements task can shorten the schedule by 1 week compared to the Build Form's 0.5 week.

■ **WARNING** Crashing a task can change the critical path on the project, even adding a task to the critical path that wasn't there before. To accurately evaluate your crash decisions, you should review the critical path after every crash.

Figure 6-18 illustrates the benefit of crashing the least costly tasks first. As you can see, the initial reductions shorten the schedule without much of an increase in overall cost. But as you dig deeper for more reductions, each additional week comes at a higher and higher price.

Reducing Scope

If the project stakeholders want a shorter schedule, a lower budget, or both, cutting scope may be answer. However, decisions like these can change, so you want to keep the original plan as well as the new, leaner one. Inactive tasks in Project 2010 can help you do just that.

When you make tasks inactive, Project removes their values from the project's rolled-up duration and cost. In addition, resource assignments for inactive tasks have no impact on the assigned resources' availability.

The tasks, their fields' values, and resource assignments, are still available and editable in the plan. If you reactivate the tasks, you don't have to reenter any information. and Project recalculates the rolled-up duration and cost to include the reactivated tasks' values.

TIP Inactive tasks are also helpful for documenting optional work. You can create tasks and assign resources, and then make the tasks inactive. The duration and cost are visible and editable, but don't appear in the total duration and cost for your project. If you decide to add the work to the project, you can make the tasks active.

To make tasks inactive, select the tasks in a task-oriented view and then on the Task tab, in the Schedule group, click Inactivate. The inactive tasks change to gray text with a strikethrough line drawn through their values, as you can see in Figure 6-19. You can edit an inactive task's values directly in table cells or in the Task Information dialog box. To re-activate a task, select it and then on the Task tab, in the Schedule group, click Inactivate.

⊖ Inactivate

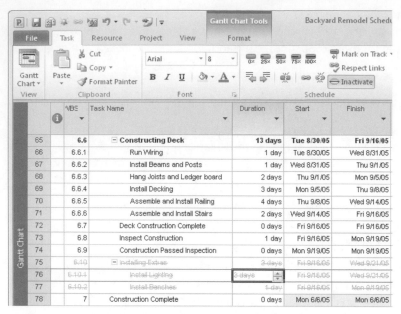

FIGURE 6-19 Inactive tasks are editable, but their values don't roll up into the project's duration and cost.

Summary

To build a project schedule, you need not only the tasks to perform and the resources assigned but also how long you expect the tasks to take. The estimating method you choose depends on the type of project, your experience with similar projects, and other factors.

With work estimates in place, you can start to build your project schedule: first, by linking tasks to show the flow of work; and second, by assigning resources to tasks to determine their duration. Unfortunately, project schedules rarely finish soon enough to satisfy stakeholders. If you must reduce the project duration, you can use techniques such as optimizing the schedule, fast-tracking, or crashing.

CHAPTER 7

Working with a Budget

IN THIS CHAPTER, YOU WILL:

- Understand financial measures for evaluating project performance

- Understand capital budgeting

- Learn methods for calculating costs for a project

- Learn how to compare project costs to the project budget

- Learn how to export costs from Microsoft Project

" *Why is there so much month left at the end of the money?* " — JOHN BARRYMORE

PROJECTS, like most people, have to live within their means. When someone proposes a project, you can be sure that at least a few stakeholders will ask "How much will this cost?" or "How much money will this project make (or save) us?" In fact, by the time you receive your assignment to manage a project, its stakeholders probably have a number in mind, be it the price tag for the project, the return on investment (ROI), or the net present value (NPV).

As you'll see in this chapter and other chapters in the book, cost estimates, budgets, actual costs, and financial measures such as ROI, are all interrelated. One of your tasks as a project manager might be to set—or reset—expectations and an estimate of project cost can help. An initial estimate helps win approval to get a project off the ground. More detailed estimates of the initial investment that a project requires, what it will cost as time passes, and how much money it generates or saves become part of a set of calculations, known as *capital budgeting*. Capital budgeting can be used to answer questions such as "What ROI will this project deliver?" and "If we commit resources to this project full-time for eight months, what other projects will we not take on—and is that the right thing to do?" If the capital budgeting analysis shows that the project's forecast financial measures warrant moving forward, estimated costs become the target that the project manager compares with actual costs as work is performed.

Cost estimates help stakeholders gain a better understanding of the scope of the project. They might start with an idea of what a project is likely to cost, and that understanding might become the financial goal (the budget and target measures) for the project manager and project team. However, with thorough and realistic estimates as ammunition, you might convince stakeholders to reconvene to agree on changes to the scope to fit the budget they set.

Performance compared with budget is one of the key measures of whether a project was successful. So, you need to set up a realistic budget from the start—a budget that reflects the project scope and goals defined by major stakeholders and decision makers. Corralling the costs for human and material resources as well as other costs helps flesh out your project plan. Moreover, these costs serve as the foundation of a baseline budget that you monitor and control throughout the life of the project.

This chapter begins with an introduction to capital budgeting and financial measures used to evaluate projects. A few project managers are lucky enough to not be held to financial performance measures. However, by understanding the budgeting process that your organization uses, you are better equipped to manage stakeholders' expectations and use resources effectively to make your projects a success.

This chapter describes how to add cost rates to labor, material, and other resources in your Microsoft Project schedule to coax Project to calculate costs. You also learn how to set up and use Project's budget resource feature to compare your project's costs against your budget. If you use another tool to evaluate financial performance in detail, be sure to read the last section in this chapter to learn how to export task costs from Project.

SEE ALSO The section "Estimating Methods," on page 116, describes how to estimate the work for project tasks that in turn helps define the duration of those tasks. To learn about managing a project budget after a project is under way, see Chapter 14, "Balancing the Budget and Other Project Variables."

Understanding Financial Measures

Many project managers who are new to their jobs think that project management is mainly about scheduling and tracking progress. But experienced project managers know that project financial measures are crucial for obtaining and maintaining executive support. Financial measures for projects are similar to the measures that investors use to evaluate investment opportunities. Although executives choose from several different project financial measures, they all boil down to which project makes the most of the available money. Considering that you invest an amount of money over a period of time, executives want to know which project provides the best return on that investment. This section introduces the most common financial measures for evaluating projects and explains their pros and cons.

Payback Period

The *payback period* measures the length of time it takes for a project to earn back what the organization pays to complete the project. For example, suppose that a project to revamp a production line costs $200,000, but the new and improved production line saves $20,000 each month that it operates. The payback period is the initial investment divided by the payback per period:

Payback period = $200,000/$20,000 per month, or 10 months

The attraction of the payback period as a project measure is its simplicity and that the data needed to calculate it are reasonably easy to obtain. The measure is easy to understand—even for people who aren't familiar with business finance.

The payback period measure has a few disadvantages:

- **Ignores cash flows beyond the payback period**   The payback period measure rewards projects that generate money early on. A project that produces savings more slowly but for a longer period of time would lose in a payback period contest. For example, a project that pays back the $200,000 investment in 10 months and earns a total of $500,000 over 60 months beats a project with a 24-month payback period, even if the second project earns $2 million over 60 months.

- **Assumes that cash comes in long enough to pay back the investment**   Suppose the product that you build on the revamped production line becomes obsolete before you reach the end of the payback period. Your company doesn't earn some of the savings that the payback period calculation takes into account.

- **Ignores the time value of money**   The payback period doesn't take into account the cost of money over time. For example, if you borrow money to carry out a project, the interest you pay is the cost of money, which increases the longer you owe on the loan. As you'll see in the next section, accounting for the time value of money produces a more accurate financial picture.

Net Present Value or Discounted Cash Flow

You know that inflation gradually nibbles away at the purchasing power of your money, which is one example of the time value of money. Net Present Value (NPV) takes the time value of money into account, so it provides a more accurate measure of financial performance than that of the payback period. NPV tells you whether your project meets, exceeds, or underperforms the target rate of return you use.

The net present value measure gets its name from the components that go into the calculation:

- **Net**   The calculation takes into account the money invested and the earnings or savings. The net amount is income minus expenses.

- **Present**   The calculation uses the rate of return that the organization requires from investments to determine today's value for the dollars that the project spends or earns at different times in the future. For instance, a company might specify that projects must provide a 10 percent rate of return.

- **Value**   If the NPV is positive, the investment earns a return greater than the one required by the company. If the NPV is negative, the project return falls short of the required return.

NPV requires more information than the payback period measure, but it's still readily available. The big drawback to NPV is the learning curve for people who aren't familiar with this method of financial analysis.

Here's an example of NPV using the revamped production line. The assumptions about the revamped production line are as follows:

- For simplicity, the company pays for the new production line in a lump sum of $200,000 when the production line begins operation.

- The production line saves $20,000 each month of operation.

- The production line equipment is worth $10,000 (salvage value) at the end of the second year when the production line equipment becomes obsolete and the investment and its returns end.

A financial calculator is a big help in calculating NPV. Microsoft Excel makes short work of NPV calculations with the XNPV function. It accepts the required rate of return, a series of cash flows in or out, and the dates on which they occur. Money that you spend is negative, and savings or income is positive. As you can see in Figure 7-1, the production line NPV is $243,528, which shows that the project exceeds the 10 percent return the company requires.

A chart showing cash inflows and outflows helps to calculate the result. Figure 7-1 shows the cash flows and the NPV for the production line.

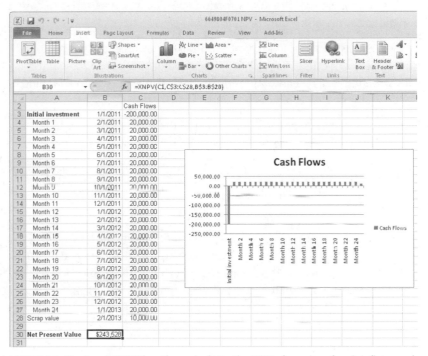

FIGURE 7-1 The Excel XNPV function calculates the NPV of a series of cash inflows and outflows.

TIP

If you have a regular series of cash flows, you can use the NPV function in Excel. Although you don't have to enter dates for this function, it accepts no more than 29 values, which can crimp calculations based on monthly cash flows. The rate you enter must equal the rate for the period between each cash flow.

Internal Rate of Return

In finance circles, *internal rate of return (IRR)* is the annual return that a project delivers, taking into account the time value of money. The IRR is the equivalent of the *annual percentage yield (APY)* that you earn on a savings account that pays a fixed interest rate (annual percentage rate, or APR). If the IRR is greater than the return the organization requires, the project is in good shape. The XIRR function in Excel accepts a series of cash flows in or out, and the dates on which they occur.

As with NPV, the timing of cash flows is important for IRR. For example, early income increases the return you earn because money now is more valuable than money in the future. However, if you spend money early, you reduce your return more than spending money later on.

IRR has its disadvantages. If you have one initial outlay and the rest of the cash flows are money coming, this measure works perfectly. However, if cash flows switch between positive and negative values, this calculation can produce several mathematically correct answers, so you can't tell what the return really is. You calculate IRR by calculating NPV with different rates of return. When the answer is zero, that return is the IRR.

NOTE

If you borrow money to run your project, the first cash flow is positive because money is coming in and the remaining cash flows are negative to pay for the project. In this situation, you want to see an IRR that is *less than* the required rate of return.

Understanding Capital Budgets

"Money isn't everything, but it ranks right up there with oxygen."
— RITA DAVENPORT

Most organizations and executives use capital budgeting to make financial decisions—including which projects to undertake. Similar to the analysis that investors use to evaluate investment opportunities, capital budgeting calculates financial measures such as a project's IRR and the period of time that will elapse before the project benefits offset its initial investment.

Calculating potential financial results helps identify the projects that meet an organization's financial goals and those that are likely to fall short. Capital budgeting can help an organization decide which projects seem the wisest to pursue and which ones should be removed from the docket. Because organizations usually don't have the financial or human resources to take on every project, they turn to capital budgeting to find the projects that provide the greatest cost-benefit trade-offs.

Putting Capital Budgeting into Practice

Not every project you manage goes through a capital budgeting process. And you might not be responsible for performing the capital budgeting analysis. But understanding these concepts puts you in a better position to influence and defend decisions about which projects are approved and which ones are rejected or postponed. Executives generally end up choosing the projects that make the most of the money available. With capital budgeting in your toolbox, you'll be able to obtain the support of decision makers—or know that a project isn't worth the effort.

Capital budgeting is more than just a financial modeling tool. The forecasted financial returns for a project might *look* favorable, but you must evaluate those measures in the context of potential risks and other factors such as resource constraints. Capital budgeting can help pin down the benefits and risks associated with a project, with the ultimate aim being to accurately quantify benefits, costs, and risks for the project in both the short term and the long run.

Using a Capital Budgeting Tool

Most organizations use some sort of capital budgeting tool to evaluate investments and projects. A template helps keep analysis consistent from project to project so stakeholders can compare results with confidence. If your organization doesn't have a tool for capital budgeting or you want to experiment with one to learn how capital budgeting works, you can download a capital budgeting Microsoft Excel template, shown in Figure 7-2, from Microsoft Office Online (*http://office.microsoft.com/en-us/templates/ TC011589891033.aspx*). After you enter your data, the spreadsheet calculates the rate of return on an investment, the NPV of the investment, and the payback period (in years).

In the template, you identify benefits that the project delivers and quantify the costs and financial benefits for three years after the project is complete. For example, benefits might include cost savings due to increased productivity, additional revenue from increasing customer satisfaction; and earning more repeat business; or, in the manufacturing world, savings from streamlining production and reducing errors and waste.

The worksheet calculates overall project costs based on the values you provide for the initial investment (Year 0) and the costs you expect to incur in the three years that follow (Year 1, Year 2, and Year 3). The example shown in Figure 7-2 includes costs for implementation, training, and support, but you can change these categories to reflect the costs for your project. For example, you could add costs for the new computers you must purchase or the salary for the high-paid systems architect you've hired.

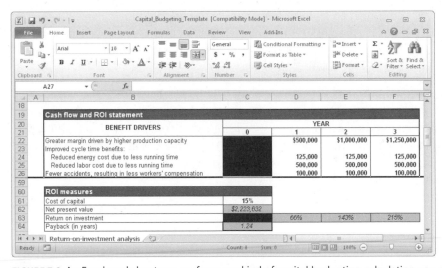

FIGURE 7-2 An Excel worksheet can perform any kind of capital budgeting calculation you need.

The other value you provide is the cost of capital. In most cases, cost of capital represents the rate of return your organization pays for the money it invests in the project. For example, if the company borrows money at 6 percent to fund the project, the cost of capital is 6 percent. The project has to provide a ROI of at least 6 percent to come out ahead.

Alternatively, you might use *opportunity cost* as the cost of capital. For example, if your company keeps its project bankroll earning interest in short-term notes paying 4 percent, taking money out of those notes to fund a project means the 4 percent return is history. The project has to provide more than a 4 percent return for the company to come out ahead. But opportunity cost is usually higher than low-risk returns. Most organizations measure opportunity cost as the highest return provided by alternative investments. In this case, the opportunity cost is the highest rate of return for other projects competing for part of the project bankroll.

■ **WARNING** Of course, you can't ignore capital budgeting measures after your project starts. Higher than expected costs reduce the NPV and IRR on which the project was originally approved. If your project falls behind, its financial benefits also lag, either because the project takes longer (which almost always costs more) or, more drastically, because the scope of the project is reduced to get the project back on track.

QUANTIFYING QUALITATIVE BENEFITS

How do you quantify benefits such as fewer errors? Suppose that a project to improve manufacturing processes is planned to reduce errors made in assembly by about 20 percent each month. From quality assurance reports, you know that approximately 1,000 errors occur on the assembly line each month and that correcting each error takes about half an hour. You also know that the burdened hourly rate for workers on this assembly line is $60. Using these numbers, you can quantify the benefit as follows:

Errors eliminated per month: 20% of 1000 = 200

Time saved per month: 200 errors * .5 hour = 100 hours

Cost savings per month: $60 * 100 hours = $6,000

Calculating Costs in a Project Schedule

"If your outgo exceeds your income, then your upkeep will be your downfall." — BILL EARLE

Most project costs come from the resources that a project requires. The people assigned to perform tasks and the equipment and material resources needed to get the work done all have costs associated with them. By assigning cost data to resources in the Resource Sheet view in Microsoft Project, you can let the program calculate a good deal of labor and material costs you need for capital budgeting. Projects often incur other costs, such as training and travel, that don't fall into the labor, equipment, or material categories. In Project, you can use *cost resources* to track these costs.

SEE ALSO	Chapter 5, "Project Resources," describes the different types of resources that Project offers and when to use them.

The type of cost information you provide for project resources depends on the types of resources and how you pay for them. Here are the different types of costs that Project supports and how you use them:

- *Standard rate* (Std. Rate in the Project Resource Sheet view) and *overtime rate* (Ovt. Rate) usually represent how much a resource costs for a unit of time. Whether you use employees or contractors, they have a labor rate, whether it's $50 per hour, $6,000 per month, or $60,000 per year. In the backyard remodeling project, work resources such as carpenters and crew members have hourly rates. Equipment sometimes has a daily rate. For example, if you rent a backhoe, you might pay $500 per day.

  When you add rates to work resources and then assign them to tasks, Project multiplies the number of hours (or other time units) by the rate to calculate the cost of the time you use the resources on those tasks. The more hours the resources spend, the higher your labor or equipment costs will be.

The Std. Rate field works just as well at calculating costs for material resources. For example, suppose that your crew members go through drill bits like water and you want to include the cost of those bits in your estimates. You can create a resource for a drill bit and enter the cost for each one in the Std. Rate field. Then, when you assign the crew members to a drilling task, you can add the drill bit resource to the task as well. In the Units field for the task assignment, enter the number of drill bits you expect the crew members to mangle. Project multiplies the cost per drill bit by the number of units to calculate the total cost of drill bits.

> **NOTE** If you pay more to use resources past the end of a standard workday, you have to fill in the overtime rate. For instance, if the standard workday is 8 hours, you might pay a carpenter $40 per hour. The $40 goes into the Std. Rate field for the carpenter. If you assign the carpenter to work 8 regular hours and 2 overtime hours in one day, his rate for the last 2 hours might jump to $60 per hour. By entering $60 in the Ovt. Rate field, Project uses the overtime rate to calculate the cost of overtime hours you assign.

- Cost/Use is another field for the costs of material resources (and some work resources). This type of cost is perfect when you pay a fee each time a resource is used. For example, in the backyard remodeling project, the dumpster and the concrete truck each have a per-use fee; every time you need a dumpster for a task, you pay $450. A labor resource might come with a cost per use, for instance, when you have to pay a consultant $100 to travel to your site.

- Accrue At tells Project when you have to pay the cost of the resource. You can choose Start if you pay for a resource up front, Finish if you pay at the end, or Prorated if you pay over the duration of the task.

> **NOTE** Project also includes a task field, Fixed Cost, which used to be the answer for costs that weren't associated with labor or materials. However, in Project 2007 and later, cost resources are a more powerful way to document these types of costs. You can assign more than one cost resource to a task and you can use different cost resources to track different categories of expenses.

BEST PRACTICES

Project costs include direct costs for labor, equipment, materials, and ancillary expenses such as travel. These expenses depend on the work required or the volume of use. But you also need to account for expenses such as overhead (rent, utilities, insurance, and the like), employees working in staff roles, and capital equipment that isn't used specifically on projects. Because each project has to help pay for these indirect costs, you need to add them to your project estimates. Indirect costs remain fairly static, so the simplest way to include them is by using burdened labor rates.

A burdened rate represents the average amount that it costs an organization to employ someone—salary or wages, benefits, and a portion of overhead costs. For example, carpenters might earn $20 per hour. But by the time you include the cost of benefits and some extra money to cover overhead expenses, the burdened hourly rate for a carpenter might be $35. Average burdened hourly rates often take into account job classifications and the level within that job class. For example, an apprentice carpenter might have a burdened hourly rate of $35, whereas a master carpenter who's faster than a novice with a nail gun might carry a burdened hourly rate of $75. You can obtain burdened labor rates from the human resources department or possibly the accounting team.

If you use burdened labor rates, be sure you know the costs they cover. If they cover only labor expenses and employee benefits, you'll still have to add indirect costs to the capital budget. If burdened labor rates also include allocations for overhead, you're free and clear. Adding overhead costs separately would count overhead costs twice.

Another method for factoring in indirect costs is adding a multiplier to the total project budget. For example, you might add 10 percent to the project budget for indirect costs, much like some catalog merchants charge for shipping based on the cost of an item instead of its weight.

Specifying Rates for Work Resources in Project

You use the Resource Sheet view in Project to add rates to work and material resources. The following steps explain how:

Resource
Sheet

1. With your Project file open, on the View tab, in the Resource Views group, click Resource Sheet.

2. In the Resource Sheet table, select the Resource Name cell for the resource to which you want to add rates. To add a new resource, select the Resource Name cell in the first blank row and then type a name.

3. In the Std. Rate field, type the rate for the resource. You can enter the rate and the time period, such as $50.00/hr, as illustrated by the Carpenter1 resource in Figure 7-3, or $300.00/day for the Backhoe resource.

   Fill in the Ovt. Rate field only if you pay people a premium hourly rate for extra work hours and assign overtime hours in Project. For example, salaried employees aren't paid overtime, and some resources are paid the same hourly rate for extra hours. In these situations, you don't need to assign overtime hours to resources, so you don't need a rate in the Ovt. Rate field.

4. If a resource has a fee for each use, in the Cost/Use cell, type that value, as illustrated by the Dumpster in Figure 7-3.

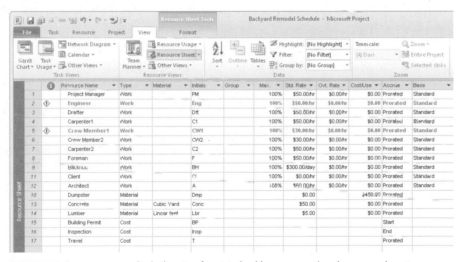

FIGURE 7-3 A resource can include rates for standard hours, overtime hours, and cost per use.

You can also create up to five *different* rates for a resource, which is helpful when a resource costs a different amount for a different type of work or to reflect increases in wages or salary that will take effect at some point in a project's schedule. For example, the carpenters cost $50 per hour in 2010, but as soon as the 2011 construction season begins, their hourly rate goes up to $55.

To add multiple rates to a resource, in the Resource Sheet, do the following:

1. Double-click the resource with the multiple rates.

2. On the Costs tab of the Resource Information dialog box, click the A (Default) tab and then type values in the Standard Rate cells.

3. In the next row of the table, type a new rate or a percentage change from the previous rate. To have this rate begin as of a specific date, in the Effective Date cell, type the date that the rate change goes into effect.

4. You can use the B, C, and other labeled tabs to define additional sets of pay rates for the resource.

5. Click OK to close the dialog box.

Entering Rates and Quantities for Material Resources

Project can calculate costs associated with material resources such as lumber, concrete, drill bits, and gasoline. In addition to specifying the rate for the material, you can also specify the units the material comes in. For example, drill bits come by the bit; concrete is priced by the cubic yard. When you assign a material resource to a task, Project calculates its cost using the material resource rate and the quantity of material used to complete the task. Here are the steps for specifying costs for materials:

1. With your Project file open, on the View menu, in the Resource Views group, click Resource Sheet.

2. In the Resource Sheet table, select the Resource Name cell for the material resource to which you want to add rates. To add a new resource, select the Resource Name cell in the first blank row and type a name.

3. Select the resource's Type cell and from the list box, select Material.

4. In the Material cell, type the unit of measure. This unit of measure might be linear feet for lumber or cubic yards for concrete, as shown in Figure 7-3.

5. In the Std. Rate field, type the price per unit of material, such as $5 for each drill bit or $50 for each cubic yard of concrete.

6. If the material resource has a cost per use, in the Cost/Use cell, type the charge for each use.

Assigning a Cost Resource to a Task

Cost resources work differently from resource and material costs. A cost resource can have a different price each time you assign it, so the airfare for a trip to New York can be $200, and airfare to Dusseldorf can be $1,100. For that reason, you set the cost for a cost resource when you assign it to a task. Here are the steps for setting a cost resource value for a task:

1. Display any task-oriented view, such as the Gantt Chart view or Task Usage view.

2. On the Resource tab, in the Assignments group, click Assign Resources.

3. In the task list, select the task to which you want to assign the cost resource.

Assign
Resources

4. In the Assign Resource dialog box, click the name of the cost resource and then click Assign.

    A check mark appears to the left of the resource's name, and the resource jumps to a location near the top of the list of resources, as shown in Figure 7-4.

5. In the Cost cell for the cost resource, type the cost for the task.

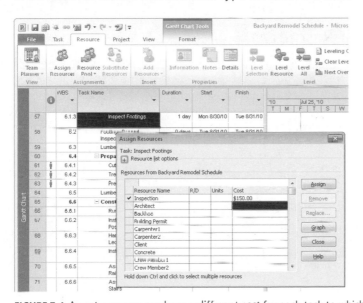

FIGURE 7-4 A cost resource can have a different cost for each task to which it is assigned.

Comparing Project Costs with the Budget

If the management team gives you budget values for costs, such as $10,000 for travel expenses and $20,000 for materials, you can use Project's *budget resource* feature to specify the budgeted values and then compare them with your project's costs.

> **SEE ALSO** Budget resources are great for comparing budgeted values with the costs for cost resources. For work resources, you enter budgeted work amounts, not costs. See the sidebar, "Budgeting for Labor Costs," on page 177, to learn how to work around this issue.

Setting up budget resources to compare with project costs comprises several steps. You create budget resources, assign them to the project summary task for your project, and fill in the budgeted values. You must also associate the other resources in your project to the appropriate budget types. Then you can group your budget and other resources so you can compare your budgeted values with the values your project delivers.

Creating Budget Resources

You use budget resources in Project to represent the budget line items you want to track. It doesn't matter whether you set up broad categories, such as Budget Labor and Budget Travel; or break categories down, such as Budget Airfare, Budget Lodging, and Budget Meals.

Creating budget resources takes place in the Resource Sheet, just as with other types of resources. You fill in a name and choose a type, such as Work, Material, or Cost. For material budget resources, fill in the Material Label field with the measurement units.

> **TIP**
> Use names that differentiate budget resources from regular resources so you can easily distinguish budget resources in the resource list. For example, start a budget resource name with the corresponding budget account number, such as 4522 Travel Budget. By starting with a number, your budget resources appear at the top of your resource list when you sort it alphabetically from A to Z.

After you create the resources, you have to designate them as budget resources. Follow these steps to quickly change this setting for all your budget resources:

1. In the Resource Sheet, right-click the column heading and then click Insert Column.

2. In the Field Name drop-down list, click Budget. Project inserts the Budget column to the left of the selected column.

3. Select the Budget cell for the first budget resource and, in the drop-down list, choose Yes. If budget resources are grouped together, drag the black square at the bottom-right corner of the cell to copy Yes to the other Budget cells.

4. Right-click the Budget column heading and then click Hide Column.

Assigning Budget Resources to the Project Summary Task

A budget resource represents the budgeted amount for a cost category for an entire project. For that reason, you assign budget resources to the project summary task:

Project
Summary
Task

1. If the project summary task (the task with row number 0) isn't visible, on the Format tab, in the Show/Hide group, select the Project Summary Task check box.

2. On the Resource tab, in the Assignments group, click Assign Resources.

3. To display only budget resources in the Assign Resources dialog box, click + to expand the Resource List Options section; select the Filter By check box; and then, in the drop-down list, choose Budget Resources, as shown in Figure 7-5.

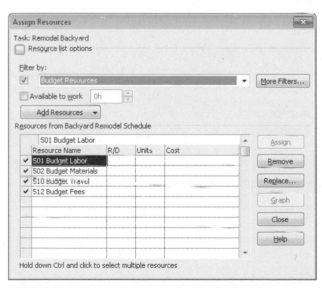

FIGURE 7-5 Filter the resource list in the Assign Resources dialog box to show only budget resources.

4. Select the first budget resource you want to assign and click Assign.

5. Repeat step 4 to assign additional budget resources to the project summary task.

> **NOTE** Budget resources are the only kind of resource you can assign to a project summary task. If you select a resource in the Assign Resource dialog box and the Assign button is grayed-out, you selected a resource that isn't a budget resource.

Filling in Budgeted Values

After you assign budget resources to the project summary task, you can add budgeted cost values for cost resources, budgeted work values for work resources, and the total number of units for material resources. You can enter budgeted values for the entire project or by time period, depending on how closely you want to track costs against the budget.

If you specify budgeted values for the entire project, the program prorates budgeted values over the duration of the project. To add budgeted values for the entire project, follow these steps:

Task Usage ▾

1. On the View tab, in the Task Views group, click Task Usage.

   The Task Usage view displays the Project summary task at the top of the task list.

2. Insert the Budget Cost field and Budget Work field into the table.

3. For a budget cost resource, type the entire budgeted value in dollars in the Budget Cost cell.

   For a budget work resource, type the budgeted work in hours or days in the Budget Work cell. For a budget material resource, type the units in the Budget Work cell.

> **TIP**   You can enter budget values only in specific locations in Project. In the Task Usage view, fill in budget amounts in the row with the budget resource name. You can also type values in a project summary task's Budget Cost or Budget Work cell. For budgeted values for a time period, fill in the Budget Cost or Budget Work cells in the time-phased grid in the Task Usage view.

BUDGETING FOR LABOR COSTS

Project calculates labor costs for work resources, but the budget resource feature can't compare budgeted costs with the labor costs that Project calculates. It compares budgeted work values with tasks' work values.

One way to represent budgeted work values in dollars is with an average labor cost. For example, if your labor budget is $100,000, and the average standard rate is $50 per hour, the work budget is $100,000 divided by $50, or 2,000 hours.

You can trick Project into showing budgeted labor costs in dollars. Set up the budget resources for work and material resources as cost resources instead of as work and material resources. By doing so, you can fill in budgeted labor cost and material cost values and compare them with the rolled-up labor and material costs from tasks.

To allocate budgeted values by time period, edit the budgeted values in the time-phased grid in the Task Usage view.

Add
Details

1. With the Task Usage view displayed, on the Format tab, in the Details group, click Add Details.

2. In the Available Fields box in the Detail Styles dialog box, click Budget Cost and then click Show.

3. Repeat step 2 for the Budget Work field.

4. Click OK.

   Budget Cost and Budget Work appear in the time-phased grid.

5. Drag the Zoom slider on the status bar to display the time period you want to use for budgeted values.

6. In the cell in the row for a budget resource's Budget Cost or Budget Work field and the column for the time period, fill in the budget cost or work amount, as shown in Figure 7-6.

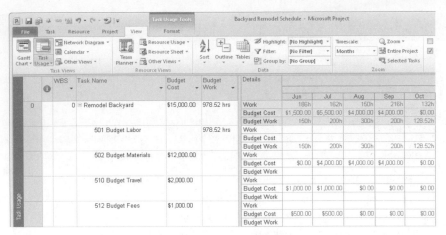

FIGURE 7-6 The Budget Cost and Budget Work columns in the table represent the project-wide budget values. The numbers in the time-phased grid are budgeted values by time period.

Flagging Resources by Budget Type

The next thing you need is a way to link your resource costs to the correct budget categories. You use a resource text field to associate work, material, and cost resources to their corresponding budget resources.

Follow these steps to customize a text field for budget categories:

1. In the Resource Sheet, insert a custom text field, such as Text1 or Text2.

2. Right-click the new column and then, on the shortcut menu, click Custom Fields.

3. In the Custom Fields dialog box, click Rename. In the Rename Field dialog box, type the name for this field, such as Budget Item. Click OK.

4. In the Calculation For Assignment Rows section, select the Roll Down Unless Manually Entered option and then click OK.

   This option distributes the budget category field values to assignments in usage views unless you manually type a value in a time-phased assignment cell.

TIP   To simplify choosing budget categories, you can set up the custom text field with a lookup table of valid budget categories. In the Custom Fields dialog box, click Lookup. In the Edit Lookup Table dialog box, you can fill in the Value cells with the categories you want.

In the Resource Sheet, click the cells in the column for the custom text field and fill in the appropriate budget category name for each one. Fill in a budget category for the budget resources, too, which is how Project knows how resource costs relate to budget categories.

Comparing Budget Resource Values

With all the setup complete, you can compare your project resource costs and work against the budgeted values that you filled in your budget resources. To compare budgeted values to project values, you group budgeted and planned fields by budget category.

Follow these steps to set up your budget comparison view:

1. On the Resource tab, in the Resource Views group, click Resource Usage.

   The Resource Usage view is best for comparing values, because you can group resources by the custom resource text field you use to specify budget categories.

2. If necessary, insert the Budget Work, Budget Cost, Work, and Cost columns into the table.

3. To group the resources by the custom resource text field, click the down arrow to the right of the Resource Name column heading. On the drop-down menu, point to Group By and then click Custom Group.

4. In the Customize Group By dialog box, in the Group By row, click the arrow in the Field Name cell; then, in the drop-down list of resource fields, choose the name of the custom text field for your budget categories. Click OK.

5. In the group summary row, shown in Figure 7-7, compare the Budget Cost or Budget Work values to the Cost or Work values.

Resource
Usage

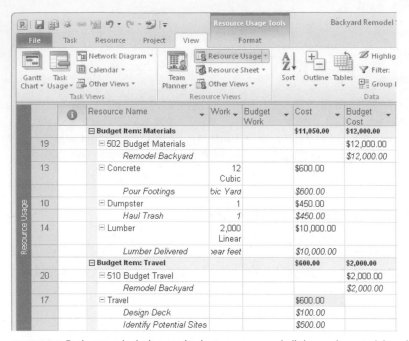

FIGURE 7-7 Each group includes one budget resource and all the work, material, and cost resources that apply to that budget line item.

The Budget Cost and Budget Work cells in the group summary rows represent the budget values for each budget resource. You see a value for Budget Cost if the budget resource is a cost resource. You see a Budget Work value if the budget resources is a work resource.

The Cost and Work cells in the group summary cells represent the rolled-up cost and rolled-up work for the resources in that particular budget category. If the Cost value is greater than the Budget Cost value, the project has exceeded the budget. If the value in the Work cell is greater than the Budget Work value, the work hours are over budget.

Exporting Costs from a Project Schedule

You can do a lot with cost information in a Project schedule: calculate the costs for summary tasks from the work packages within them, track variances between budgeted amounts and actual values, and see how the actual cost of a task compares to its percentage of completion. But some of the financial analysis and reporting that you want to do is often easier in a software application other than Project—Excel, for example. Export maps make it easy to export your costs from Project for in-depth scrutiny.

In Project, an *export (or import) map* controls the type of data you export (or import), the order in which the data transfers, and the field names at the destination. You can export data to Microsoft Access as well as to Excel or to file formats such as HTML or XML. Project comes with built-in maps for exporting information, and the one you want for your budgeting activities is Cost Data By Task.

The following example illustrates how to export cost data using the Project file for the backyard remodeling project. Because organizations use different spreadsheets and tools for capital budgeting, you'll probably have to modify the options and other settings to work with your organization's budgeting tools.

> **PROJECT FILE** The schedule for the backyard remodeling project, Backyard Remodel Schedule.mpp, is available in the Chapter07 folder on the companion website.

Exporting Costs to an Excel File

Here are the steps for exporting task costs to an Excel workbook:

1. On the Format tab, in the Show/Hide group, clear the Project Summary Task check box and the Summary Tasks check box.

   You don't want to export costs for summary tasks because you run the risk of counting costs twice—once for work package items and again within the subtotal for the summary tasks. By filtering out summary tasks before you export cost information, you prevent this double counting.

2. On the File tab, click Save As.

3. In the Save As dialog box, from the Save As Type list box, select Excel Workbook and then click Save. You'll see the Welcome page of the Export Wizard. Click Next.

4. On the Export Wizard - Data page, keep the Selected Data option selected, as shown in Figure 7-8, and click Next.

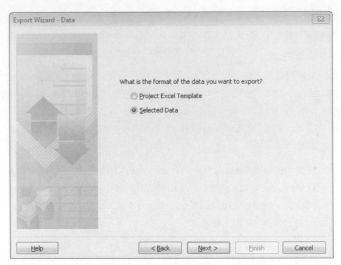

FIGURE 7-8 On the Export Wizard - Data page, the Selected Data option lets you specify the fields you want Project to export.

5. On the Export Wizard - Map page, verify that the New Map option is selected and click Next.

6. On the Export Wizard - Map Options page, select the Tasks check box, as shown in Figure 7-9, to export costs associated with tasks. Verify that the Export Includes Headers check box is selected so that column headings appear in the spreadsheet you create.

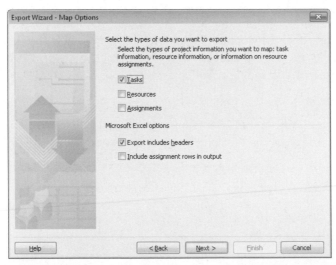

FIGURE 7-9 When you select the Export Includes Headers check box, Project exports the column headings to the spreadsheet you create.

7. Click Next. You'll see the Export Wizard - Task Mapping page.

The Task Mapping page (and a similar page for resources) is the crux of the export map. On this page, you can choose a filter for tasks. You can also specify the fields in Project that contain the data you want to export.

8. Click the first blank cell in the From: Microsoft Project Field column, click the down arrow that appears, and then click Name.

Project fills in the To: Excel Field cell with the same field name: Name.

9. Repeat step 8 to add Cost to the table.

The Task Mapping page should look like the one in Figure 7-10.

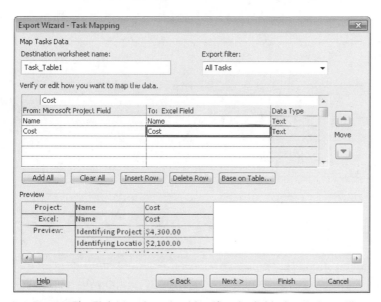

FIGURE 7-10 The Task Mapping page identifies the fields that Project will export.

10. Click Next and then click Finish. Figure 7-11 shows the resulting Excel worksheet.

Green triangles in the cost cells, shown in Figure 7-11, indicate that the values are not stored as numbers. To convert the exported costs to numbers in Excel, select all the cost cells. Hover the pointer over the yellow diamond indicator that appears, click the down arrow, and then click Convert To Number.

	A	B	C
1	Name	Cost	
2	Identifying Project Constraints	4300	
3	Identifying Locations	2100	
4	Calculate Available Sq. Ft.	400	
5	Locate Underground Lines	800	
6	Identify Access	400	
7	Identify Potential Sites	400	
8	Choose Location	100	
9	Location Selected	0	
10	Developing Budget	1000	
11	Develop Desired Budget	200	
12	Obtain Interest Rate and Loan Qualification	400	
13	Build Target Budget	400	
14	Target Budget Created	0	

Task_Table1

Ready

FIGURE 7-11 The Excel file includes the task names and costs from the Project file.

TIP ✓ Getting the export map right could take a couple of tries, as you experiment with its options and the fields you want to include. When the Excel workbook contains what you want, run the wizard one last time, and on the End Of Map Definition page, click Save Map so that you can use the map again in the future.

▇ Summary

Chances are your organization uses some form of capital budgeting to decide which projects to undertake. Although you might receive a budget along with a project management assignment, understanding capital budgeting and financial measures can help you keep your projects on track to meet stakeholders' expectations. As you develop your project plan, you can enlist Project to help calculate estimated costs. You can use Project's Budgeting feature to compare project costs to the budget you're aiming for. You can also export costs to another program, such as Excel or your company's budgeting tool, for further analysis.

3

Carrying Out a Project

CHAPTER 8

Executing the Project Plan

IN THIS CHAPTER, YOU WILL:

- Learn about procuring resources for a project

- Understand the process for kicking off a project

- Learn the steps to perform to begin execution of a project

"Pray that success will not come any faster than you are able to endure it."—ELBERT HUBBARD

AFTER ALL THE ACTIVITY and excitement of the project planning phase, project execution sounds simple: carry out the plan. Before you can do that, you have a few activities to perform.

First, you need the members of your project team in place to do the work that comprises the project. If you already lined up the people you need within your organization, getting the team on board may be as simple as telling their managers that the project is starting. However, if you require resources from outside your organization or never went farther than identifying skill sets and the number of resources you need, you have to procure your project resources.

Once your team is in place, members look to you for instructions or guidance. You can take advantage of their attention and start the project off right by holding a kickoff meeting. In addition to introducing the players to one another, the kickoff meeting is the perfect time to review the project schedule, lay out the ground rules, and complete other team-oriented activities.

This chapter explains how to work with vendors to obtain the resources you need. It also describes how to use a kickoff meeting to get a project off the ground successfully. The rest of the chapter describes other items that you should complete before you start work, such as an approved project plan, a filing system for your project documents, and a baseline of the plan to which you'll compare progress.

Procuring Resources

The people who helped you plan the project are already on board. Now, it's time to corral the rest of the team. If you're using people within your organization (or your client's), you can notify the resources' managers that the project is starting and when people's assignments are due to start. To obtain people, equipment, or materials from other companies, you have to go through a procurement process.

A procurement process comprises several steps, although you can make it as robust or as informal as your project requires. The process boils down to the following steps:

- **Solicitation**   The first step is to identify potential vendors and ask them to bid on your work.

- **Evaluation and selection**   When the vendors you solicit respond with proposals or bids, you have to evaluate their responses and choose the vendor or vendors you want to work with.

- **Contracting**   After you select vendors, you have to negotiate and sign contracts for the work.

- **Vendor management**   You supervise the vendor's work until it's complete and then you close out the contract.

If your organization has a procurement department, you can provide them with your requirements and let them handle the rest. If you aren't so fortunate, this section introduces procurement basics.

TIP   Procuring resources often takes significant time. For that reason, it's a good idea to include procurement tasks in your project schedule. That way, you have a better idea of when the actual work on the project can start.

Soliciting Vendors

A request for proposal (RFP) is a common method for obtaining bids from vendors. An RFP spells out what you need and acts as the basis for the contract you and the vendor sign.

> **NOTE**   If you need to research vendors before you send out an RFP, you can start with a request for information (RFI). An RFI is a short document that asks vendors for more information about the services and products they provide.

An RFP gives vendors the information they need to respond to your request. Typically, an RFP includes the following information:

- An overview of the project.

- A description of the services or resources you require, when you need them, and your budget, all of which you can pull from your project plan.

- Selection criteria, so vendors can determine whether they have a shot at winning before they prepare a proposal or bid. Typical selection criteria include a vendor's track record, financial stability, location, experience with your requirements, how well the proposal matches your needs, and lowest bid.

- The deadline for responding to the RFP and when you plan to make your decision.

You have to identify the vendors you want to solicit. Vendors you have worked with successfully in the past are a good starting point for your vendor list. You can check out several vendors in a short period of time by attending trade shows. Other methods for identifying potential vendors include reading ads in trade magazines, placing ads in magazines, and renting company lists.

After you send RFPs to vendors, you wait for the responses to pour in. In the meantime, you'll probably receive questions from vendors. It's important to provide all the vendors with the same information so you can compare apples to apples. For small RFPs, you may choose to answer questions individually. A bidders' conference is an effective way to handle questions. At a bidders' conference, every vendor has an opportunity to ask their questions and hear your answers. Posting your RFP online allows vendors to post their questions electronically. Then, you answer the questions on the same electronic forum so all vendors can review your answers.

Selecting Vendors

After you receive responses from vendors, you have to evaluate them and decide who you want to work with. Choosing a vendor boils down to using some sort of algorithm to score the responses. For example, you can rate each vendor on each criterion, add up the vendors' scores, and choose the vendor with the best score.

> **NOTE** You may have to go through more than one round of evaluations. For example, you can whittle the list of vendors down by evaluating their responses. In many cases, the vendors that pass the first round make a presentation or provide a demonstration.

Contracting

After you select your vendors, you must negotiate and sign contracts with them. For small projects or simple requests, contracts can be short and sweet. Sometimes, contracts are long and complicated. If your organization has a legal department, you provide the information from the RFP, and the legal folks generate a contract. An alternative is to ask an attorney to draw up a contract. If your needs are simple, you may be able to use a boilerplate agreement with a statement of work as an attachment.

Most vendor contracts include a statement of work, terms and conditions, deliverables, deadlines, and price. You should also include acceptance criteria and a description of your acceptance process, so you and the vendor can easily determine whether the work has been completed successfully. The contract should also spell out your vendor management and change management processes. Include specific processes, procedures, methods, tools, and any other guidelines that you want the vendor to follow.

Contracts come in several flavors:

- *Fixed price* contracts are effective when your requirements are well-defined and you anticipate few changes. A fixed price contract places most of the risk on the vendor, who is paid a fixed price regardless of how much time and expense they incur to perform the work.

- *Time and materials* contracts pay vendors for time worked and expenses incurred. The vendor submits timesheets and documentation for materials and expenses. This type of contract places the bulk of the risk on the client. These types of contracts often include a not-to-exceed clause to place an upper limit on the cost.

- *Cost plus* is similar to a time and materials contract with an added feature for rewarding or penalizing based on the vendor's performance and quality.

- *Retainers* are useful if you can't specify detailed work ahead of time that you want the vendor to perform. With this type of contract, you contract a vendor to work a specific number of days or hours during a period for a specific amount of money. Then, you assign work to the vendor to complete within a timeframe. If the work requires more time than the retainer covers, you either pay more during that period or delay the delivery date.

Kicking Off a Project

A kickoff meeting is a good way to get a project off to a good start. Your team is assembled, but most of the members have never met. A kickoff meeting is the perfect venue for introductions. This first (and perhaps only) project-wide meeting is also a great opportunity to review key information about the project. The following are some of the items to include on the kickoff meeting agenda:

- **Introductions**   Whether you meet face to face, via teleconference, or online, you can introduce all the players: the project sponsor, the client, you (the project manager), and the rest of the team.

- **Project purpose and mission**   You can increase commitment to the project by asking the project sponsor to explain why the project is important and discuss the objectives that the project is supposed to achieve.

- **Review of the project plan**   The project plan is approved, so the kickoff meeting is a good time to review the plan with the entire team. This review is the perfect opportunity to find out if the team thinks the plan is realistic, if you didn't have the chance to involve the entire team in the earlier planning activities.

- **Review processes**   You can use the kickoff meeting to review communication ground rules, and other processes such as change management.

> **SEE ALSO**   Chapter 11, "Communicating Information," and Chapter 12, "Managing Project Changes," describe these processes in detail.

■ A Final Checklist

To start managing the project that you've so carefully planned, you need a few key components. Most of the time, you'll complete these items during the planning phase, and you'll be all set to start. However, just as you pat your pockets for your house keys before you lock the front door, it's a good idea to ensure that you have everything you need to launch project execution.

Approvals and Commitments

During planning, you worked hard to get people to agree on the plans and commit to the project. As you reached agreements and obtained commitments for resources, you asked the project sponsor, customers, and other stakeholders to formally sign documents to approve the plan.

If you're glancing around nervously and shaking your head no, don't panic. Many projects have to start before the project plan is complete and approved. It's risky, but it's a common occurrence in the world of project management. You have to execute and control the project according to the plan as it is, while continuing to push to complete the plan and obtain approval on it.

The following checklist includes the items that are (ideally) complete with signatures that represent stakeholder support:

- The project sponsor has signed and distributed the project charter to everyone involved with the project.

> **SEE ALSO**   Page 51 explains the purpose of the project charter and what it conveys.

- The project sponsor and all stakeholders have signed the project plan, including completion criteria, indicating their approval and support for it.

- The functional managers for the resources you need have notified you of the resources they are providing to the project.

- Any contracts that are required, for instance with subcontractors or vendors, have been signed by both parties.

- Any additional steps or procedures that your organization has for obtaining funding or budget approval are complete, and project funding is officially available.

The Project Notebook

The project plan is a collection of text documents, spreadsheets, project schedules, diagrams, memos, and more. Moreover, after you begin managing project execution, you'll be awash in more paperwork: status reports, change requests, email with questions from team members, and so on. If you haven't done so already, now is the time to create a repository for the project notebook, whether it's a set of ring binders with tabbed separators, hanging folders in a filing cabinet, or electronic folders on a computer.

> **SEE ALSO**   Chapter 18, "Archiving Historical Information," describes different ways to store project information electronically. Figure 18-1, on page 388, shows a sample index for a project notebook.

The best approach to a filing system depends on the type and size of the project, your dedication to keeping information organized, and the technology your organization has available. Setting up the ring binders or computer folders beforehand ensures that you have a home for every piece of information you generate or receive. However, if time is already tight, set up the following binders or folders as a minimum:

- *A project plan binder* contains all the documents that comprise a project plan: the text document for the overall plan, the project schedule, the budget, text documents for component plans, and so on.

>
> **TIP**   If you make major changes to the entire plan or to parts of it, don't place the revisions in chronological order. Keep the most recent versions in the front of a physical binder and store the older versions in the back. If you store files on a computer, use one folder for the current version of a document and a second folder as an archive of previous versions.

- *A communication binder* covers so much of a project that it is sure to expand as the project progresses. You can include tabs (or subfolders) for status reports, variance reports, all forms of correspondence, and meeting minutes. Or you can set up separate binders for each one.

- *A change management binder* stores the documentation for change requests and their status. Depending on how you manage changes, this binder can include the original change requests, estimates, approvals, rejections and the reasons for them, and a regularly updated status of all changes requested so far.

- *A risk management binder* contains risk plans, reports, and status for risks that have occurred or are still only potential problems.

| **SEE ALSO** | Chapters 11, 12, and 15 describe communication, change management, and risk management, respectively, in more detail. |

Project Baselines

You're anxious to start managing your project and comparing progress to the plan. But before you can track progress, you need to save the numbers from the plan so you can compare your actual results to them. The numbers you've planned for are called *baselines*, and Microsoft Project can save them for values you track in the program.

Project includes baselines for both the schedule and costs, but it doesn't set them automatically. When you receive approval for the project schedule, you can set a baseline in Project to save baseline values for start and finish dates, duration, work, and cost. To save your initial baseline in Project, do the following:

Set
Baseline ▾

1. With the schedule open in Project, on the Project tab, in the Schedule group, click the down arrow to the right of the Set Baseline button, and then click Set Baseline.

2. In the Set Baseline dialog box, make sure that the Set Baseline option is selected.

3. In the drop-down list underneath the Set Baseline option, choose Baseline, which indicates the baseline that Project uses to calculate variances.

| **SEE ALSO** | The section "Modifying Baselines," on page 323, provides instructions for saving additional baselines. |

4. Under the For heading, verify that Entire Project is selected.

5. Click OK. Project stores the values in fields for the baseline.

BEST PRACTICES

Because Project calculates variances based on the values in the Baseline fields, consider reserving Baseline for the values from your most recent baseline. After you save your original plan values to Baseline, immediately save the same values to Baseline1 to keep a permanent copy of this baseline. (On the Project tab, in the Schedule group, click the down arrow to the right of the Set Baseline button. In the Set Baseline drop-down list, choose Baseline1 and click OK.) By doing so, you store your original baseline values in Baseline1 and your most recent baseline (which at this point is the same as the original) in Baseline.

When you save a revised baseline, for instance to incorporate a major change to the project, save it to the next empty baseline—Baseline2, Baseline3, and so on. At the same time, save a copy of those values in Baseline, so your variances are based on the most recent baseline values.

If you save a baseline for the entire project, you can be sure that Project dutifully copies your estimated values to its baseline fields. However, if a few small changes come in or you want to check that you've saved the correct baseline values, the Baseline table in Project includes every field for the primary baseline: Baseline Duration, Baseline Start, Baseline Finish, Baseline Work, and Baseline Cost, as shown in Figure 8-1. Here are the steps for applying the Baseline table to a view, such as the Gantt Chart view:

1. With the Gantt Chart view visible, on the View tab, in the Data group, click the down arrow to the right of the Tables button and then choose More Tables.

2. In the More Tables dialog box, select Baseline, and then click Apply.

You can see baseline dates for tasks in the Task Details Form, also shown in Figure 8-1. Here are the steps to display the Task Details Form:

1. On the View tab, in the Split View group, select the Details check box if it isn't already selected.

2. In the drop-down list, click More Views.

3. In the More Views dialog box, select Task Details Form, and then click Apply.

   Initially, the Task Details Form opens with the Current option selected, which shows your current estimates for task start and finish dates. However, when you select the Baseline option, the dates in the Start and Finish boxes change to your baseline dates.

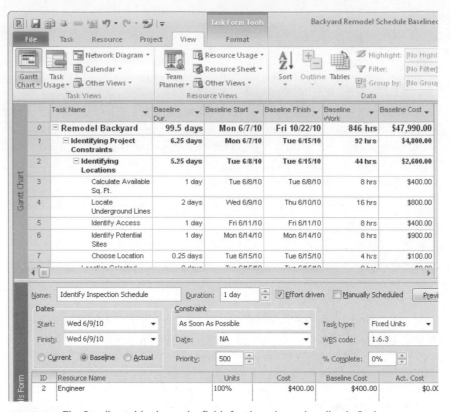

FIGURE 8-1 The Baseline table shows the fields for the primary baseline in Project.

Summary

The goal for project execution is simple: carry out the project plan to achieve the project objectives. As project manager, you start by lining up any team members who aren't already on board. A kickoff meeting helps the team get to know one another and prepare to start their work on the right foot. After that, you make sure that people are working on what they should be; you see whether they're making progress as they should; and if they aren't, you come up with changes to the plan to recover.

CHAPTER 9

Evaluating Project Performance

> "*An unsophisticated forecaster uses statistics as a drunken man uses lamp-posts—for support rather than illumination.*"—ANDREW LANG

THE MORE TIME you have to correct the course of a project, the more likely you are to succeed in getting things back on track. As a project manager, you can prevent unpleasant jolts of adrenaline by regularly reviewing your projects for early signs of trouble. Knowing where a project is relative to the planned schedule and budget helps answer questions such as "Are the hours allocated to tasks realistic?" and "Are team members working as productively as we estimated?" which, in turn, can help you decide how to rectify any problems. And with a bit more analysis, you can answer the questions the stakeholders ask, such as "Will the project meet our objectives?" and "What's the return on investment?"

This chapter describes how you go about analyzing project performance. The first task, of course, is to collect information about actual progress to compare to the plan. Then, you can update task status so you can evaluate schedule and cost performance—reviewing the current schedule and cost versus the baseline values, for example. Microsoft Project provides several tools, such as views, tables, filters, and reports, for tracking progress and spotting early warning signs. You'll learn which ones to use and when. You'll also learn how to use Project's visual reports to analyze project performance from different perspectives. This chapter also introduces a technique known as *earned value analysis*, which indicates whether your project is on time and within budget by comparing the relationships among actual costs, budgeted costs, scheduled work, and completed work.

Gathering Data

The cost and schedule for a project is an extension of the resources that it requires. To determine where a project stands, you mainly need to know how much time resources are spending on their tasks and when. If you have costs other than those for labor and materials, you need to know how much of those your project has incurred as well. As difficult as it can be to gather numbers for time and cost, you also need to know other, less easily quantifiable measures of project progress—how closely the work conforms to the project requirements and quality, and whether the project is making the customer happy. This section describes the information you need to gauge progress and provides some guidelines for how to obtain it.

The Data You Need

The data you need to evaluate progress depends on what's important to you and project stakeholders. Because "Are we on time?" and "Are we within budget?" are the most frequently asked questions, you know you need information about the work that's been done, how much work remains, how much money has been spent, and how much it will cost to complete the job. But there's more to progress than time and money. This section introduces some of the data you might want to collect to evaluate project performance.

Progress on Work Packages

When all the work packages are complete, the project is done, so tracking progress on work packages is a great place to start. Work packages that are completely finished are comparatively easy to measure. Each work package should have completion criteria, so a work package is complete when it has met those criteria. You also need to know how much time team members spent, when they did the work, and any additional costs beyond labor that the work incurred.

SEE ALSO   The section "Detailing Work Packages," on page 85, describes how you document the work that must be performed to complete a project.

But because you gather data while work packages are in progress, you also need to know how much work team members have completed to date as well as what it's going to take to finish. Besides providing accomplishments to include in your status report, work the resources have finished can help you determine whether their forecasts for completion are realistic.

Here is the data that give you a good picture of where a task stands:

- **Actual start**   This is the date when the assigned resources began work on the task.

- **Actual duration or work**   If people usually work on one task at a time, you can ask for the number of business days they have worked on the task so far. But resources don't always work full-time on their assignments and sometimes don't work consecutive days, for example, to perform other work or for sick days. For these reasons, asking for the number of hours the resources worked usually provides a more accurate picture of completion.

- **Remaining duration or work**   In order to tell whether a task is on schedule and within budget, you also need to know how long it will take to finish the work that remains. In addition to the actual duration or work, ask the assigned resources how many work hours or days they estimate it will take to complete their assignment.

TIP   If a vendor is delivering work on a fixed-price bid, all you really need to know is when the vendor achieves major milestones in addition to when the vendor expects to finish, because the actual hours and cost don't affect your project at all.

Quality

Quality measures can alter the picture of the progress you've made. For example, if you find defects faster than you can fix them, you might not be as far along on completed software as your team members are telling you.

TIP   One way to maintain quality throughout your project is to schedule reviews. For example, reviewing the project plan is essential for your project to solve the right problem in the right way. Reviewing requirements is another way to keep your project on track. Work that delivers the wrong or unnecessary requirements wastes time and money—and decreases morale when team members find out the work they did was for naught.

For product-related projects, keep your eye on defect statistics, such as the number of open defects, closed defects, and new defects found or reopened. In addition, watch trends in quality measures. For instance, the number of open defects usually increases during the early part of testing, when the most defects exist and testers find the most obvious ones. Eventually, the number of open defects hits a peak and begins to decline.

User feedback is another way to measure quality. You can ask people who will use the final product to test it and provide feedback.

TIP   The cost to fix a defect is an important measure, but it can be misleading. For example, if you plan a project to prevent defects, the cost per defect is higher, but the total cost of fixing defects is lower. Moreover, if the cost per defect increases with time, team members might be fixing the easiest defects first, which means that the rest of the defect-fixing iceberg could still be waiting.

Problems That Could Lie Ahead

Another key category for determining true progress is what can and could go wrong. (You need to know what issues team members have and what risks have arisen.) For example, for the backyard remodel project, tasks in the planning phases could be ahead of schedule, but then you find out that the hippopotamus that took up residence in the homeowners' backyard mud hole is a bigger problem than anyone imagined. Until you know how many permits you have to obtain and how long it's going to take to relocate the creature, your project progress could be stuck.

As well, when risks occur, you have to snap your risk management plan into action. Depending on the risk, your response might include dipping into the project's contingency funds and time. Or you implement your other responses, such as submitting an insurance claim for the tree that the bulldozer knocked down. And for some risks, you'll have to rework the schedule.

> **SEE ALSO** Chapter 15, "Managing Risk," describes techniques for identifying, tracking, and handling risks that turn into reality.

Obtaining Time and Status

Obtaining time and status is essential to tracking progress. Some people are happy to oblige, but others might be reluctant to report time in the way you require. Perhaps they don't see the value of recording the hours they've spent on a task. Or they could be so busy that a few minutes to track time are minutes they don't get to sleep. To make matters worse, you might need to understand the ins and outs of your organization's time-tracking system to see whether it helps or hinders collecting the information you need.

Work resources that bill and are paid by the hour should have plenty of incentive to report the time they spend on tasks. But salaried employees are paid the same amount whether they spend two days or two weeks completing a task. People offer lots of reasons for failing to accurately report the time they spend on project tasks. For one thing, work resources might divvy up their days among several tasks. Remembering to account for 30 minutes preparing a report for one task, an hour-long meeting to plan work for three other tasks, and half a day to finish still another task is tedious at best. And performed in hindsight, keeping track of relatively short periods of time on several tasks can involve more guesswork than accuracy.

> **TIP** Many organizations use compensation systems, such as pay-for-performance and reviews, to ensure that salaried employees perform the work for which they're responsible. Rewarding people for doing what you want is a big motivator. If your organization doesn't include project results as employee compensation goals, talk to management about adding these new measures.

The first step to getting the time-reporting accuracy you want is to explain the benefits of recording actual labor hours to team members. Accurate time reporting can help to do the following:

- Improve estimates in the future

- Persuade the customer and stakeholders of the time required to produce quality work

- Negotiate additional money and time for change requests

- Identify potential problems with a project schedule and budget early enough to take corrective actions

Asking people to track their time to a meaningful increment of time might be the most successful approach. You probably don't need to know how each minute of the work day is spent. You might get better results and more participation by asking team members to estimate their time to the nearest hour (or day for long tasks).

WHEN THE ACCOUNTING SYSTEM IS AN ADVERSARY

The accounting or time-tracking application that you and your team members must use can present problems for tracking project work hours. The systems and programs that many organizations use track time by role, by customer, or by entire project. They aren't designed to track time for discrete tasks within a project, which is, unfortunately, exactly the information you need. As a result, you might need to ask team members to track their task time separately so that you can incorporate it into the project schedule and budget.

Suppose someone asks you to record hours that you've spent on one task to a different task. For example, the actual hours exceed the estimated hours (or the number of hours specified in the contract). The accounting department might want to record the hours against different tasks rather than amend the contract or track variances. If you follow this advice, you won't know whether your estimates are over the budget, under budget, or right on track. You might not have any choice but to do what the accounting department says. However, if you track detailed task time outside of the accounting system, you have a record of actual hours. The challenge in this situation is to keep track of both the actual project hours and the numbers that accounting uses so you can explain any discrepancies between your project performance calculations and accounting's calculations.

Updating Tasks in Your Schedule

Before you can evaluate progress, you have to update your Project file with actual progress and the work that remains. This section describes several methods for tracking progress in Project. Some techniques are quick and easy, but don't provide much accuracy. Other techniques take more effort, but give you a better view of where things stand.

Setting the Status Date

Before you begin to update tasks, you should set the status date in Project to the date through which you have collected progress information. For example, you can set the status date to Friday of the previous week, even if you prepare your status report on Monday of this week. If you don't set the status date, Project uses today's date.

To set the status date, follow these steps:

1. On the Project tab, in the Status group, click Status Date.

2. In the Status Date dialog box, choose the status date, as shown in Figure 9-1.

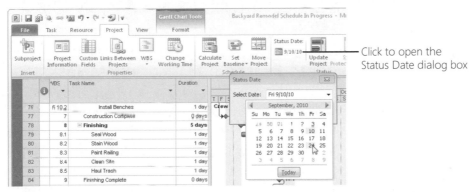

FIGURE 9-1 When you set the status date, you can update tasks through a date other than today's date.

You can display a vertical line at the status date in the timescale to make it easy to see the current status date. To do so, follow these steps:

1. On the Format tab, in the Format group, click Gridlines, and then choose Progress Lines.

Status Date:

📅 9/10/10

Gridlines
▾

2. In the Progress Lines dialog box, on the Dates And Intervals tab, select the Display check box, and then select the At Project Status Date option.

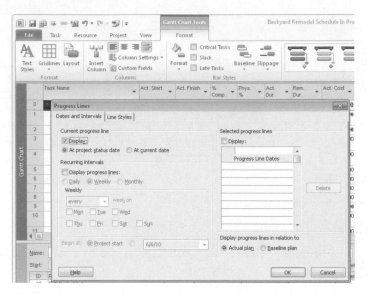

3. Click OK.

Setting Up Project to Reschedule Incomplete Tasks

If a task is incomplete, you want the incomplete portion of the task to move to after the status date. You can tell Project to automatically record completed work prior to the status date and move incomplete work to after the status date.

To reschedule incomplete work, you have to split tasks that are in progress. To set the option for this behavior, follow these steps:

1. On the File tab, choose Options.

2. In the Project Options dialog box, click Schedule.

3. Under the Scheduling Options For This Project label, select the Split In-progress Tasks check box.

Select this option to split tasks
that have already started

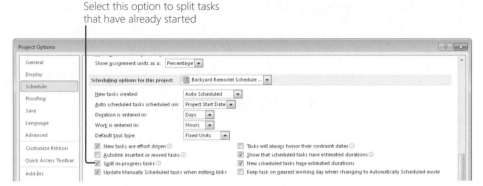

4. Click OK.

TIP   You can also move complete and incomplete work manually. In the task
view, select the task. On the Task tab, in the Tasks group, click the down
arrow to the right of the Move button. On the Move drop-down menu,
choose Completed Parts To Status Date to record the completed work
before the status date. Choose Incomplete Parts To Status Date to re-
sume the incomplete work after the status date.

 Move ▾

Quickly Updating Tasks

In Project 2010, the Mark on Track command is the quickest way to update tasks. It sets the
actual start and finish dates to the task's scheduled start and finish dates, and changes the
percent complete to 100% complete. This command provides accurate results only when
you use it to update tasks that are complete and have finished according to plan.

NOTE   The Mark On Track command can help you quickly catch up on task
updates. However, the start and finish dates and the work values won't
be accurate.

To update a task with Mark On Track, follow these steps:

1. In the Gantt Chart table, select the task or tasks that you want to update.

2. On the Task tab, in the Schedule group, click Mark on Track.

Mark on
Track

Recording Progress

You can update progress for individual tasks, several tasks at once, or even individual assignments within a task. Project offers several places for updating tasks, each with its pros and cons. This section explains how to use each one.

Using the Update Tasks Dialog Box

The Update Tasks dialog box helps you update task progress, including the percent complete, actual start and finish dates, actual duration, and remaining duration. However, it doesn't update actual work, so use one of the other two methods if you want to record actual and remaining work. Follow these steps to update tasks with this dialog box:

1. In a task view, such as Gantt Chart, select the task you want to update.

    If several tasks have the same progress values, you can update them all at once. Select all the tasks with the same update values before you open the dialog box.

2. On the Task tab, in the Schedule group, click the down arrow to the right of the Mark on Track button and then choose Update Tasks.

    The Update Tasks dialog box displays any existing actual values, as shown in Figure 9-2.

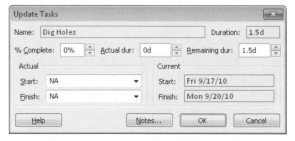

FIGURE 9-2 The Update Tasks dialog box can update the percent complete, actual start, actual finish, actual duration, and remaining duration.

3. If the task started on a date other than its scheduled start date, below the Actual label, click the down arrow in the Start box and then choose the actual start date from the calendar.

    You don't have to set the actual start date if the task started on its scheduled start date. Project automatically changes the Actual Start to the scheduled start date when you update other fields without filling in the Actual Start box.

4. If the task is complete and finished within its scheduled duration, you can update the task by entering 100% in the % Complete field and clicking OK.

   Project automatically sets the actual duration to the scheduled duration and calculates the finish date based on the start date and the actual duration.

5. If the task isn't complete, in the Actual Dur box, enter the actual duration, such as 10 days or 3 weeks.

6. In the Remaining Dur box, enter the remaining duration.

7. Click OK.

Using the Tracking Table

The Tracking table in a task-oriented view is a quick way to enter progress. You update the values in a task's cells and you can see the changes that Project calculates for other fields based on the values you enter. For example, depending on the value you update, Project may recalculate the actual start and finish dates, percent complete, actual duration, and remaining duration. If the task has assigned resources, Project updates the actual work and actual cost. To apply the Tracking table to a view, on the View tab, in the Data group, click Tables, and then choose Tracking on the drop-down list.

Tables

> **TIP** If you want to update Actual Work and Remaining Work, insert those fields into the table. Right-click the heading row of the table and choose Insert Column on the shortcut menu. Then, in the drop-down list, choose the field you want to insert, such as Actual Work or Remaining Work.

Using the Task Details Form

The Task Details Form is handy if you want to update Actual Work, Remaining Work, and Overtime Work for each assigned resource. You can also update the actual start, actual finish, and percent complete. Follow these steps to update a task or its assignments in the Task Details Form:

1. To display the Task Details Form in the bottom pane of a task view, on the View tab, in the Split View group, select the Details check box. Click the down arrow to the right of the Details box, and then choose More Views. In the More Views dialog box, click Task Details Form, and then click Apply.

2. Select a task in the top pane of the view.

   The Task Details Form displays the values for the task you selected.

3. In the Task Details Form, select the Actual option.

4. To set the actual start date, click the down arrow to the right of the Start box and then choose the date on which the task started.

   If you update other fields without setting the Actual Start date, Project automatically changes the Actual Start to the scheduled start date.

5. If you want to update actual and remaining work, right-click the Task Details Form, and then choose Work on the shortcut menu.

6. To update a resource's work, fill in the values in the Actual Work and Remaining Work cells in the resource's row, as shown in Figure 9-3.

   If you modify the % Complete field, Project calculates Actual Work and Remaining Work.

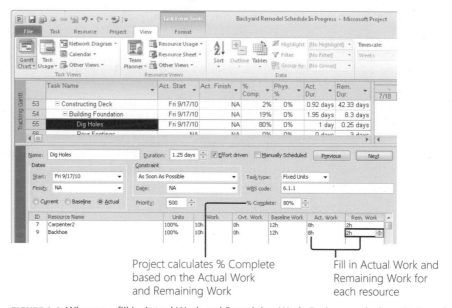

Project calculates % Complete based on the Actual Work and Remaining Work

Fill in Actual Work and Remaining Work for each resource

FIGURE 9-3 When you fill in Actual Work and Remaining Work, Project recalculates % Complete.

Recording Actual Costs

Most project costs come from the cost of labor, equipment, and materials. For any ancillary costs, such as travel, you use Project cost resources. If you specify standard rates, overtime rates, and costs per use for the work resources that represent people and equipment, you don't have to record actual costs for these resources. Project calculates actual costs based on the actual work you record for resources assigned to tasks. (You record actual quantities for material resources in the Actual Work field for a material resource assignment.) On the other hand, you do have to record actual costs for cost resources.

When you assign a cost resource to a task, you fill in a planned cost. However, Project doesn't calculate cost for cost resources when you enter progress for tasks because cost resources aren't based on time spent on a task.

> **SEE ALSO** The section "Creating Resources in Project," on page 99, describes how to create work, material, and cost resources in Project and specify cost fields. You learn how to specify planned costs for cost resources in the section "Assigning Resources to Tasks," on page 137. The section "Using the Task Details Form," on page 207, shows how to record actual work.

To record actual costs for cost resources, follow these steps:

1. On the View tab, in the Resource Views group, click Resource Usage.

2. In the table, double-click the cost resource assignment you want to update.

3. In the Assignment Information dialog box, click the Tracking tab.

   As shown in Figure 9-4, you can update either % Work Complete or Actual Cost. It's usually easier to fill in the Actual Cost box. However, if you fill in a percentage in the % Work Complete field, Project calculates the corresponding actual cost.

   If you enter less than the planned amount, the remainder transfers into the assignment's Remaining Cost field for the assignment. This field doesn't appear in the Assignment Information dialog box, but it is available in the Cost table if you need to modify it.

Resource
Usage

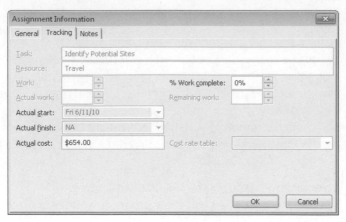

FIGURE 9-4 Fill in the Actual Cost box with the actual value for the cost resource.

Tracking Schedule Progress

Progress on the schedule is your first measure of progress, because the longer a project takes, the more it usually costs. However, to get an accurate picture of schedule progress, you have to track what's been accomplished, not just how much time has passed or how many hours have been billed. This section introduces some techniques for reviewing schedule progress in Project as well as how to use some of its built-in reports to do the same. As long as you enter the information that Project needs to calculate remaining duration and finish dates for tasks, you can view progress in a couple of ways.

> **NOTE** If the scope of your project has changed, tracking progress against your original schedule doesn't give a clear picture of progress.

> **SEE ALSO** See Chapter 12, "Managing Project Changes," and "Modifying Baselines," on page 323, to learn how to update your schedule to reflect the current scope.

The quickest way to see an overall picture of project completion and cost is in the Project Information dialog box. On the Project tab, in the Properties group, click Project Information. In the Project Information dialog box, click Statistics to see high-level status for duration, work, and cost, as well as the project start and finish dates. As you can see in Figure 9-5, the Project Statistics dialog box shows baseline values, Project's current estimate at completion, actual amounts so far, and remaining amounts.

Project
Information

Project Statistics for 'Backyard Remodel Schedule In Progress'

	Start	Finish
Current	Tue 6/8/10	Wed 11/24/10
Baseline	Mon 6/7/10	Fri 10/22/10
Actual	Tue 6/8/10	NA
Variance	1d	23.25d

	Duration	Work	Cost
Current	121.75d	942h	$51,410.00
Baseline	99.5d	846h	$47,990.00
Actual	61.02d	444h	$21,520.00
Remaining	60.73d	498h	$29,890.00

Percent complete:
Duration: 50%   Work: 47%

[Close]

FIGURE 9-5 At the bottom of the Project Statistics dialog box, if the percentage of work that's complete is less than the percentage of duration that's passed, your project is falling behind.

PROJECT FILE You can view a schedule with actual values added in Backyard Remodel Schedule InProgress.mpp in the Chapter09 folder on the companion website.

HOW PROJECT CALCULATES VALUES AND VARIANCE

Project keeps track of several sets of start dates, finish dates, durations, work, and cost, which it uses to calculate performance. You provide baseline and actual values, and Project uses those to estimate values at completion and how much remains. By understanding the difference between these values, you can track and interpret your progress more easily.

Baseline information, also called *planned information*, represents the estimates that you put together and to which stakeholders have agreed. When you save a baseline, you copy the current scheduled values to baseline fields.

SEE ALSO   The section "Project Baselines," on page 194, describes the steps to save a baseline.

Scheduled values are always the most up-to-date values for your schedule regardless of whether you are still planning or work has begun. As you build and fine-tune your schedule, the values that you see in fields in the Task Form are your current scheduled values. (The Task Details Form lets you choose the values you see by including three options for Current, Baseline, and Actual.) After you begin tracking actual values, scheduled values represent Project's estimates of the values at completion based on actual dates, effort, and costs for completed work and the estimated dates and costs for the work that remains. Project subtracts scheduled values from baseline values to determine variance.

Actual values, of course, are the values that come true: the dates that tasks actually started and finished, the work hours that team members actually spent, and the resulting actual durations and costs.

Remaining values are merely scheduled values minus actual values—how much duration, work, or cost remains.

Reviewing Schedule Progress

As you might expect, you can view progress for your schedule in several ways in Project. But by far the easiest way to see where tasks in the schedule stand is with the Tracking Gantt view. This view shows two sets of taskbars, as demonstrated in Figure 9-6: one using baseline start and finish dates, and the other using scheduled start and finish dates.

Gantt
Chart ▾

The Tracking Gantt view is great for viewing schedule status. It displays baseline and scheduled taskbars above each other and shows critical tasks in red, so it's easy to spot critical tasks that are running behind schedule. To switch to the Tracking Gantt view, on the View tab, in the Task Views group, click the down arrow next to the Gantt Chart button and then choose Tracking Gantt.

SEE ALSO   The section "Shortening a Project Schedule," on page 150, describes
several methods for bringing your schedule back on track.

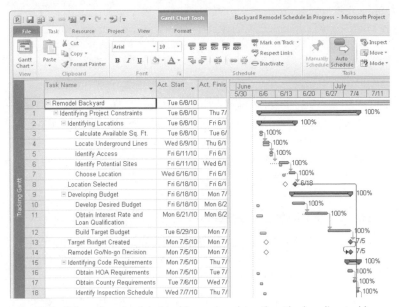

FIGURE 9-6 When the scheduled taskbars occur later than the baseline taskbars, you know that your
tasks are running later than you planned.

VIEWING SCHEDULE STATUS

Project 2010 makes it easy to see schedule status, such as the critical path, baseline information, and slack. Commands for formatting a task-oriented view are
available on the Format tab:

- **Critical tasks**   In the Bar Styles group, select the Critical Tasks check box to
  display critical tasks in red. (If you select the Late Tasks check box, critical tasks
  look the same whether they are on time or late.)

- **Slack**   A slack bar shows how much a task can be delayed before it delays its
  successors. In the Bar Styles group, turn on the Slack check box to display narrow black slack bars from the right end of a taskbar.

- **Late tasks**   In the Bar Styles group, select the Late Tasks check box to display
  tasks that are late using black taskbars.

- **Baseline**   In the Bar Styles group, click the Baseline down arrow and then choose the baseline you want to use for the Baseline taskbars.

- **Slippage**   Slippage bars shows how far tasks have delayed from their baseline start dates. Click the Slippage down arrow and then select a baseline to draw narrow black bars from the baseline start dates to the current scheduled start dates.

In Project, views, tables, and filters work together to help you spot potential problems. Views, such as the Tracking Gantt view, format data so progress is easy to see. The fields in tables come in handy for identifying estimated finish dates, finding tasks with slack time, or seeing whether the schedule variance is getting worse or better. And filters restrict the tasks that appear to ones that might require attention.

Tables with Schedule-Related Fields

To apply a table to the current view, on the View tab, in the Data group, click the Tables button, and then click the name of the table you want. Here are tables in Project that include different fields for evaluating schedule performance:

- **Summary**   The Summary table shows the scheduled values for the most common progress measures: Duration, Start, Finish, percentage complete (% Complete), Cost, and Work. If a stakeholder asks when the project will finish or how much it will cost, this table has the answers.

- **Variance**   This table includes both scheduled and baseline start and finish dates, and also shows the time variance between those dates.

TIP   One way to spot schedule trends is to display the Variance table and then sort tasks by finish date. If the values in the Finish variance field continue to increase, your project is falling further and further behind schedule.

- **Schedule**   The Schedule table includes the Free Slack and Total Slack fields, which are helpful when you're looking for tasks whose resources you can reassign to shorten tasks on the critical path.

TIP   A checklist for progress analysis can remind you of the views you want to see and the filters you want to apply, particularly if you create customized views and filters. One way to keep your checklist nearby is to store it as a note attached to the top-level summary task in your project file. Right-click the summary task and then, on the shortcut menu, click Notes. In the Summary Task Information dialog box, type the checklist points you want to perform.

Filters for Checking Schedule Progress

Many tasks run without incident, so you can reserve your attention for the ones that are falling behind or are at risk of doing so. Project includes several built-in filters for finding these at-risk tasks. To apply a filter, on the View tab, in the Data group, click the Filter down arrow and then choose the filter you want to apply. Here are a few filters for checking the schedule:

NOTE   If the filter you want doesn't appear in the filter drop-down list, click More Filters. In the More Filters dialog box, click the filter you want and then click Apply.

- **Slipping Tasks**   Use this filter to check for tasks whose finish dates have slipped. This filter shows tasks that are already in progress and whose scheduled finish dates are later than the baseline finish.

- **Slipped/Late Progress**   This filter looks for potential schedule slippage in two ways. The filter looks for baselined tasks whose scheduled finish is later than the baseline finish or those whose work performed is less than the work scheduled.

- **Should Start By**   You can look for delayed tasks with this filter, which shows tasks that should have started, but haven't. For this filter, you type the start date you want.

- **Should Start/Finish By**   This filter looks for delays in both start and finish dates. It filters for tasks that should have started or finished by the date you specify, but haven't.

- **Work Overbudget**   The Work Overbudget filter shows tasks whose actual work is greater than the baseline work, which usually translates into delays.

- **Slipping Assignments**   This is a resource filter that you can apply to views such as Resource Usage to show resources that might need help. The filter shows tasks in progress whose scheduled finish date is later than the baseline finish.

Reviewing Cost and Cost Variance

By tracking actual costs, you can compare them to the original estimate (the baseline). The simplest measure of cost performance is whether actual costs are more or less than baselined costs, whether you look at a few tasks or the project as a whole. As you keep an eye on the status of tasks as resources work on them, the actual cost and cost variance are easy ways to spot problems.

This section describes some straightforward procedures you can follow to review costs in Project as well as how to use its built-in budget and cost reports.

SEE ALSO   The section "Comparing Project Costs to the Budget," on page 174, describes how to compare project costs to budgeted costs using Microsoft Project budget resources.

EVALUATING FINANCIAL MEASURES

Project cost performance isn't limited to how much you spend. Sometimes, it depends on how much more money your organization makes or how much it saves. You should check all the financial assumptions included in the project's capital budget. For example, has the project met the revenue projections used to establish its return on investment? If you assumed that the project would reduce the cost of processing orders by 15 percent, has the project saved that amount of money? If the capital budget assumed that the cost to support and train users for the first three months after project completion would be $75,000, what were the support and training costs?

Project calculates cost based on resource rates and the amount of work performed or the percentage of the task's duration that's complete. You set up resource rates in Project when you build your project team in the Microsoft Project Resource Sheet. When you assign resources to tasks and specify the amount of work they do, Project can calculate the projected task cost. Now that work has begun on those tasks, you and the project team must track the amount of work done and the percentage that's complete so that Project can also calculate the actual task cost and the variance from your estimate.

SEE ALSO   For more information about capital budgeting, see Chapter 7, "Working With a Budget." The sections "Specifying Rates for Work Resources in Project," on page 171, and "Assigning Resources to Tasks," on page 137, describe how to set up rates for resources and then assign those resources to tasks.

Viewing Cost and Cost Variance

Baseline costs represent the costs approved by a project's stakeholders. In a perfect world, the actual costs are equal to or less than the baseline. But in reality, some tasks cost more than you estimated, and some cost less. As long as you enter the information that Project needs to calculate estimated and actual costs, you can view costs in a couple of ways.

Applying the Cost table to a task-oriented view displays columns for all kinds of costs as well as the variance between the baseline and actual costs, as described in the next section. Project recalculates the scheduled cost as you enter work or task completion percentages, and actual costs for cost resources, so the costs and variances you see are always up to date. To display the Cost table, on the View tab, in the Data group, click the Tables down arrow and then choose Cost.

TIP   You can also apply a table to a view by right-clicking the blank cell immediately above the first ID cell and then choosing the name of the table you want to apply, such as Cost.

Figure 9-7 shows the backyard remodel project with the Cost table applied. Here are the fields that the Cost table includes by default:

- **Fixed Cost**   Although cost resources are a better way to track costs other than work or materials costs, the Cost table still includes the Fixed Cost field. To hide this column, right-click its column heading and then, on the shortcut menu, choose Hide Column.

SEE ALSO   To learn about how to use cost resources, see the section "Types of Resources," on page 99.

- **Fixed Cost Accrual** If you use the Fixed Cost field to document any project costs, this field tells Project when to apply the fixed cost to the schedule. Prorated means that the cost is distributed over the duration of the task. Start and End represent the cost occurring at the start or the finish of the task, respectively.

- **Total Cost** This field is the scheduled cost and includes all costs for the task.

- **Baseline** This field represents the baseline cost for all task costs, including labor, material, and cost resources.

- **Variance** Project calculates variance by subtracting the baseline cost from the total cost. If the variance is positive, the project is over budget.

- **Actual** This field represents the actual cost for labor, material, cost resources, and fixed costs.

- **Remaining** Project calculates the remaining value by subtracting the actual cost from the total cost.

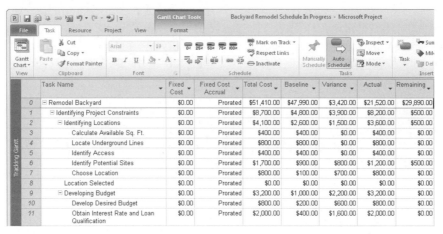

FIGURE 9-7 The Cost table provides a quick view of the status of costs and variances.

> **NOTE**   If your variances are all zero, you aren't necessarily right on track. You can view cost variances only if you've entered pay rates for resources and saved a baseline.

Finding Costs That Are Over Budget

One of the first steps to controlling costs is regularly checking the tasks and resources that have exceeded their baselined amounts. Project includes both views and reports for examining costs that are over budget. Here are the steps to view cost overruns by applying a filter to a task-oriented view:

1. On the View tab, in the Task Views group, click Task Usage to see values for each resource assigned to each task. By using this view, you can evaluate task overruns and which resources are over and under budget.

2. On the View tab, in the Data group, click the Tables down arrow, and then select Cost.

3. To view only over budget tasks, on the View tab, in the Data group, click the Filter down arrow and then, in the Filter list, choose More Views. In the More Views dialog box, select Cost Overbudget, and then click Apply.

With large projects, you probably don't want to spend time on tasks that are only slightly over budget. You can show the tasks with the largest cost overruns in a table. First, hide summary tasks (on the Format tab, in the Show/Hide group, select the Summary Tasks check box). On the View tab, in the Data group, click the Sort down arrow and choose Sort By. In the Sort dialog box, in the Sort By box, choose Cost Variance. Select the Descending option and then click Sort.

> **NOTE** To view cost overruns by resource, follow the same steps, except choose Resource Usage in step 1.

Reporting on Project Performance

Reports come in handy when you want to review project performance to see whether you need to take corrective action. They're also great for communicating project status and performance to others. Project offers a plethora of built-in reports, whether you want high-level status for the management team or detailed reports to pinpoint problems.

Project has two types of reports. *Text-based reports* use a static format. They're easy to run and you can customize them if you want to see information in slightly different ways. *Visual reports*, on the other hand, are dynamic. They grab data from your Project file and bring it into a Microsoft Excel PivotTable or a Microsoft Visio PivotDiagram, so you can change your perspective of project performance on the fly.

This section tells you about a few text-based and visual reports you can use to evaluate project performance. You'll learn how to generate and configure visual reports to view results from different angles. You'll also learn how to use earned value analysis to review project schedule and cost performance.

Looking at High-Level Status

Project has text-based and visual reports for high-level status:

Reports

- **Project Summary** This text-based report shows the same high-level information as the Project Statistics dialog box. You can see baseline, scheduled, and actual values for the project start and finish dates, duration, work, and cost. The report also shows the number of unstarted, in progress, and completed tasks, the number of resources, and the number of resources that are overallocated. To run the report, on the Project tab, in the Reports group, click Reports. In the Reports dialog box, click Overview, and then click Select. Click Project Summary and then click Select.

> **SEE ALSO** Figure 9-5, on page 211, shows the Project Statistics dialog box.

Visual Reports

- **Task Status** This Visio-based visual report shows work, cost, and percentage complete for top-level tasks, but you can include other fields like baseline work, actual work, baseline cost, and actual cost to evaluate project progress, as shown in Figure 9-8. You can also expand summary tasks in the report to evaluate progress in more detail.

  The Visio shapes display icons that indicate status. For example, happy, sad, or neutral faces appear when completed work is ahead, behind, or equal to the baseline schedule. A progress bar in the box indicates the percentage of work complete.

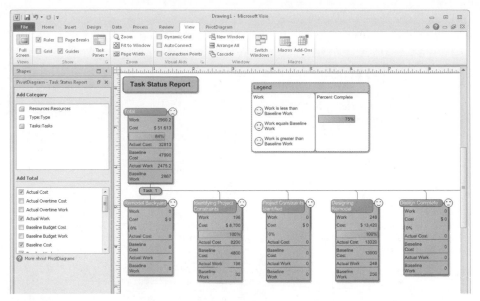

FIGURE 9-8 You can turn on check boxes in the Add Total section to display fields in the Visio shapes.

SEE ALSO   To learn how to generate and configure visual reports to view information in different ways, see the section "Working with Visual Reports," on page 233.

- **Critical Tasks Status**   Another Visio-based visual report, the Critical Tasks Status report shows work and remaining work for critical tasks. To see whether the tasks on the critical path are on track, you can include fields like baseline and actual work.

Evaluating Cost and Work

Project offers several visual reports with information on cost and work. Here are two that help you evaluate cost performance at a high level or in detail:

- **Baseline Cost**   You can take your pick between the Excel or Visio Baseline Cost visual reports to see planned, actual, and baseline costs. Because you can change these reports on the fly, you can analyze cost for the entire project, drill down to see cost by phase or summary task, or modify the report to show cost by quarter. The Excel Baseline Cost visual report initially shows costs by summary task, as shown in Figure 9-9. The Visio Baseline Cost report initially shows cost by quarter.

However, you can rearrange either report to show costs by the category or time period you want.

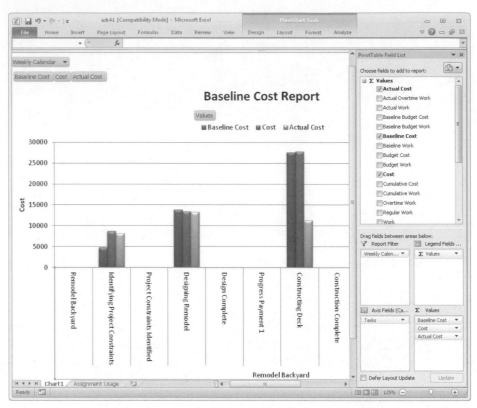

FIGURE 9-9 Although the Excel Baseline Cost visual report initially shows cost by summary task, you can rearrange the report to show cost by time period or other categories.

TIP   The Baseline Work visual report is a bar graph of baseline, planned, and actual work.

- **Cash Flow**   The Excel Cash Flow report shows cost by quarter. A line in the graph shows the cumulative cost as time passes. The shapes in the Visio Cash Flow report display orange exclamation points if the current scheduled cost is greater than the baseline cost.

SEE ALSO   The next section, "Earned Value Analysis: Schedule and Cost Performance," describes how you can use earned value to evaluate where your project stands in both schedule and cost.

Earned Value Analysis: Schedule and Cost Performance

The comparison of how much you've spent to what you've planned to spend can be deceiving. For example, suppose a project is through half of its scheduled duration and you've spent roughly half the budget. If half the work is done as well, you're right on track. But if the budget and schedule are half spent and the team has finished only 30 percent of the work, the picture isn't as bright. You have 50 percent of the budget and duration left but you still must complete 70 percent of the work. *Earned value analysis* takes into account not only actual and budgeted costs but also how much actual and estimated work is complete to give you a better idea of where your project stands. For example, if you've spent more than was budgeted for the current status of the project, you could be ahead of schedule rather than over budget. Because you performed more work than you planned in the time that's passed, the higher costs are to be expected.

NOTE   Earned value analysis gets its name because you identify the value that the project has earned so far (the money that's been spent to perform the work that's complete). The U.S. Department of Defense and other government agencies require an earned value analysis for their projects, but businesses use it to evaluate projects as well.

Earned value analysis calculates how much of a budget should have been spent given the amount of work that's been performed to a specific date. Earned value uses the following concepts to measure status:

- Project tasks earn value as work on the task is completed.

- The earned value compared to actual and planned costs shows cost performance and forecasts future costs.

- Work completed is measured in dollars so that cost performance and schedule performance are money-based measures.

Earned Value Status Measures

The measures that initiate earned value analysis are budgeted cost of work scheduled (BCWS), actual cost of work performed (ACWP), and budgeted cost of work performed (BCWP). Here is what each one of these measures represents:

- *Budgeted cost of work scheduled (BCWS)* is sometimes referred to as planned value (PV) because it is the baseline cost up to the status date for tasks as they were originally scheduled in the project plan. It is how much of the money you planned to spend by the status date. For example, if the cost of work that you planned to complete by September 23, 2011 is $10,000, BCWS on that date is $10,000.

- *Budgeted cost of work performed (BCWP)* is also called *earned value (EV)* because it measures the value of the worked performed, thus earned, up to the status date. This measure calculates how much of the cost should have been spent given the work that's actually been done. It has nothing to do with when the work is performed. For example, if the budgeted cost for all the task work completed so far is $8,000, BCWP is $8,000. Although you calculate BCWP for each task individually, you analyze earned value at the project level.

- *Actual cost of work performed (ACWP)*, which is also known simply as *actual costs*, represents the actual costs for the work performed up to the status date, whether you've completed more or fewer tasks than you had planned so far. ACWS is whatever you've spent up to September 23, 2011 in this example.

Analyzing an Earned Value Graph

An earned value graph is the best way to view earned value because you don't even have to see any numbers to know whether your project is on schedule and within budget. You'll typically see BCWS, ACWP, and BCWP compared, as shown in Figure 9-10. By plotting each measure over time, you quickly see how your project is doing compared to your planned schedule and budget. The *y*-axis in the earned value graph represents cost, whereas the *x*-axis shows time.

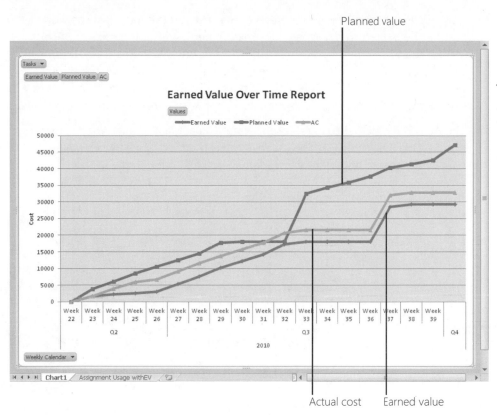

FIGURE 9-10 An earned value graph visually depicts the relationships among earned value, planned value, and actual cost, so you can easily identify trends.

Here's how you read an earned value graph to determine both the schedule and budget status for a project:

- The BCWS line (planned value) represents the amount of money you planned to spend over the course of the project, so it's no surprise that it continues to rise throughout the project's duration. As the BCWS line in Figure 9-10 illustrates, the budgeted cost increases until it reaches its planned budget ($47,240) at the end of the project.

> **NOTE**   In this example, the flat section in the middle of the graph is due to a several-week wait to obtain the construction permit from the county. And the big spike in cost represents the cost of the materials delivered just before construction.

- The BCWP line (earned value) represents the cost you estimated for the work that has been performed. When construction begins (after the spike in price), the earned value line is below the planned value line. Mathematically, this means that the cost of the work you've done is less than the cost of the work scheduled to be completed. In project status terms, this translates into *the project is behind schedule.*

- The ACWP line (actual cost) represents what you actually spent. When construction begins, the actual cost line is above the earned value line, which means that you spent more to complete the work than you had budgeted—in short, your project is over budget.

> **TIP** Here's a summary of what you *want* to see in an earned value chart. The project is ahead of schedule when the earned value line is above the planned value line. The project is under budget when the actual cost line is below the earned value line.

> **SEE ALSO** You can create an earned value graph by generating a visual report in Project, which is described in detail in the section "Creating an Earned Value Graph in Project," on page 231.

Earned Value Performance

Earned value analysis also calculates variances and indexes to help you determine whether you have enough money left in the budget to complete the project or whether the project is on track to finish on time. The following are other earned value measures you can calculate and what they tell you:

- **Cost variance (CV)**   The budgeted cost of work performed (BCWP or earned value) for a task minus the actual cost of work performed (ACWP). If the variance is positive, the actual cost is under the budgeted amount; if the variance is negative, the task is over budget.

> **NOTE** The CV and Cost Variance fields in Project represent different things. For example, in the Cost table, the Variance column is the Cost Variance field, which is the actual cost minus the baseline cost, so a positive variance means that the task is over budget. However, the CV field is BCWP minus ACWP, so a positive CV means that the task is under budget.

- **Schedule variance (SV**)   The budgeted cost of work performed (BCWP or earned value) minus the budgeted cost of work scheduled (BCWS or planned value). A positive schedule variance means that the project is ahead of schedule.

- **The cost performance index (CPI)**   An indicator of whether a project might go over budget. CPI is the ratio of budgeted costs of work performed (earned value) to actual costs of work performed (BCWP / ACWP). The CPI for the entire project is the sum of BCWP for all tasks divided by the sum of ACWP for all tasks. A CPI greater than 1 indicates the project is under budget, because actual costs are less than earned value. A CPI less than 1 means the project is over budget. For example, a CPI of 0.7 means that the earned value is 70 percent of the actual cost.

- **The schedule performance index (SPI)**   An indicator of whether a project will be on time and can help you estimate the project completion date. SPI is the ratio of the budgeted cost of work performed (BCWP or earned value) to the budgeted cost of work scheduled (BCWS or planned value). An SPI greater than 1 indicates that the project is ahead of schedule because the work performed exceeds the work scheduled. An SPI less than 1 indicates that the project is behind schedule.

- **Budget at completion (BAC)**   Simply the baseline cost approved for the entire project.

- **Estimate at completion (EAC)**   An estimate of the total cost of a task or project based on progress as of the status date. EAC is calculated using the formula EAC = ACWP + ((BAC − BCWP) / CPI).

- **Variance at completion (VAC)**   The difference between the budget at completion (BAC) and the estimate at completion (EAC). In Project, the Total Cost field represents EAC and the Baseline Cost field is BAC.

- **Estimate to complete (ETC)**   The amount of money needed to finish the project. To calculate ETC, subtract ACWP from EAC.

- **To complete performance index (TCPI)**   The ratio of the work remaining to the budget remaining (as of a status date). The formula for TCPI is (BAC − BCWP) / (BAC − ACWP). The numerator for TCPI is the baseline cost for the work remaining. The denominator is the unspent baseline dollars for the project. If TCPI is greater than 1, the remaining baseline cost is greater than the remaining dollars, that is, the remaining work costs more than the money that's left. If TCPI is less than 1, the baseline cost for the remaining work is less than the available dollars and you have a surplus.

BEST PRACTICES

Earned value analysis might sound a little daunting, and when you throw in acronyms like BCWS, BCWP, and the like, you might think that the calculations must take more time than you have available. The good news is that Project can calculate earned value measures for you. To obtain Project's assistance, you must assign costs to tasks, set a baseline, set a status date, keep track of actual costs in Project, and set up tasks that don't run from the project start to project finish. (Project uses completed tasks to calculate earned value unless you instruct it otherwise.)

Although you certainly want to find out why a CPI is less than 1, don't panic. For example, the CPI might have improved from last month's report, which means that the project is coming back closer to the original budget.

Finally, even if your analysis reveals a positive schedule variance, take a look at the tasks that must be completed to reach major milestones. If secondary tasks are all on track, but a few major tasks are behind, that positive schedule variance could disappear.

Earned Value in Microsoft Project

Project can calculate values for BCWS, BCWP, ACWS, and the other earned value measures, but you have a few tasks to complete first. You must check that options related to earned value are set the way you want. You must save a baseline (at least one). If you save more than one baseline, you must know which baseline you want to use for earned value comparisons. And you must choose between using the % Complete field or the Physical % Complete field as the basis of the calculations, which is described in the following sidebar, "The % Complete and Physical % Complete Fields." After you've completed these steps, you can view earned value analysis in several ways.

THE % COMPLETE AND PHYSICAL % COMPLETE FIELDS

The PMI Body of Knowledge (PMBOK) suggests two definitions of complete for earned value calculations. However, you can define complete in three ways:

- **All or nothing**   This is the most conservative definition because a task is either complete or incomplete. Any less than 100 percent complete represents incomplete, which means the task is not included in earned value calculations. Project initially uses this method. If a task's % Complete field is 100 percent, then Project calculates its earned value fields. % Complete less than 100 percent means earned value fields are 0 percent.

- **Unstarted, started, or complete**   A more moderate approach is to keep unstarted tasks at 0 percent and completed tasks at 100 percent, while recording tasks in progress at 50 percent. Another moderate method is to break the percentages into quadrants: 0 percent for unstarted, 25 percent for started, 50 percent for halfway, 75 percent for almost complete, and 100 percent for complete.

- **Completed work**   A more accurate approach is to define complete as the specific percentage of work that's complete.

Here's an example of how % Complete and Physical % Complete differ. % Complete is the percentage of task duration that has passed. It doesn't indicate how much work has been done. For example, you estimate that pouring 100 concrete pads will take 10 days. Because it rained, you've poured 30 concrete pads at the 5-day mark. % Complete is 50 percent, because 5 of the 10 days have passed. % Physical Complete is 30 percent because you've poured 30 of the 100 concrete pads.

Physical % Complete is a value you enter, so you can make it as accurate as you want. For example, you can set Physical % Complete to 0 percent, 25 percent, 50 percent, 75 percent, or 100 percent, depending on the relative completion of a task. Or, you can enter the value from the % Work Complete field into Physical % Complete.

If you don't want to use the all or nothing method, you must tell Project to use the Physical % Complete field to calculate earned value.

SEE ALSO   To learn how to change the field Project uses to calculate earned value, see the next section, "Setting Options for Earned Value."

Setting Options for Earned Value

Here are the steps for setting up options for earned value calculations:

1. On the File tab, click Options.

2. In the Project Options dialog box, click Advanced.

3. Below the Earned Value Options For This Project label, in the Default Task Earned Value Method drop-down list, choose Physical % Complete.

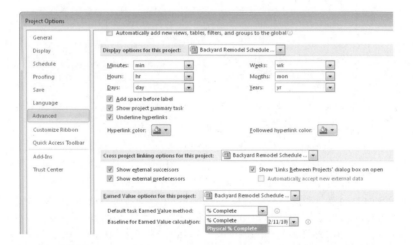

NOTE   Changing the value of this option affects only the tasks that are added to your Project file *after* the option is changed. To change this setting for a task that already exists, double-click the task to open the Task Information dialog box and then click the Advanced tab. Choose the field you want in the Earned Value Method list.

4. In the Baseline For Earned Value Calculations list, select the baseline you want Project to use when it calculates earned value totals.

5. Click Close.

6. In the Project Options dialog box, click OK.

Viewing Earned Value in a Table

In a Project schedule, you can see earned value in the Earned Value table and in the Earned Value Cost Indicators table. (On the View tab, in the Data group, click the Tables down arrow, and then choose More Tables. In the More Tables dialog box, double-click either the Earned Value or Earned Value Cost Indicators table.)

- **Earned Value table**   Shows the fundamental earned value measures, including BCWS, BCWP, ACWP, SV, CV, EAC, BAC, and VAC. You can use this table to spot variances and the different values at completion.

- **Earned Value Cost Indicators table**   Includes some of the same columns as the Earned Value table, but also includes indexes, such as CPI and TCPI. Check the values of CPI and TCPI to see whether the project is on budget and schedule. If CPI is less than 1, the task or project is over budget. The value of TCPI indicates how much you need to increase project performance on remaining work to stay within the budget.

Creating an Earned Value Graph in Project

The Earned Value Over Time visual report automatically generates an earned value graph. To generate this visual report, follow these steps:

1. On the Project tab, in the Reports group, click Visual Reports.

2. In the Visual Reports–Create Report dialog box, on the All tab, shown in Figure 9-11, click Earned Value Over Time Report.

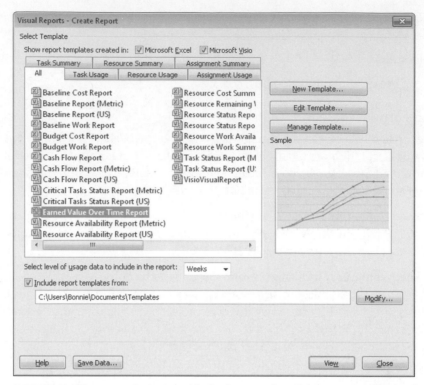

FIGURE 9-11 When you select a report in the list, a preview of the report appears on the right side of the dialog box.

3. In the Select Level Of Usage Data To Include In The Report drop-down list, choose Days, Weeks, Months, Quarters, or Years to specify the smallest time periods you want to evaluate in the report.

4. Click View.

> **SEE ALSO**   To see an example of an earned value visual report, see Figure 9-10, on page 225.

Working with Visual Reports

Visual reports are powerful tools for evaluating project performance, so it's a good idea to learn how to put them through their paces. You can change how you categorize the results, expand or collapse detail, and change the fields of information you see. This section begins with the steps for generating a visual report. Then, you learn several methods for modifying Excel and Visio visual reports.

Generating Visual Reports

Here are the steps for generating a visual report:

1. On the Project tab, in the Reports group, click Visual Reports.

2. In the Visual Reports–Create Report dialog box, on the All tab, click the report you want to generate.

    On the right side of the dialog box, the preview displays a sample of the visual report you selected.

    > **NOTE** Visio-based visual reports appear in the Visual Reports dialog box only if Visio is installed on your computer.

3. In the Select Level Of Usage Data To Include In The Report drop-down list, choose Days, Weeks, Months, Quarters, or Years to specify the smallest time periods you want to evaluate in the report.

4. Click View.

Modifying Excel-Based Visual Reports

This section describes methods for configuring Excel-based visual reports, which are nothing more than Excel pivot charts.

Choosing Fields to Display

The Excel pivot chart for a visual report doesn't automatically display every field that the visual report contains. With the visual report opened in Excel as a pivot chart and table, you can add, remove, or change the fields that appear. The fields that you select show up as vertical bars in the pivot chart and as columns in the pivot table worksheet. If you change the type of chart, the values may appear as 3-D bars, a series of line segments, data points, or other formats.

The PivotTable Field List is a task pane that appears to the right of the pivot chart, as shown in Figure 9-12. Use the following methods to choose and order the fields in the pivot chart:

Select to add a field
to the report

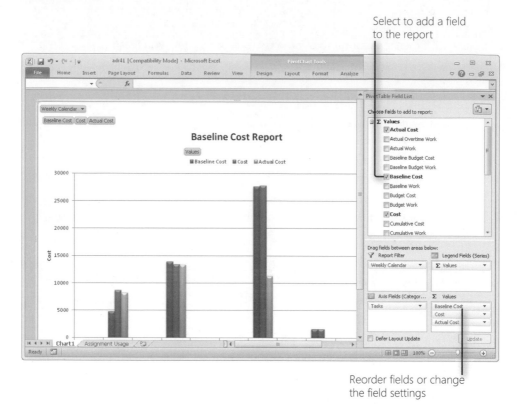

Reorder fields or change
the field settings

FIGURE 9-12 The PivotChart Tools tab and the PivotTable Field List provide commands for configuring an Excel pivot chart.

TIP If you don't see the PivotChart Tools tab or the PivotTable Field List, click anywhere in the Excel chart. If the PivotTable Field List doesn't appear, under PivotChart Tools, click the Analyze tab and then, in the Show/Hide group, click Field List.

- To add a field, in the Choose Fields To Add To Report section, select the field's check box. To remove a field, clear the check box. You can also add a field by dragging the field name into the Σ Values box in the task pane.

- To change the order of fields, drag a field to a new location in the list in the Σ Values box.

- To change how the field is calculated, in the Σ Values box, click the field name and then, on the shortcut menu, choose Value Field Settings. In the Value Field Settings dialog box, click the Summarize Values By tab. In the Summarize Value Field By list, click the type of calculation you want. Depending on the field, the calculations you can choose include sum, average, minimum value, maximum value, count, and so on.

Filtering the Information That Appears in the Chart

You can filter the information that appears in a visual report to show data for specific time periods, tasks, resources, or based on the values in fields. The following steps use the Baseline Cost visual report as an example:

1. Drag the field or category you want into the Report Filter box in the task pane. To filter by tasks, for example, drag Tasks from the Axis Fields (Categories) box into the Report Filter box.

   The Baseline Cost report initially filters by time, which is represented by Weekly Calendar in the Report Filter box.

   > **NOTE** When the pivot chart is visible (the Chart1 tab is selected), the filter label is Axis Fields (Categories). When the pivot table is active (in this example, the Assignment Usage tab is selected), the filter label reads Row Labels.

2. Click the Assignment Usage tab to display the pivot table.

   > **NOTE** The name of the tab depends on the visual report you're working with. For example, the Cash Flow report is in the Task Usage visual report category, so the Excel spreadsheet tab name is Task Usage.

3. To choose the tasks you want to display, click the Tasks down arrow at the top of the pivot table.

   At first, the drop-down list displays only the top-level category, which is the name of the project if you filter by tasks. If you filter by time, the table shows calendar years.

4. To select multiple items in the pivot table, choose the Select Multiple Items check box. Select the check boxes for items you want to include, as shown in Figure 9-13, and then click OK.

   To expand a higher-level to show the next lower level, click the plus sign to the left of the category.

FIGURE 9-13 Select check boxes to include the items in the chart. Clear check boxes to omit the items.

5. To filter by other fields in the pivot table, click the down arrow to the right of the field name, and then choose a filter to apply, as shown in Figure 9-14.

FIGURE 9-14 Choose a filter on the shortcut menu or select check boxes to include items in the chart.

TIP   When the pivot chart is visible, click the buttons at the bottom of the chart to apply filters. For example, to filter by time, click the Weekly Calendar button. You can choose filters on the shortcut menu or select and clear check boxes for specific items.

Categorizing Information

Tasks, time, and resources are the most common ways to categorize a visual report. For example, you might slice up a visual report to see results by project phase, by time period, or by resource.

Visual report categories are represented by the rows in the report's pivot table (on the Assignment Usage tab in the Baseline Cost visual report), and they show up as groups on the pivot chart's x-axis (on the Chart1 tab). For example, the Baseline Cost visual report categorizes by task initially. It starts with one row for the entire project, but you can expand that category to show additional rows for each top-level task, and expand those tasks to see lower-level tasks. In the default Baseline Cost visual report, each top-level task appears along the x-axis with a set of field bars for the fields you display.

You can break down results by more than one category and you don't have to use the same category for each level. For example, you can categorize by tasks first, and then by time period to evaluate cost for each summary task per time period.

To add or remove a category, add or remove fields in the task pane's Row Labels box (called Axis Fields if the pivot chart is active). For example, to further break down the Baseline Cost report by time periods, drag the Weekly Calendar from the Report Filter box into the Row Labels box below Tasks. By doing so, each time period has its own set of field bars. For example, you can see a set of field bars for each calendar quarter for each summary task, as shown in Figure 9-15.

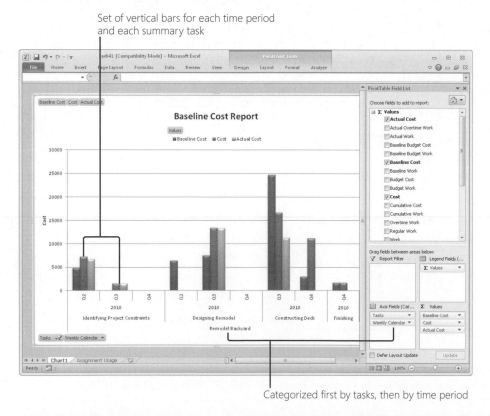

FIGURE 9-15 In this example, the report results are categorized by task and then by time period, so the report includes a set of vertical bars for each time period and for each top-level summary task.

TIP

You can drag fields between the Report Filter and Row Labels (or Axis Fields) boxes to reconfigure the report. For example, to filter by time and group by tasks, simply drag Weekly Calendar from the Row Labels (or Axis Fields) box into the Report Filter box. Then, drag Tasks from the Report Filter box into the Row Labels (Axis Fields) box.

Summarizing and Showing Detail

Showing summaries or detail in a visual report is as easy as clicking the + and - buttons in the pivot table. The pivot chart changes to reflect what you see in the pivot table. For example, the Baseline Cost report in Figure 9-15 shows cost by top-level summary task for calendar quarters. Figure 9-16 shows how the year 2010 is expanded in the pivot table to show each calendar quarter.

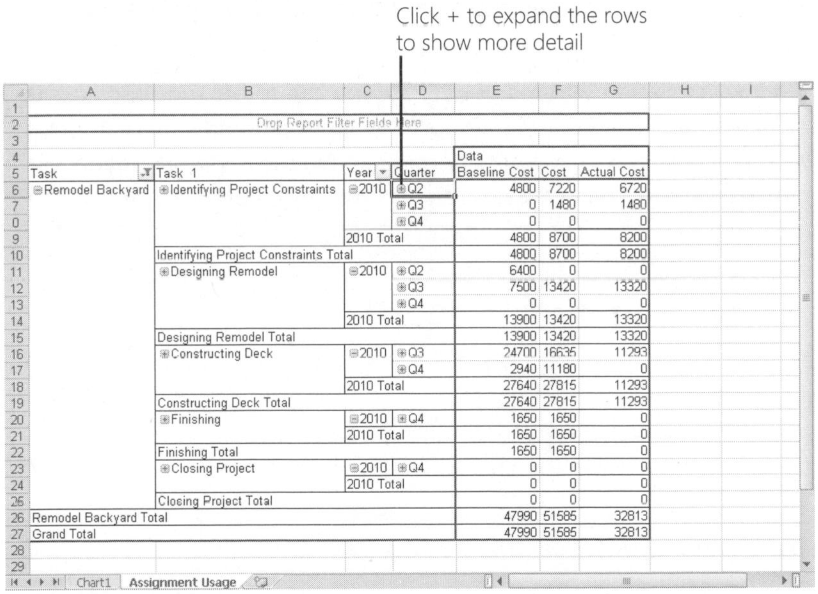

Click + to expand the rows
to show more detail

Task	Task 1	Year	Quarter	Baseline Cost	Cost	Actual Cost
Remodel Backyard	Identifying Project Constraints	2010	Q2	4800	7220	6720
			Q3	0	1480	1480
			Q4	0	0	0
		2010 Total		4800	8700	8200
	Identifying Project Constraints Total			4800	8700	8200
	Designing Remodel	2010	Q2	6400	0	0
			Q3	7500	13420	13320
			Q4	0	0	0
		2010 Total		13900	13420	13320
	Designing Remodel Total			13900	13420	13320
	Constructing Deck	2010	Q3	24700	16635	11293
			Q4	2940	11180	0
		2010 Total		27640	27815	11293
	Constructing Deck Total			27640	27815	11293
	Finishing	2010	Q4	1650	1650	0
		2010 Total		1650	1650	0
	Finishing Total			1650	1650	0
	Closing Project	2010	Q4	0	0	0
		2010 Total		0	0	0
	Closing Project Total			0	0	0
Remodel Backyard Total				47990	51585	32813
Grand Total				47990	51585	32813

Chart1   Assignment Usage

FIGURE 9-16 You can expand the time periods further to show each week in a quarter by clicking the plus sign to the left of a quarter.

To expand a quarter to show cost by week, click the + to the left of the quarter (Q2, for example). You don't have to expand or collapse the entire report to the same level. For example, you can expand the time periods that are complete to show weeks and keep future time periods at quarters.

Formatting the Appearance of the Chart

Pivot charts can perform more tricks than regular Excel charts, but they are still charts, so you can use the same formatting tools to make them look the way you want. For example, you can change the chart type, choose bar styles, and format the chart axes. Here are a few of the formatting tasks that you can use:

Change
Chart Type

- **Chart type**   To change the chart type, right-click the pivot chart, and then choose Change Chart Type. In the Change Chart Type dialog box, select the type of chart in the list and then click the button for the specific appearance you want. Alternatively, on the ribbon under PivotChartTools, click the Design tab, and then click Change Chart Type.

- **Labels**   To format chart labels, on the ribbon under PivotChart Tools, click the Layout tab and then choose a command, such as Chart Title, Axis Titles, Legend, Data Labels, and so on. You can also format a specific element of the chart by right-clicking it (the x-axis, for example), and then choosing a command like Format Axis.

- **Text**   Often, the labels along the x-axis overlap. You can rotate the axis labels to vertical to remove these overlaps. Right-click the x-axis and then choose Format Axis. In the Format Axis dialog box, click Alignment. On the Alignment page, click the down arrow in the Text Direction box and then choose Rotate All Text 90° or Rotate All Text 270°.

Modifying Visio-Based Visual Reports

Visio-based visual reports generate Visio pivot diagrams. A Visio pivot diagram starts with a single node, which represents your entire project. You can expand the diagram to additional levels by adding categories. The nodes in a pivot diagram show field values, but you can also display icons in them to make status easier to see.

With Visio pivot diagrams, you can choose the fields you want to include and the categories you want for your project breakdown. The following are a few of the tools you can use to configure a pivot diagram:

- **Show fields**   You can add or remove fields to show the information you want in the nodes on the diagram. In the PivotDiagram task pane Add Total section, select the check boxes for the fields you want to include. Clear check boxes to remove those fields from the nodes.

- **Categorize**   To expand a node to show more detail, you add a category to that node. Right-click the node, and then choose Add Category. On the submenu, choose Resources:Resources, Time:Weekly Calendar, Type:Type, or Tasks:Tasks, as shown in Figure 9-17. For example, if the first level is categorized by tasks, you can add additional levels with the category Tasks:Tasks to build a work breakdown structure (WBS) diagram. You can also add a category by selecting the node and then clicking the category in the Add Category section of the PivotDiagram task pane to the left of the pivot diagram.

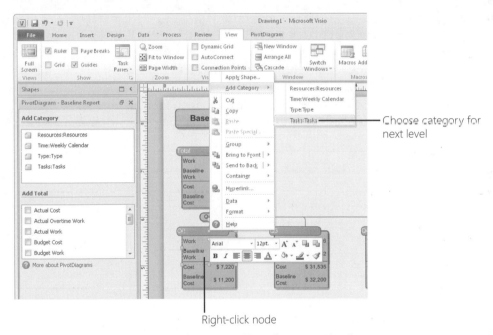

Choose category for next level

Right-click node

FIGURE 9-17 Add a category to a node to expand it to show more detail.

To remove a level, right-click the node to which the level is attached (for example, Resources) and then, on the shortcut menu, choose Collapse.

- **Filter**   You can filter a level in the diagram to show information for specific portions of your project. Right-click the small shape between levels, which represents the category for that level, such as Quarter, Week, or Task; and then choose Configure Level on the shortcut menu. In the Configure Level dialog box, you can specify the criteria that the nodes must meet to appear in the diagram. For example, you can define a test so that Resources does not equal Material, so that the report shows costs only for Work and Cost type resources.

- **Combine nodes**   You can combine nodes with the Merge, Promote, and Collapse commands. For example, to combine two summary tasks, select each node and then choose the Merge command. The values in the newly merged node represent the total for both summary tasks. On the PivotDiagram tab on the ribbon, in the Arrange group, click the command.

Summary

Regular checkups are the best way to keep a project healthy. If you spot signs of trouble early, you have time to make changes. To review progress, you need information. Team members must provide accurate data about what they've accomplished, the time they've worked, and how much time remains. Project includes tools for looking at your schedule and costs in detail. But to see the big picture of project performance, you need the indicators that earned value analysis provides, comparing baseline costs to how much of the budget has been spent and how much should have been spent for the completed work.

CHAPTER 10

Managing Project Resources

IN THIS CHAPTER, YOU WILL:

- Understand the importance of motivating people

- Learn how to develop a team

- Identify ways to evaluate people's performance

- Learn how to compare resource performance to your plan

> *Pull the string, and it will follow wherever you wish. Push it, and it will go nowhere at all.*
> —DWIGHT EISENHOWER

MANAGING A PROJECT TEAM is a tough job. The people who work on your project usually report to other managers who have more control over their salaries and chances for promotion. Although you work with team members for relatively short periods of time, optimizing their performance on your project means you must work with them as if you've known them for years. Furthermore, you must lead the group to turn it into a team in more than just name.

Managing people is a skill that's enhanced over time, but never truly mastered, so this chapter introduces a few approaches to managing people on a project. What's important is that there's no one way to manage team members. Your goal should be to continually increase your repertoire of people skills.

Part of managing people is evaluating their performance. In this chapter, you'll learn how to review resource progress in Microsoft Project. More important, you'll also learn about performance factors that no software program can help with.

Motivating Project Resources

> "*A leader is best when people barely know he exists, not so good when people obey and acclaim him, worse when they despise him. But of a good leader who talks little when his work is done, his aim fulfilled, they will say: We did it ourselves.*"—LAO-TZU

Demanding, dictating, wresting, or wringing work out of people might deliver results—at least, initially. Over the long term, however, your project performance will deteriorate along with your relationships with your team members. Leading people is a big part of a project manager's job. Ideally, you'll entice them to do their best without making them cringe every time they see you. Building good relationships is especially important in today's business world, as team members try to juggle multiple projects in addition to day-to-day responsibilities. Team members are more responsive to project managers who get to know them and respect their expertise and time.

The challenge, of course, is determining how to get the best out of each person on the team because everyone is different. Some people want nothing more than to develop an elegant solution to a problem. To them, the achievement is its own reward. Others might want interesting work, recognition, advancement, or personal and professional growth. Still others might crave more tangible results: more money, more vacation, fewer hours at the office, less stress, or never ever having to speak in public.

Sitting in your office, collecting status from team members and assembling it into project status reports will not tell you what's really going on in your project. You need to get out and talk to people. Much of your job is about communicating *effectively*, and that can change depending on who you're talking to. Here are some guidelines for developing strong working relationships with most, if not all, of the people who work, albeit temporarily, as part of your project team.

- **Clearly delineate and communicate roles and responsibilities**   If you've ever dodged left and right as you and someone else try to get out of each other's way, you know that deciding what you're going to do and communicating it clearly can solve or prevent a lot of problems. The same approach is equally effective for working with project team members. Work flows more smoothly, and relationships are stronger when team members know what *they* are supposed to do, as well as what *you*, the project manager, do. For example, change requests can turn scope creep into a scheduling scramble if team members speak directly to the customer and make changes without telling you. But if team members know that they should report change requests to the person in charge of the change management process, you can manage change requests and work with the customer to handle them properly. At the same time, team members need to know that they are also part of the change management process because they must estimate the effect of requested changes and estimate the time it will take to complete them.

SEE ALSO	Chapter 12, "Managing Project Changes," discusses the components of a change management plan and describes sample steps for a change management process.

Similar to building a responsibility matrix with stakeholders, discussing roles and responsibilities with team members helps identify points on which you disagree. There's no guarantee that you can resolve those disagreements, but knowing that they're there helps you work around them.

SEE ALSO	You learn what a responsibility matrix is in the section "The Responsibility Matrix," on page 90.

TIP	Many team members have no idea what a project manager does or, worse, remember only what the last project manager did—good or bad. By explaining your role to team members and how you plan to help them accomplish their work, you begin to build trust and respect.

- **Assign specific and attainable goals** Whether you assign a single work package to someone or assign a major section of a project to a team leader to manage, specific goals give them a target on which to focus. Telling a group to develop an eye-catching advertisement won't help if the group doesn't know the product being advertised or the audience you're trying to reach. Assigning specific goals isn't difficult because they're much like project plans in miniature; they have their own objectives, completion criteria, due dates, and budgets.

> **NOTE**   Don't be afraid to set challenging (yet attainable) goals for your people. Objectives that are *too* easy to accomplish can make team members think you doubt their capabilities. Eventually, thoughts like those become self-fulfilling prophecies, as demoralized team members do less or deliver lower-quality work. On the other hand, if you find out what your team members like to do and give them tasks that fit their work preferences, you barely have to direct them at all.

- **Provide the tools people need to do their jobs**   Trying to perform surgery with a butter knife wouldn't be pleasant for a doctor *or* a patient. Part of your job is to ensure that team members have what they need to do their work, whether that's the proper equipment, enough time, or a sufficient budget.

- **Treat team members as valued and important individuals**   There are a few people who are driven from within and don't need motivation from others, but most people want to know that they are of value to the project. Of course, you can tell people directly that they're important, but simply treating them with respect is a more sincere and powerful approach. For example, saying "thank you" is simple, quick, and incredibly effective.

   ■ **WARNING**   In contrast, treating people as if they are incompetent or untrustworthy is a fast track to poor project relationships. And bureaucratic procedures with unending forms, reports, checkpoints, evaluations, and rules tend to convey that message. One challenge to project management is balancing your need for information with team members' needs to do their work and feel as if they are in control of their assignments.

- **Remove obstacles**   Suppose your project is falling behind schedule, tasks are taking too long, or quality is an issue. You might wonder if team members are shirking their responsibilities, but chances are good that obstacles are getting in the way. The best way to uncover obstacles is to ask team members what's standing in their way. Then, go to work removing those hurdles so that team members can focus on their jobs.

BEST PRACTICES

Obstacles aren't necessarily easy to eliminate. You might have to find a way to obtain equipment that the accounting department cut from the budget, protect team members from a salesperson who wants to know every five minutes when the product will ship, or streamline administrative procedures that are consuming a few hours of each work day.

You can't remove every barrier that stops team members' progress. The important point is that your team members know that you're there to help if they run into trouble.

One common problem is that people are asked to work on several projects at the same time without any guidance on project priority from management. Don't let your team members flounder over which task to do first or struggle to complete all project tasks at once. As project manager, investigate the priorities of different projects and urge management to formally communicate those priorities.

Paying attention to and acting on team members' requests doesn't only remove the obstacles in their way. You also gain team members' gratitude and support, which comes in handy when you do have to ask for favors.

- **Provide frequent feedback**   Your team members are adults. Nonetheless, some techniques that work for training children are equally effective for helping team members succeed. Give people positive reinforcement as soon as they do something good. And if they do something wrong, quickly explain the problem and how they can perform better in the future. By providing feedback to people quickly, they can use it immediately to improve or continue their performance.

- **Be honest**   Face it. From time to time, getting project work done isn't fun—or optional. If you need results from team members, tell them the truth. At the same time, you can use the opportunity to also remind them that you have faith in their abilities. People respond more favorably when they know *why* you're asking for them to push. For example, "Getting this project done in one more month is clearly a challenge, but I know that we can do it. Our customer benefits from reduced inventory and faster payments. I will do everything I can to provide what you need to meet this goal. Just ask."

- **Have fun**   Project work can become very serious, so finding ways to have fun while meeting project goals is a great morale booster. Small gestures can mean a lot, such as hanging a miner's helmet on the wall of the tester who found the most interesting defect the past week. Casual competitions are another approach. Because project teams enjoy turning the tables on managers, prizes that involve managers making fun of themselves are extremely popular. For example, if someone finds that the project manager made an error, a fun and harmless way to relieve stress is to have the entire project team bombard the project manager with marshmallows for 30 seconds as "punishment."

- **Enable excellence**   Everything might be going well, but why not strive to do even better? Besides asking about obstacles in people's way, ask team members what you can do to help them excel.

BEST PRACTICES

People like to know that their work is appreciated. Public acknowledgements of jobs done well and small, thoughtful rewards, such as commemorative plaques and coffee mugs, can be very effective. However, more creative rewards can motivate teams long after they are awarded. Arthur P. Thomas, PhD, a professor at Syracuse University, once worked for a company that believed in rewarding employees for their effort. A fellow manager wanted to recognize the IT team's effort by doing something special and unexpected.

Dr. Thomas and his colleague planned the reward, estimated the cost, and presented it to senior management to obtain approval. They told the team to dress up a little for a group portrait as part of a publicity campaign. On the designated day, a midweek work day that didn't coincide with any project milestones or events, the team came in dressed in smart casual attire. Just before lunch, three white limousines pulled up to the door. The managers confessed that the photo shoot was a ruse and that the limos were there to take the team to lunch. Other groups rushed to that side of the building to gape at the team entering the limos. The team enjoyed a long lunch at an upscale restaurant and returned to the office two hours later to walk proudly past the gauntlet of employees anxious to learn what happened.

The Limousine Lunch became a legend at the company and inspired other managers to come up with creative ways to turn ordinary rewards into something special. From then on, motivation always ran high within the staff and people clamored for a chance to be recruited to work for this group. In addition, the staff seemed to dress up more for work—just in case.

TIP As you get to know team members, make a point of finding out what they enjoy doing. If you can assign them the type of work they like, they'll work harder and enjoy it more. For example, ask people who love to fix things to troubleshoot problems.

BEST PRACTICES

Some people have the technical skills you need, but they may not fit your project or don't work well with the rest of your team. Robyn Odegaard, president and owner of Champion Performance Development, recommends interview questions to help you determine how well someone will fit in. She also suggests steps to integrate a new member into your team to help them acclimate and become productive quickly.

You can get a sense of someone's style and approach to teamwork during the interview. Here are some questions you can try:

- How do you set expectations or how do you like to have expectations set out for you?

- What is your leadership style? What style of leadership is easiest for you to follow?

- How do you handle conflict when you have an issue with someone?

- Have you had a serious disagreement with someone? How did it turn out?

- If a member of your team made a mistake, how would you handle it?

- How open are you to adapting your methods?

If these questions are new to interviewees, they may stumble over the answers, particularly under the pressure of an interview. While their composure is an indication of how they respond to stress, it's more important to listen to their answers. If the fit seems good or someone is adaptable, you can iron out differences when you bring them on board. On the other hand, someone whose approach is at odds with your culture is likely to sap your team's energy and productivity.

How you bring someone on board is the second key to success. You need to convey the important aspects as well as the nuances of your culture. Perhaps the five on the locker room keypad sticks. Maybe there is an unwritten rule that the first person in makes coffee and the last person out rinses out the pot, whether or not they drink coffee. Chiding new team members for breaking unspoken rules doesn't make them feel welcome or a part of the team.

New team members bring skills and strengths to the team. They need to know who has complementary strengths to offset their weaknesses and who is open to helping them get up to speed. If they have questions or concerns, answer their questions and help address their concerns. Assign someone on the team as a mentor.

Developing a Team

Teams don't start out as well-oiled machines. Nor do they become effective by accident. Teams of people mature just as individuals gain wisdom and better judgment over the years. And, yes, teams go through awkward adolescent stages on their way to high performance. You can choose from several models of team behavior, such as Bruce Tuckman's "Forming, Storming, Norming, and Performing," but the models all describe similar stages. Typically, teams mature over time; they increase their abilities as relationships develop between team members; and leaders of teams must adjust their leadership style as their teams move through each stage.

BEST PRACTICES

Team members often have widely disparate work styles, from workaholics to regular folks to those who don't quite carry their fair share. To strike a balance, you may have to ask some team members to temper their expectations and approach, while asking others to step up their contributions. As vice president of Open Information Systems Security Group, Niloufer Tamboly addresses this issue by reaffirming with a team that a project's timeline is achievable and that each team member has a personal stake in the success of the project.

If a group consistently misses its deadlines, Ms. Tamboly reminds the group that holding up the project isn't fair to others. In many instances, this reminder uncovers information about the source of the problem. For example, a team member had a family emergency, but the group did not have the skills to cover the team member's work. When asked about the delay, the team finally communicated the issue. With that information, she found a replacement to get the project moving again.

Sometimes, talking and inspiration isn't enough. If a group has a history of missed deadlines, Ms. Tamboly monitors progress very closely. In most cases, groups don't like the level of monitoring and work hard to ensure that they don't miss deadlines in the future.

At the other extreme, she once worked with a group that worked with amazing speed. However, the group expected everyone else to do the same, which caused friction with other groups on the project. Telling this highly productive group to slow down didn't work. In this situation, she adjusted the group's deadlines to reflect a work pace more in line with the rest of the groups.

Teams that deliver the highest performance tend to be small groups of people, so you shouldn't expect an entire project team to become a close-knit group. Nonetheless, as a project manager, you can help your team become more effective by understanding each stage of team behavior and changing how you interact with the team as it matures. For example, giving inexperienced team members detailed task instructions is a good idea, but the reaction when you give an expert the same directions will be totally and unpleasantly different. Here is an introduction to the stages using Bruce Tuckman's nomenclature and the most effective leadership style for each:

- **Forming**   During the forming stage, teams aren't yet teams, so they rely on the leader for direction. The team members haven't sorted out their roles and responsibilities with each other and often don't agree on their goals as a team. As the leader, you must define the goals clearly, direct the team members, and answer their questions about what they are supposed to do and how they fit into the big picture of the project. What's more, forming teams resist authority, so you can expect them to challenge your leadership and the guidelines you've provided.

- **Storming**   Many situations have to get worse before they can get better, and team performance is one of them. As team members establish their relationships with other team members, you can expect some power struggles over who does what. As the leader, your authority is a target for challenges from members. Factions often form within the group, which makes decisions difficult to reach. However, the struggles and disagreements mean discussion, and that communication helps the group clarify its purpose. However, if the team begins storming over issues not related to the project at hand, you, as project manager, must help them focus on more productive discussions. The tension and emotions are distracting, so the leader must coach the team to focus on its purpose and objectives. Furthermore, the leader must help the team reach decisions—and compromises, if necessary.

- **Norming**   When the storm quiets down, you'll find that the team is finally a team. The team members understand the purpose of the group and their roles and responsibilities in achieving the team objectives. The team makes major decisions while leaving smaller decisions to individuals or subgroups. The team continues to grow by refining how the group works together and by having fun together. At this point, you, as the leader, can back off and delegate some of the leadership to the team. Your role becomes facilitation—someone who takes action only if the team requests it or gently guides the team if it veers off on an inappropriate tangent.

- **Performing**   A team at this level has a clear vision of what it is doing and why, so it has little need for a leader. In fact, the team leads itself, so you simply delegate tasks or subprojects to the team and let it work out how best to meet your criteria. Although disagreements don't disappear, the team can resolve them effectively and even modify the team processes or relationships to improve team performance.

BEST PRACTICES

Many teams reach the norming phase, but the leap to a performing team is a big one. Depending on your generation, you might think of the Harlem Globetrotters, the Blue Angels, Cirque du Soleil troupes, or other groups that perform at a level of perfection that's hard to believe. Leaders don't take an active role within these performance teams, but they can engender their development.

To achieve high performance, teams need two ingredients that only management can provide:

- **A direction or challenge**   Teams reach a high level of performance in part by shaping their purpose, which is a direct response to a challenge or opportunity that the team receives from the project manager, project sponsor, or customer.

- **Specific performance goals**   Similar to individuals, teams thrive when they receive specific goals that are challenging, but attainable. Challenging goals are what pushes a team to increase its performance. Otherwise, any team at the norming level will do.

Evaluating People's Performance

Evaluating people's performance is more challenging than evaluating the performance of a project because human performance is not always easy to quantify. For example, do people work well with others on the team? Do they build a level of synergy with other team members that enhances the performance of the entire team? Or, do they disrupt the team by complaining or not delivering what they're supposed to? This section describes what you can do to evaluate the qualitative performance of people on projects and how to handle problems if they arise. It also provides a few techniques for reviewing people's performance using Project.

Watching for People's Performance

Management by walking around is the best way to see how people are performing on your project. Team members don't necessarily announce that they have problems with other people and, when the project is going well, they often simply keep their heads down and pump out work. You can tell a lot just by talking to team members. With a few insightful and open-ended questions, you can learn about what's going well and what could be better. And reading between the lines in those responses, you might also learn about people who are doing well or not so well. Symptoms vary with the people on the project. Problems can lead to more bickering than usual, but an unusual silence can be the indicator as well.

Status meetings and lessons learned sessions provide additional opportunities for learning about performance. The mood of the group, people joking with each other, strained discussion, and other interaction can tell you how work is going.

<table>
<tr><td>SEE ALSO</td><td>The sidebar "Initiate Discussion with Open-Ended Questions," on page 363, describes the difference between open-ended and closed-ended questions and provides tips on using open-ended questions to obtain the information you need. The section "Collecting Lessons Learned," on page 360, describes techniques for obtaining information about what went well and what could have gone better. Identifying and resolving issues is much easier when you focus on improvement, not who is to blame. See the sidebar "Getting Better, Not Blamed," on page 366, for some techniques that can help keep a positive focus.</td></tr>
</table>

What to Do with Problem People

Despite all your efforts to build an effective project team, some people problems are bound to arise. Team members might not deliver what they're supposed to, might not get along with other members of the team, and could exhibit any of an almost infinite variety of performance-deteriorating behaviors. As you learned in "Motivating Project Resources," on page 244, attending to the problem quickly is crucial. In many cases, people don't understand what you expect of them or don't realize the effect their actions have on others. You can often resolve these issues with a clear yet tactful discussion.

The first step is determining whether people have the capability to perform satisfactorily. Are they qualified for their assignments? If not, you have to decide whether your project can handle the additional time, additional cost, or reduced quality that the resources can deliver. (Of course, you must review your work packages and communication with functional managers to ensure that you were clear about assignments and skills you needed.) If your project can't afford the burden of someone who doesn't have the qualifications you need, you must work with the functional manager to transfer the person to a more suitable assignment and get someone else for your project. If transferring the person isn't possible, you must work with stakeholders to reset their expectations for cost, quality, or schedule. Another option is to assess the impact of dismissing team members and *not* replacing them. Although this option puts a burden on other team members and you, it may be easier than working with team members who aren't qualified for their assignments.

If people's qualifications are acceptable, the next step is determining whether they want to perform. If someone *doesn't* want to meet your expectations—of productivity, quality, team spirit, attitude, or whatever else—it isn't fair to the rest of the team to keep that person on board. Poor performance and negative attitudes can be disruptive to both the team and your project. When people don't want to perform, you must work with the functional manager, project sponsor, and perhaps the human resources department to decide what to do and how to proceed.

■ **WARNING** Solving people problems can require documentation. If you plan to ask the project sponsor for help, be prepared to provide a brief summary of the problem, what you've tried, and what you recommend. If the problem is more severe and could lead to dismissal, the human resources department can tell you and the functional manager the steps you must perform.

Reviewing People's Performance Compared to the Plan

Project includes several built-in resource filters for finding assignments that aren't sticking to your plan. However, these filters can't pinpoint schedule problems due to resource assignments. For example, a resource filter can show assignments that are scheduled to finish later than you planned, but it can't tell if the delay is due to the resource's productivity, the resource not being available to work on the task as much as you estimated, or that the task itself started late.

A better way to look for resources who might need help is to use the Overbudget Resources report. This report shows resources whose actual costs on their assignments exceed the baseline costs and sorts the report with the highest variances first, as shown in Figure 10-1. Because you see overbudget costs by resource, you know that the person is spending more time than you budgeted. But you'll still have to talk to the person to unearth the real problem.

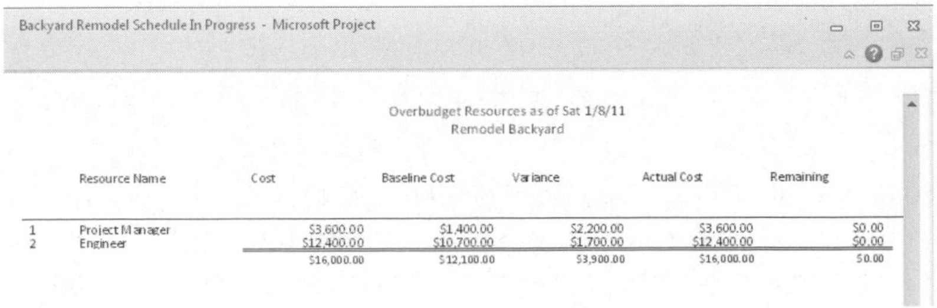

FIGURE 10-1 The Overbudget Resources report shows resources whose assignments cost more than you planned, whether the problem is an optimistic task estimate or the productivity of the assigned resources.

Reports

Here are the steps for generating the Overbudget Resources report:

1. On the View Project tab, in the Reports group, select Reports.

2. In the Reports dialog box, double-click Costs.

3. In the Cost Reports dialog box, select Overbudget Resources, and then click Select.

> **TIP** ✓ If you want to modify the Overbudget Resources report before you generate it, select Overbudget Resources, and then click Edit. For example, you can choose a time frame in the Period list to show variances for days, weeks, months, the entire project, or several other time frames. To display different fields in the report, choose the table you want to apply in the Table list.

Resource Usage

[No Filter]

To apply resource filters, you must first display a resource-oriented view, such as Resource Usage. (On the View tab, in the Resource Views group, click Resource Usage.) Then, in the Data group, click the Filter list down arrow, and choose the filter you want to apply. (If the filter doesn't appear on the drop-down list, choose More Filters, and then, in the More Filters dialog box, double-click the filter you want.) Here are some of the resource filters that help you evaluate progress by resource:

- **Slipping Assignments** This resource filter shows assignments whose scheduled finish date is later than the baseline finish. Slipping assignments could indicate that the resource isn't making progress as quickly as you had planned. However, this filter doesn't check whether the task has started or, if it's in progress, whether it started on time, so the late finish might be due to a delayed or late start date, not the assigned resource's productivity or availability.

- **Work Overbudget** This filter shows assignments whose scheduled work is greater than the baseline work. Although the problem might lie with your estimate, you can review these assignments to see whether the assigned resources need help.

- **Cost Overbudget** This filter shows any assignments in which scheduled cost is greater than baseline cost (and a baseline cost exists). The problem could be a low estimate, higher material costs, or resources who are taking longer than you planned. You must review these assignments in more detail to see whether the assigned resources need help.

Summary

Managing the team members for a project is challenging for several reasons. People report to other managers, so you must share management responsibilities with someone else. In addition, you work with people for short periods of time. Finally, each person is different, so you must tune your techniques depending on who you're working with. You can use Project to gauge how people perform on delivering their assignments according to your plan. And you might use other tools to measure productivity. But evaluating people has more to do with understanding them and motivating them than it does with numbers.

CHAPTER 11

Communicating Information

IN THIS CHAPTER, YOU WILL:

- Identify the components of a communication plan

- Understand guidelines for good communication

- Learn how to run effective meetings

- Identify what to include in good status reports

- Learn how to keep email under control

> ❝*The greatest problem in communication is the illusion that it has been accomplished.*❞
> —George Bernard Shaw

AS A PROJECT MANAGER, you use tools such as a work breakdown structure (WBS), Gantt chart, and earned-value graph, but communicating with people is a huge part of managing a project. Project communication helps ensure that customers, stakeholders, and team members know what they need to do their jobs, whether you're trying to get stakeholders to agree on project objectives, telling team members about their assignments, or working with a group to resolve an issue that's delaying the project. But keeping everyone informed about project status is an important part of project communication, too.

You can spend years learning to communicate effectively. Ideally, what a project needs is effective communication between every person involved. An impossible goal? Yes, but you, as the project manager, can do a lot to improve communication on your projects. This chapter discusses methods for communicating information to people on the project. You'll learn about who needs information, what they usually need to know, when they need to know it, and the best way to get it to them. This sums up the purpose and contents of a project communication plan, a project planning document that describes the tools and techniques you will use to communicate on your project. But you'll also learn how to communicate effectively, whether you're talking to people, running meetings, authoring reports, or sending email.

Knowledge Is Power

Many people think that the person with the knowledge is the one who has the power. For projects, power comes from *everyone* being in the know. Here are a few ways that good communication contributes to project success:

- **Focus on the goal**   After stakeholders define the problem that a project is supposed to solve and what constitutes success, they must communicate these items to the entire project team to gain their support and help them understand what they are supposed to do.

- **Better decisions**   Everyone on a project—from the sponsor to individual team members—needs information to make good decisions. With project information readily available, people can make the right choices, take advantage of opportunities, and fend off problems.

- **Increased productivity**   Team members can get more done if they have the information they need or know how to find it easily. By communicating effectively, you can ensure that team members are doing the right work the right way. To the contrary, when communication is lacking or unclear, time spent delivering the wrong results or duplicating effort hurts the project schedule, budget, and team morale.

- **Fewer errors**   Team members make fewer mistakes, and if problems do arise, team members can identify and fix them quickly.

- **Better project management**   As a project manager, you have a selfish reason for sharing information—your job is easier. When people don't know what's going on, they usually ask questions—often with a great deal of impatience and at the worst possible moment. The other reaction to not knowing is not acting; people sometimes ignore tasks if they aren't sure what they should do and don't want to ask. By distributing the information that people need to know *before* they need to know it, you can spend more time proactively managing your projects.

- **Continuous improvement**   Communication doesn't stop at the end of a project. By documenting information about completed projects, you can provide guidelines for project teams to follow on future projects.

> **SEE ALSO**   Chapter 16, "Learning Lessons," provides techniques for acquiring and documenting information about completed projects.

- **Enhancing collaboration**   Sharing information helps build teamwork and increases people's satisfaction with their work.

The Communication Plan

For small projects, communication can be quite simple. Communication for the project of heading home after the holidays might be no more than "Call us when you get there." But good communication grows complex as the scope of the project increases, more people are involved, and teams are scattered around the world. For example, a conference call that includes people in Europe, Asia, and North America is going to keep someone up late and get someone else up early, and you don't want to make those decisions at the last minute. By planning your approach for communication in advance, you can provide the right information to the right people, at the right time, in the right format, and with the right emphasis. Your road map is the project *communication plan,* illustrated by the first page of a sample communication plan in Figure 11-1. This section describes the components of a communication plan, how you choose the communication methods appropriate for your project, and how to create a communication plan.

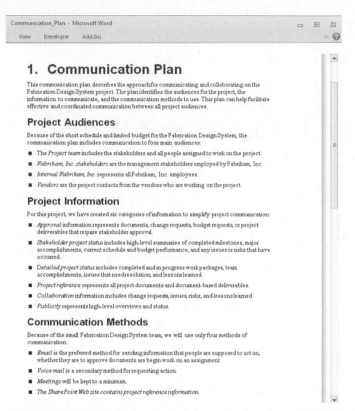

FIGURE 11-1 A communication plan can be as simple or as sophisticated as your project requires for delivering information to the people who need it.

> **PROJECT FILE**   A sample communication plan, Communication_Plan.docx, is available in the Chapter11 folder on the companion website.

Who Needs to Know?

The first step to creating a communication plan is identifying who needs to know something about the project. Stakeholders are obvious audiences for project communications, but other groups often need—or want—project information. As you build your communication plan, ask stakeholders and other groups you've identified as audiences if there's anyone else who needs to know something about your project. Here are some typical audiences, both stakeholders and ancillary groups, you might include in a communication plan:

- *The project team* is the core of communication. Team members work on the project every day. They need to know what's going on with the project, but they also contribute a lot of the information that you communicate to others.

- *Management stakeholders* aren't dedicated to the project, but they make key decisions about it. Management stakeholders share similar needs for project communication and can include customers, the project sponsor, a steering committee or leadership team, members of the change management board, functional managers, and so on.

> **NOTE**   *The customer* is part of the management stakeholder group, but often wants different information delivered in different ways.

- *The project sponsor* is also part of the management stakeholder group, but is usually involved more intimately with the project. For example, you might send the project sponsor the same information that you provide to other management stakeholder groups, but also meet face to face for in-depth discussions.

- *Supporting groups* might be involved in your project from time to time and need to know specific information. For example, sales and marketing might want to know what the product features are and when it'll be ready to sell. The legal department gets involved only to work on contracts or to review documents for legal issues. Other supporting groups include operations, manufacturing, IT, and other departments.

- *External audiences* can be very involved in your project. For example, vendors, suppliers, partners, and the project managers who work for them can belong to your core team. However, you typically don't tell external audiences as much as you do internal team members. For example, if you're trying to resolve issues, you'd include external audiences in those discussions only if they are directly affected. Investors and regulatory agencies (such as the IRS or a public utility commission) might represent additional external audiences. For these audiences, the format and schedule of communication is often already specified, such as the financial statements that the SEC requires.

> **TIP** ✓
>
> As you develop your communication plan, the golden rule is to give the audience what it wants. Just as a Gantt chart might make perfect sense to you and not one whit to the customer, the methods of communication you choose must actually get the message through to your audience. And if that means you have to prepare a Microsoft PowerPoint presentation for the steering committee, a Microsoft Excel spreadsheet for the accounting department, a Microsoft Word document for project teams, and a Microsoft SharePoint site for the developers, so be it. After all, your job as project manager is to make the project a success, and communicating information successfully is a big part of that.

BEST PRACTICES

It's better to send information to too many people than too few, suggests Ron Taylor, founder of the Ron Taylor Group and PMI's 2008 Leader of the Year. Mr. Taylor's approach is to give people the opportunity to opt out of receiving specific types of information. However, opting out has one downside that he makes sure everyone understands up front. To make sure responsibility lies where it belongs, anyone who opts out of receiving communications must abide by decisions that are made without their input.

What Do You Communicate to Audiences?

Sad but true, people hear only what they want to hear. Your customer might care deeply about the return on investment (ROI) of the project, but using ROI to inspire team members to complete their tasks more quickly probably won't deliver the results you're hoping for. For all audiences that you've identified, the next step is to determine what they *need* to know, what they *want* to know, and what information *you* want to tell them. For example, the customer, project sponsor, and management stakeholders need status reports, but they also want information about the project strategy and issues and risks that might affect the business objectives for the project. Functional managers need status information in order to plan their people's time.

Usually, you want to distribute some information that audiences don't think to ask for. For example, you communicate the benefits of your project, the problem statement, and the project objectives to everyone involved, even though team members might *want* to know only what their task assignments are. For another example, if a project is going to change how processes in your organization are going to work, you can begin to tout the benefits of the changes.

You can categorize project information in different ways. For example, you might categorize information based on what different groups need to know: planning, day-to-day detailed status, high-level status, and general information. You might also categorize information by whether it's required, desired, or merely for reference. This section describes information you typically communicate in projects and then categorizes it by the groups that use it.

TIP   Keep track of each type of information that you provide to each audience because the distribution method and timetable you choose may vary based on the information. For example, you might distribute project status every week while the stakeholders want a thorough financial update once a month.

Types of Project Information

The information that you communicate varies depending on whether you're planning, executing, or closing the project. Here are types of project information that you distribute by phase in a project:

- **Project planning**   The components of the project plan help people involved with the project understand the purpose of the project and their roles in completing it successfully. From the problem statement to the schedule and the communication plan, each component describes how you plan to run the project. Some audiences review planning documents in detail and approve them, whereas other groups use them simply as direction for the work they perform.

    SEE ALSO   The section "The Components of a Project Implementation Plan," on page 62, describes the information that goes into a project plan.

- **Project execution and control**   Once the plan is approved and you begin to execute that plan, people need to know the rules. You have to provide people with procedures, such as reporting time and expenses, requesting time off, escalating issues, and so on. For most of the project duration, people need to know the status of the project and what's planned for the near future.

   The status you provide varies by the needs of the audience. For example, the elegant programming shortcut that is helpful and fascinating to the development team would put management stakeholders to sleep. On the other hand, the financial measures that the management stakeholders can't live without would be equally boring to most technical folks.

- **Project closure**   You wrap up projects with reports that summarize the performance of the project.

> **SEE ALSO**   The section "Project Closeout Reports," on page 378, describes what you document in the close-out reports you generate when a project is complete.

- **Project publicity**   Regardless of the phase a project is in, you want to build enthusiasm and commitment for it. Publicizing a project early on might include announcements in the company newsletter, contests to name the project, or road shows that describe the purpose and benefits of the project. During project execution, you might use a project newsletter to publicize accomplishments, host celebrations upon completion of significant milestones, or distribute pens or coffee cups emblazoned with the project logo. And nothing beats meeting stakeholders and team members one-on-one to build commitment.

Management Stakeholders

Management stakeholders, including the customer, project sponsor, and other high-level stakeholders, typically care about the overall business goals of a project. Early on, they evaluate the project plan to ensure that it meets their needs. During project execution, they frequently review performance, such as how much progress has been made, how much money has been spent, and the quality of the results that have been achieved. Most of the time, they don't want to know the details, although they will for significant issues, such as someone absconding with project funds.

> **NOTE**   As internal customers, company executives often require more detailed project information than external customers. They must evaluate project performance compared to the entire portfolio of the company's projects and business objectives.

Here is some of the information that management stakeholders want to receive:

- **The project plan**   During planning, management stakeholders must ensure that the proposed plan satisfies their needs. Later, if requirements or criteria change, these stakeholders revisit the project plan while negotiating change orders, contract revisions, or modifications to the project goals.

- **Project status**   Executive summaries of project status focus on high-level performance and accomplishments. Management stakeholders want to know about major milestones that have been completed, summaries of costs and schedule performance (the project is one month behind schedule and $20,000 over budget), and major issues and risks that could prevent the project from achieving its goals. If you are measuring other aspects of project performance, such as lines of code written or statistics about defects found and fixed, they want to know whether the metrics are good or bad and about the trends in performance.

> **SEE ALSO**   The section "Project Status Reports," on page 291, provides some guidelines for the information to include in status reports.

- **Financial information**   These stakeholders understand and care about the financial measures for projects, so they want to know the current financial results, including performance compared to the budget and other metrics, such as ROI.

- **Change requests**   Some management stakeholders need to know about change requests. For example, the customer, project sponsor, and members of the change management board must evaluate change requests to see whether they should be approved or rejected.

> **SEE ALSO**   Chapter 12, "Managing Project Changes," describes the purpose of the change management process and provides one example of how manage change.

TIP   Executives plan for the long term, so they also want to know what is in store for the project in the future. Is the project going to deliver on time and under budget? Will it deliver the financial results they want? Will it achieve its objectives? Or are changes necessary?

Functional Managers

Functional managers usually provide the people who perform the project work, so they need to see project plans to understand the skills required, to know when their people are needed, and to be aware of any constraints, such as cost or availability. Once people are working on assignments, functional managers want to know how much longer those people are needed or might ask if they can substitute someone else.

Here is typical information you might communicate to functional managers:

- **Project plan**   During planning, functional managers must understand the big picture of the project, but they focus on work packages, the skills needed, and when assignments are scheduled to occur.

- **Project status**   Functional managers need to know when their people will be done with their assignments, so they can line up more work for them in the future.

Team Members

Initially, team members must understand the work they are supposed to perform as well as how that work fits into the big picture of the project. This information helps them make good decisions in their day-to-day work. As work progresses on the project, team members need to know detailed status about completed work and the work that's scheduled for them in the near future. Here are some types of information that team members need:

- **Assignments**   Team members want to know what work they are supposed to do and when.

- **Status**   Team members need to know the status of their work and related tasks. With status updates, team members can collaborate with their colleagues and help devise solutions to problems.

- **Issues**   Team members need to know about issues that might affect them, proposed solutions, and how closed issues were resolved.

- **Lessons learned**   Team members can work more effectively if they can take advantage of tips, shortcuts, or practices to avoid.

- **Decisions**   Team members must know about any decisions that affect the direction or objectives of the project, so they can conform to the new guidelines.

What Communication Method Should You Use?

The last step to developing a communication plan is to determine the best methods for getting each type of information to your audiences. You must decide how often audiences need information, the best method for delivering information, and the best format in which to deliver it. For example, everyone involved in the project needs a project status report, which you might distribute via email to the entire team but review in a meeting with stakeholders. Your organization's executive team meets once a month and wants an executive summary of project status with emphasis on the budget and financial measures. The project sponsor prefers to meet in person to review status, issues, and risks. And team members have asked you to distribute the detailed status reports of team accomplishments every week.

Communication methods come in many guises and each one has its advantages and disadvantages. For example, face-to-face communication is best for delicate discussions or to brainstorm solutions. Conference calls and email come in handy for teams that are distributed geographically. Documents in paper or electronic format are ideal for communicating large amounts of information that require study.

Here are some considerations for communication methods:

- **Status reports**   These can contain different types of information depending on the audience. Moreover, whether you produce paper or electronic status reports depends on the audience as well. Sending status reports to people makes it easy for them to read the information, and they can choose to scan the reports for pertinent topics—or ignore them if time is at a premium.

> **NOTE:** When you distribute documents electronically, you have to consider the software formats that your audiences can read. For example, if some team members have older versions of Word, you might choose to distribute reports in Adobe Acrobat or Microsoft XPS Document Writer format. Don't forget that most people in your audiences won't have Microsoft Project, so you should save Gantt Charts and other Project views as pictures, PowerPoint files, or web pages.

■ **Meetings**   These can vary from one-time kickoff meetings to daily meetings of small groups of team members, weekly or monthly executive updates, or occasional all-hands meetings. Although you can't guarantee that people will pay attention in a meeting, getting people in the same room is ideal for discussions, brainstorming, and decision making.

> **SEE ALSO**   The section "Meetings That Work," on page 283, describes several techniques for running effective meetings.

You have options for how you deliver information in face-to-face meetings. For example, an executive update meeting might start with a presentation of project status followed by an energetic discussion. Other meetings, such as lessons learned sessions, can be completely dedicated to group discussion.

■ **Conference calls and videoconferencing**   These are options for meetings when people are distributed geographically; however, they are not ideal if you are working through issues or dealing with a team that is "storming." In situations in which tension is high, a videoconference or Microsoft Office LiveMeeting provides more effective interaction.

> **SEE ALSO**   The section "Developing a Team," on page 250, describes the different phases that teams pass through on their way to working together effectively.

■ **Sending documents to people**   This is preferable if you want the recipients to take action. For example, if you want stakeholders to review and approve your project plan, you should send the plan to them for review. However, the best way to obtain approval and signatures is to hold a meeting.

■ **Storing documents**   This is a reasonable solution for information that only some people need only some of the time. For example, you can store any document-based deliverables, such as the current project plan, requirements, specifications, change requests, and other project information in a shared folder, on a web page, or in a shared workspace. People who need the information can retrieve it when they need it.

SEE ALSO   The section "Ways to Build a Project Archive," on page 388, describes several methods for storing project documents.

- **Newsletters and email distribution lists**   These work well for announcements and other information you want to disseminate to broad audiences. You can distribute information to many people without much effort, but the readers can skip the message if it doesn't apply to them.

RESOLUTION IS WHAT'S IMPORTANT

If you want someone to do something, sending an email or leaving a voice message is *not* the same as getting something done. If you have an issue that's delaying your project, you can't afford to wait until the person you contacted decides to act. The most effective way to obtain a response to a request is to tell people up front what you want them to do and when. For example, an email that scrolls for pages before you get to the point will be deleted long before the recipient knows what you're asking for. Put requests in the first paragraph of an email, memo, or other written communication. State requests in the first sentence of voice messages. You can follow up with the whys and hows after that.

After you've sent requests for action, you must follow up if you don't receive a response when you expect. If a return email doesn't arrive, follow up with another email or a telephone call. (Emails get caught in spam filters all the time, so don't begin your follow-up with an accusation.) If a voice message goes unanswered, find the person or someone else who can help.

Some folks don't respond no matter what you do. One way to coax responses from people who do that is to tell them what you plan to do if you don't hear from them by a specific time or day. If your contingency plan is something you know they don't want, you're almost guaranteed to receive a response when you need it. For example, "Hi, Dale. I really need the graphic for the brochure by tomorrow morning at 9:00 A.M. If I don't have it by then, I'm going to use the photograph of the meerkat. Thanks for your help." If someone still doesn't respond, diplomatically escalate your request. If you do ask for help, it's a good idea to tell the managers you ask what you would like them to do. Otherwise, they might apply more pressure than you intended. Of course, you must be willing to go with the picture of the meerkat if you still don't get a response.

When you choose communication options, opt for the ones that get information to audiences with the least amount of effort. For example, don't send hard copies of status reports if everyone on the project checks email every day. An email distribution list is much easier than printing and distributing dozens of hard-copy memos. However, for some information, such as reports that government agencies require, you have to use their format and transmission methods.

TIP   Although the ideal approach is to provide every audience with exactly what they want, some communication methods can be extraordinarily time-consuming. If communication demands threaten to consume every workday, try suggesting to stakeholders alternatives that require less time.

Building a Communication Plan

The communication plan begins with sections that list the audiences for the project, the information you plan to communicate, how you will compile the information, and the communication methods you plan to use. But the heart of the communication plan is a matrix that shows how you plan to communicate information to each project audience, as illustrated in Figure 11-2.

TIP   Although the communication plan is often a part of the project plan, it's a good idea to publish the communication plan as a stand-alone document. That makes it easy to keep a copy handy for quick reference.

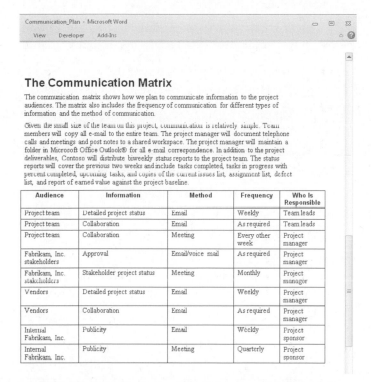

FIGURE 11-2 A matrix like the one included on page 2 of the sample communication plan is helpful for showing the information you communicate to audiences and the methods you plan to use.

Creating Communication Reminders

After you complete your communication plan and begin executing the project, days and weeks can pass before you realize it. As project manager, you can set up your communication tasks as milestones in Project so you see reminders about communication along with the rest of the tasks you review regularly. If you prefer more obvious reminders, you can create tasks with reminders in Microsoft Outlook so you don't forget to send important information to project audiences or schedule meetings.

In Outlook, you can set up recurring tasks for email, reports, and regularly scheduled meetings. In fact, you can send meeting requests to attendees to schedule meetings and keep track of who has accepted and who can't attend.

New
Items ▾

Recurrence

Here are the steps for creating a communication reminder:

1. In Outlook, on the Home tab, in the New group, click New Items, and then choose Task.

2. In the Untitled – Task dialog box, in the Subject text box, type the name of the communication task, such as Prepare stakeholders status report.

3. On the Task tab, in the Recurrence group, click Recurrence.

4. In the Task Recurrence dialog box, choose the option for the time period. For example, to set up a status report that you send every other week, select Weekly.

5. In the Recur Every . . . Week(s) On text box, type the number of periods between each occurrence. For example, for every other week, type 2.

6. Select the check box for the day of the week on which you perform the task.

7. In the Range Of Recurrence section, you can keep the No End Date option selected, as shown in Figure 11-3, to receive reminders until you decide to delete the task. If you're certain that the project will end when you expect, you can choose either the End After . . . Occurrences option when you know the number of occurrences or the End By option when you know the last date for the task to occur.

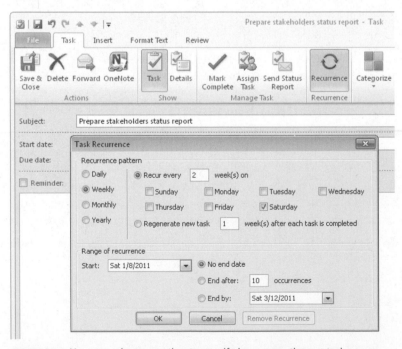

FIGURE 11-3 You can select an option to specify how many times a task occurs.

8. Click OK to close the Task Recurrence dialog box. Click Save And Close to save the recurring task.

■ Guidelines for Good Communication

"Most conversations are simply monologues delivered in the presence of a witness."—MARGARET MILLER

You listen to team members explain something and you answer the question that they ask only to have them blurt out in disgust, "You just don't understand!" Years ago, you learned to pronounce words and found out what they meant. You learned how to string them together into sentences, written and spoken. And you learned how to recognize the words that other people say or write. So, why don't you understand? For that matter, why does *everyone* have so many problems with miscommunication? The answer is that most people aren't taught to communicate effectively.

What Is Communication?

Communication is actually a *two-way* process with information successfully passing from one person to another. Effective communication entails several achievements, each one more useful—and more difficult—than the last. If you're having a problem with communication, review these steps to see where the breakdown might be.

- **Transmitting information** This is the first and easiest step. Speaking to someone, sending a letter or an email, and folding your arms over your chest while scowling all represent transmitting information. But, similar to the television broadcasts we've transmitted into space, there's no guarantee that someone hears your speech or reads your message. Recipients can block out what you say or delete your email messages without reading them.

- **Receiving information** This is the next step after transmitting, but it still doesn't guarantee communication. Someone can play a voice mail or open an email, which is, in principle, receiving information. After all, a read receipt in Outlook can confirm that someone received and opened your email message. But the person still might delete the voice mail without really listening to it or delete the email without reading the words.

- **Understanding the message**   This is the first step that represents communication and it can be a big challenge, as illustrated here in Abbott and Costello's famous give-and-take about baseball players:

Costello: *Well then who's on first?*
Abbott: *Yes.*
Costello: *I mean the fellow's name.*
Abbott: *Who.*
Costello: *The guy on first.*
Abbott: *Who.*
Costello: *The first baseman.*
Abbott: *Who.*
Costello: *The guy playing...*
Abbott: *Who is on first!*
Costello: *I'm asking YOU who's on first.*
Abbott: *That's the man's name.*
Costello: *That's who's name?*
Abbott: *Yes.*
Costello: *Well go ahead and tell me.*
Abbott: *That's it.*
Costello: *That's who?*
Abbott: *Yes.*

In a *successful* communication, someone transmits a message and someone else receives the message *and understands* its contents. Understanding what someone else is trying to convey can involve a lot more than grasping the meaning of their words. You might have to learn something new, interpret the hidden meanings in messages, or ask questions to clarify points that aren't clear to you.

> **SEE ALSO**   Listening is the key to good communication. The section "Learning to Listen," on page 280, provides some tips for improving communication by listening more effectively.

- **Obtaining agreement**   This is the next step toward effective communication. If you ask the project steering committee for more money and its members say no, they've understood your message, but they don't agree with it. In order to turn communication into decisions and results, you must obtain agreement from the other party. Similar to understanding, obtaining agreement can be a complicated undertaking. Negotiation, compromise, collaboration, and many other approaches all strive to reach some kind of agreement so that work can continue.

- **Acting on communication**   This is nirvana. In project management, you communicate to move your project to completion. Every communication is about getting something to happen. For example, suppose the project steering committee tells you that you can have more money, but it never gives the accounting department the approval to disburse the money. You obtained agreement but still didn't get the money you needed.

BEST PRACTICES

According to a UCLA study, 93 percent of communication is nonverbal. Tres Roeder, president of Roeder Consulting, recommends reconciling *what* people say with *how* they say it in order to gain a more accurate understanding of situations. Instead of focusing on the words alone, pay attention to nonverbal cues, such as facial expressions, arm and head positions and movements, hand and foot movements, eye contact or avoidance, posture, and tone of voice.

Mr. Roeder suggests practicing to increase your awareness of all forms of communication. For example, when you attend a meeting, make note of both the verbal and nonverbal behavior of the attendees. Or, in any situation, take some time to identify the input from your senses. What do you see? What do you hear? What about touch or taste? Is your gut sending you signals? Do you have a hunch about the situation? With practice, these techniques become second nature, and you will automatically incorporate this additional information into your analysis of situations.

How to Get Messages Through

"Diplomacy is the art of letting someone have your way."
—DANIELE VARE

If you are trying to make a point or convince someone else to do something, the responsibility for communicating well is yours alone. Of course, communication is easier if the other person cooperates. But the hard truth is that no one else cares as much about what you want than you. Here are some guidelines for getting your messages through to your audience:

- **Talk in the audience's terms**   Stephen Covey describes this approach as "Seek first to understand." If you want to convince others to see as you do or to do what you want, you must first understand what's important to them and what they are concerned about. Only then will you have any chance of showing them why your request is important to them. For example, if you want functional managers to provide or keep people on your project, first understand the pressures that they face. If they're measured by the group's billable income, you might focus on how your project needs their people full time for several months. On the other hand, if you know that the biggest challenge is a heavy workload, you can show the functional managers how you've planned the project to prevent overtime and last-minute deliveries.

- **Be accurate**   Check the accuracy of the information you are presenting and avoid speculation or gossip at all cost. If you don't know an answer, don't bluff. Admit that you don't know, promise to find the answer, and then do as you promised. Credibility is much easier to keep than to gain back.

- **Be persuasive**   Although accuracy is important, dry facts and pages of data will lose your audience faster than a fire alarm in the building. Try telling stories (relevant to the topic, of course) or using interesting analogies.

- **Be brief**   No one enjoys a presentation that seems to go on forever. Take the time to prepare your message, so you can present it clearly and succinctly. Follow the lead of newspaper reporters and assume that no one will read past the first paragraph.

- **Accentuate the positive**   Publicize project successes frequently and make sure that the customer, key stakeholders, managers, and project team hear about them. Back up project success stories with performance data.

On the other hand, if people make mistakes, work with them individually to help them improve. Blaming others or targeting the person instead of the behavior ruins any chance of effective communication. If people on the team begin to blame others, jump in and redirect their conversation to the issue at hand. If *you* make a mistake, admit it, explain how you will prevent it in the future, and then do just that.

SEE ALSO	The section "Accentuating the Positive," on page 364, provides some tips on how to focus on positive information. In "Motivating Project Resources," on page 244, you can learn more about how to communicate effectively with team members, including being clear about roles and responsibilities, and treating people with respect.

DON'T ASSUME ANYTHING

Making assumptions is one of the most common communication problems. For example, you ask someone to prepare a report and, in your mind, you know that you want to see a summary of the labor costs broken down by employees and subcontractors and that you need it before a stakeholder meeting on Monday. In fact, you know what you want so clearly, you forget to tell the person these important details. If you stomp into his office on Friday demanding the report, you're likely to meet a blank stare or the question, "Well, when do you need it?" If you respond with a huffy "In two hours," you're still in trouble. If he didn't know when you needed the report, it's likely he doesn't know what should be in the report either.

The best approach for getting what you want is to clearly state what you expect and be proactive about confirming that the person understands your request. For instance, "Joe, what questions do you have about the report content?" or "Joe, tell me how you plan to present the information for the report." However, if a miscommunication occurs, it's more productive to start a conversation by clarifying the request instead of yelling or accusing the person of dropping the ball. "Have you completed the report I asked you to prepare? I need it today so we have time to revise it, if necessary, before the stakeholder meeting."

You might be forgiven for poor or inappropriate communications, but your message will never be forgotten. Before you communicate, consult the following checklist to see whether you need to say anything at all, and if you do, whether the message you're sending will produce a positive result:

- Is my message necessary?
- Is my message true?

- Is my message considerate?

- Is my message better than no message at all?

BEING RESPONSIBLE

Some people feel as if they are controlled by events. Others make a point of choosing their responses. People who say "He doesn't understand," or "You didn't tell me to do that," push responsibility for their action (or inaction) onto someone else. People who accept responsibility for their actions say instead "I'm not making myself clear," or "I forgot to ask about that."

As a project manager, choosing your responses is an important part of dealing with the challenges you face every day. Eventually, it might even make you a little more comfortable in uncomfortable situations. If you tend to blame others for your choices, you must learn to accept responsibility for your actions. The easiest way to recast your comments is to start your sentences with "I" and complete them with what you can do to improve the situation.

Learning to Listen

Because communication is a two-way process, listening to the messages you receive is as important as sending your own. Unfortunately, hearing and listening are two very different things. Your ears might sense the sound waves from your team members talking, but without your brain listening to the message, you'll have no idea how to respond to their questions. Here are some suggestions for improving your listening skills:

- **Give your full attention to the speaker**   As a project manager, you've learned to work on multiple tasks at once. However, when you're meeting with someone or talking to them on the phone, you must switch gears and give them your undivided attention. Try to meet in a quiet place and turn off your cell phone or pager. (Taking calls in the middle of meetings doesn't demonstrate importance—only rudeness.)

TIP

If someone interrupts a meeting with you, say something like "Well, I assume the meeting is over, so I'm going to get back to work." The person will either confirm your statement or refocus his attention on you.

- **Listen for unspoken communication** Only a small percentage of meaning is in the words that are spoken. In fact, facial expressions convey the majority of a message, and the *way* words are said contributes almost all the rest. For this reason, you must focus even more on telephone calls even though the temptation is to work on other tasks at the same time because the other person can't see you.

- **Keep an open mind** If you enter a conversation with preconceived notions and predetermined responses, there's little point in the discussion because you've already made up your mind. Concentrate on what other people have to say and make your decisions only after you've listened to their points.

- **Repeat or paraphrase what you have heard** The best way to acknowledge that you've listened is by repeating what the other person has said. If you put it into your own words, you can demonstrate that you listened and that you understand. In the worst case, you give the other person a chance to correct any misunderstanding you might have.

TIP	Body language says a lot. If you meet with people face-to-face, make eye contact and avoid distracting habits, such as yawning and fidgeting.

FROM EDUCATION TO COMMUNICATION

Communicating project information is a challenge when the rest of the organization is not familiar with project management practices. And if you're new to project management as well, communication practically comes to a halt. You probably know the drill. You're happily mixing chemicals in the lab and mostly not blowing things up when your boss tells you you're going to manage a project to expand the lab. Little do you know that without project management training or knowing how to communicate with project teams, you can watch something really explode—your project and the folks on the team.

You have to understand the benefits of the project management practices you use before you can convince team members, customers, functional managers, and anyone else involved in a project to follow your example. Of course, your first tentative explanations and answering the questions that arise can increase your understanding, too. As your knowledge of project management grows, so should the success of your projects. And that success provides even more fuel for convincing people in your organization to use project management.

EFFECTIVE COMMUNICATION WITH VIRTUAL TEAMS

Face-to-face communication has become a luxury for many organizations and project teams. Because so much communication is nonverbal, virtual teams make it difficult to communicate effectively. Several techniques can help your teams communicate better and become more productive:

- **Develop a team culture**   A culture is a set of mores that everyone learns to follow until they become second nature. A common culture builds trust and a feeling of belonging that is essential if the going gets tough. Culture also helps everyone produce consistent results. For example, standards for response time help people know what to expect when they communicate. Set standards for how quickly people return telephone calls, emails, or other communications. Document the rules for people who are out of the office or on vacation, such as changing the message on voice mail or the email auto-reply message to specify who to contact during the person's absence.

- **Build trust among team members**   For teams to work well together, the team members must trust one another. Although face-to-face meetings can develop trust more quickly, they may not be realistic for global teams. As a substitute, you can use videoconferences or conference calls to bring the team together. Even without direct contact, you can build trust by being honest and respectful of one another. Listening and understanding what others say also helps to build trust.

- **Follow through on commitments**   With virtual teams, team members must tell others what they plan to do and then follow through on those plans. In addition to keeping everyone informed, team members come to trust that others will do what they say.

- **Store information in a central location**   Team members often have to take over for other resources. In addition to documenting everything well, store the documents where everyone can access them.

- **Focus on results**   Because you can't see what virtual team members are doing, you must focus on the results they produce. Instead of watching their day-to-day activities, you simply communicate your expectations and monitor the results. This technique empowers people to take responsibility for their work. In addition, you can also identify people who aren't able to get things done on their own.

- **Communicate on a regular schedule**   With geographically distributed teams, schedule a time convenient for most team members to meet virtually to review status.

Meetings That Work

Many team members dread meetings, and for good reason. Regularly scheduled meetings that occur without a specific purpose or framework can be boring wastes of time. Pointless meetings drive people to distraction and eventually they look for any excuse to miss the meetings you schedule. What's more, meetings are extraordinarily expensive in time and cost. A status meeting for a team of 12 that lasts for 2 hours costs your project 3 person-days and $1,200, assuming a $50 an hour labor rate. That's time that someone could spend completing a work package or money that could provide people with the equipment they need. However, if you take advantage of the interaction at meetings, you can resolve problems, make decisions, and share information more effectively than in any other method of communication. In short, if you're going to hold a meeting, make it count. This section provides some guidelines for getting the most out of your meetings and describes different types of project meetings you might schedule.

Guidelines for Good Meetings

Productive meetings don't just happen. They require foresight, facilitation, and follow-up. The sections that follow describe the steps for running productive meetings.

Setting Up Meetings

> *If I am to speak ten minutes, I need a week for preparation; if fifteen minutes, three days; if half an hour, two days; if an hour, I am ready now.*—WOODROW WILSON

One reason for unproductive meetings is lack of preparation. If you don't know what you're trying to accomplish with a meeting, and the attendees don't come prepared to discuss the topic, you can easily waste precious time with "What do you think?" and "Well, I don't know. What do you think?" Preparing for a meeting can be short, although prep time increases with the importance of the outcome. For example, a brief agenda might be sufficient for a team meeting to resolve a small issue that's come up, but you're likely to spend considerable time preparing concise yet persuasive handouts and presentations for a go/no-go meeting with stakeholders for a multimillion dollar project. Regardless of the detail involved in meeting setup, the steps are simple:

1. **Determine the purpose of the meeting**   What do you want to accomplish with the meeting? What results do you expect at the end of the meeting? For example, are you trying to obtain status information, a decision from stakeholders, or resolution to an issue?

2. **Identify the right attendees** Meetings run longer than you plan if too many people attend. To the contrary, any time spent in a meeting with the wrong people is usually wasted. Based on the reason for the meeting, decide who must attend. (And if others show up when the meeting starts, politely shoo them away.)

3. **Develop the agenda** Prepare an agenda that identifies the topics to discuss and the order in which you plan to discuss them. Estimate the time you'll need for each topic and add those estimates to the agenda. When you run the meeting, you can refer to the estimated times to cut short unproductive discussion. Or you can decide to defer a few topics to another meeting if the discussion is worthwhile. An agenda can also provide the first introduction of the ground rules you set for meetings, such as "Arrive on time" or "Keep it constructive."

> **PROJECT FILE** A template for a lessons learned meeting agenda, *Lessons_ Learned_Agenda.dotx*, is available in the Chapter16 folder on the companion website.

4. **Schedule the meeting** Choose a date and time that works for the attendees you need. Reserve the meeting location for the date and time you've selected. Then, send a meeting invitation with enough advance notice that the attendees can prepare for the meeting. For example, if you want to obtain approval for your project plan, stakeholders need enough time to fit a thorough review of the plan into their schedules.

5. **Prepare and distribute meeting materials** At least a few days before the meeting, distribute any materials that attendees must review for the meeting. Prepare any other materials, such as PowerPoint presentations, that you plan to use during the meeting.

> **TIP** ✓ You can adjust the meeting schedule and duration depending on where you are in the life of the project. For example, early on, meetings may last one to two hours as you hash out the plans and get the team up to speed. During easier portions of the project, you may hold 30- to 45-minute meetings and schedule them every other week instead of every week. As you approach major milestones, you can increase the frequency and duration of meetings if necessary.

Running Meetings Well

Although preparation is a good start for a good meeting, a group of people will quickly go astray if you don't keep them focused on the meeting objective. And maintaining focus in a meeting requires a subtle yet valuable skill called *facilitation*. As project manager, you will often facilitate meetings. However, if you have many other duties in a meeting, such as presenting status or discussing issues with stakeholders, you might choose to assign someone else to facilitate the meeting.

The meeting facilitator ensures that the time spent in the meeting is effective. Here are some of the skills and techniques that facilitators use to keep meetings under control:

- **Kick off the meeting**   Identify the purpose of the meeting, introduce the attendees, explain the ground rules, and initiate the discussion. By taking the lead at the beginning of the meeting, people will be more likely to defer to you when you direct the discussion or move the meeting on to another topic. Selecting a position of authority in the room helps you to control the meeting without overt actions. For example, the head of the table, the middle of a long table, or in the front of the room are all positions of authority.

TIP   People might be familiar with the rules by which you run meetings. However, reviewing the rules at the beginning of the meeting is always a good idea, just like paying attention to flight attendants explaining safety procedures—you never know when the rules will come in handy.

- **Direct the meeting to maintain focus on the agenda topics**   If the discussion begins to digress, quickly jump in to get it back on track. If the conversation is totally off the topic, say something like "We're supposed to be discussing the identified project risks. Let's get back to that." However, if the discussion is of value, you can interrupt and tell people that you've added the topic to the end of the agenda. Or, if the new topic is very valuable, you might ask the attendees if they want to modify the agenda to continue the discussion and eliminate another topic.

  Keep your eye on the agenda during the meeting. By following the agenda, you can ensure that you cover the important points, keep discussions on track, or make good decisions about changing the agenda to incorporate new topics.

NOTE   If it becomes clear that only a few people are involved in a discussion, you can keep the meeting on schedule and earn the never-ending gratitude of the other attendees by asking the people talking to finish their discussion after the meeting. For example, if two people disagree about the best way to resolve an issue, ask them to pick up their discussion after the meeting and notify you and the rest of the attendees of their decision.

- **Help people communicate**   Promote discussion, ask open-ended questions, make notes on a flip chart or white board, and suggest methods for setting priorities. Guide the group through making decisions. For example, "Sara, you suggested that we fast-track the project. Does everyone else agree?" If the group members get stuck on a point or conflicts arise, step in to identify the problem and help them resolve their issues.

  You can also help people communicate by paraphrasing what they say. For instance, if someone is struggling to explain a point, jump in and describe the point in a different way. For example, "Meg, I think you're asking if the engineering team can deliver a prototype before the end of the year. Is that correct?"

  ■ **WARNING** Silence is not the same as agreement. If a decision is required, be sure to get people's verbal agreement.

- **Meeting notes are an essential part of successful meetings**   Have you ever attended a meeting in which dozens of action items were identified, but nary a one written down? The chances of those action items ever seeing action are slim. It's a tough job to facilitate a meeting, present information, and take notes at the same time, particularly if the meeting includes several people enthusiastic about their ideas.

  As the facilitator, you use a white board to collect action items and commitments along with who's responsible for them. But a better solution, if it's feasible, is to appoint a scribe to take thorough notes. Someone who is familiar with the project and fast on a keyboard can take notes about discussions, disagreements, action items, and decisions.

BEST PRACTICES

To limit the length of meetings, start and end them on time. People tend to follow the unspoken lead of people in charge, so set an example and show up on time for the meetings you schedule. If people who aren't crucial to the discussion haven't shown up, you can start without them. But don't stop to review when they do appear, or else you'll teach everyone that they can be late without penalty. A more lasting approach is to publicly call laggards to the meeting—a call from a speakerphone with all the attendees who are present chiming in is a powerful incentive to show up on time for the next meeting.

If crucial attendees aren't present, try to round them up quickly—say within 10 minutes. Longer than that, you're better off rescheduling the meeting.

During the meeting, stick to the agenda. Or, if something important comes up, make a conscious decision to change the agenda. Another way to keep meetings short once everyone is present is by standing up. If possible, stack the chairs or move them to the corner of the room. If that isn't possible, purposefully remain standing with your chair pushed under the table.

Meeting Follow-Up

After the meeting is over, edit the notes from the meeting and quickly distribute them to the attendees and any other people who need to know. This gives people a chance to catch any mistakes in the notes or ask questions about the content.

SEE ALSO   Distribution methods for information are identified in the communication plan, as described in the section "Building a Communication Plan," on page 272.

Be sure to emphasize the action items and the people responsible for performing them. Follow up on action items to ensure that they're completed.

Kickoff Meetings

At the beginning of a project (and at the beginning of phases in large projects), a kickoff meeting is a great way to launch the project or next phase of work. By getting stakeholders and team members together, you can build commitment to the project, help team members get to know one another, and have a little fun before the hard work kicks in.

Take advantage of the energy that a new beginning provides. When the project plan is approved, and you're ready to begin the execution phase of the project, hold a kickoff meeting to tell people about the project, introduce all the players, and get them excited about the project. Here are a few of the activities you can schedule for a kickoff meeting:

- The project sponsor reviews the purpose of the project and why it's important to the customer and key stakeholders. In addition, kickoff meetings are a great time for project sponsors to introduce and announce their support for the project managers they assign.

> **SEE ALSO**   The sidebar "The Project Mission Statement," on page 38, discusses how to develop a project mission statement, which summarizes the purpose of a project.

- The customer amplifies the importance of the project or provides a different perspective of its benefits.

- The project sponsor can introduce team members or groups, including any vendors or subcontractors working on the project.

- Coordinate team-building activities to help people get to know each other and develop camaraderie. For example, give everyone at the meeting "project bingo" cards with the names of stakeholders on them. Give small prizes to the first several people who get signatures from the stakeholders whose names appear in a column or row on the card.

> **TIP**   ✓   If you are going to give people pens, coffee mugs, or other products, hand them out at the kickoff meeting to build team spirit before the project starts.

Project Status Meetings

Most team members don't need a meeting to understand the tasks that are complete, delayed, or overdue to start. The benefit of project status meetings is gathering team members to discuss and resolve issues, coordinate work, make decisions, and build relationships. You might have to hold one project status meeting for customers and other key stakeholders that reviews the project in less detail but with more of a business focus. You then schedule additional, more detailed project status meetings for teams within the project. Here are topics and activities you can include in project status meetings:

- **Communicate progress on work packages**   In particular, review tasks that should have started or completed, but haven't. If you distribute a report of tasks that are slipping or should have started or finished, team members can come to the meeting prepared to discuss the delays and potential changes to the project plan.

> **SEE ALSO**   The section "Filters for Checking Schedule Progress," on page 215, identifies several filters in Project that help identify work packages that might require attention.

- **Inform the team about decisions and changes from the customer, project sponsor, or other groups involved in the project**   And if stakeholders have offered positive feedback, be sure to announce that at the meeting.

- **Share lessons learned**   They will help team members be more productive.

> **SEE ALSO**   Chapter 16 discusses techniques for collecting lessons learned.

- **Brainstorm issues and solutions if they are small enough to tackle in a status meeting**   Take advantage of the face-to-face discussion to collect suggestions or find out why some solutions might not work. As you identify next steps, add them to the issues tracking log and also document them as action items for the meeting.

> **SEE ALSO**   The section "Running Meetings Well," on page 285, provides techniques for running effective and efficient meetings.

- **Discuss issues**   Issues are problems or obstacles that must be resolved for work to continue or complete successfully. If your organization uses the Microsoft Enterprise Project Management Solution (EPM), you can use its collaboration features to track issues. However, you can also easily maintain an issues tracking log with Excel. The basic information to store about issues includes ID, status (open or closed), a description of the issue, status and last action taken, next action, person assigned to the issue, date the issue was identified, and target or actual completion date.

> **PROJECT FILE**   For an issue tracking template, open *Issue_Tracking_Log.xlsx* in the *Chapter11* folder on the companion website.

Management Meetings

Meetings with management don't occur that often, but they are valuable opportunities to obtain support for your project or changes you want to make. One common mistake that some project managers make is giving executives too much information about items they don't care about. As a project manager, your job is to manage the day-to-day activities of your project, so you spend much of your time with project details. Meetings with executives require a different perspective because they want to see the big picture of progress and consider only major issues and risks.

■ **WARNING** Unlike team members who simply try to avoid meetings they find pointless, executives are quick to tell you that you're missing the mark or wasting their time. And you won't get more than a couple of chances to get your executive-level presentations right. If your first management meeting meets with disapproval, go back to your communication plan and revise it based on the executives' feedback. You can also ask your project sponsor for some assistance putting the right emphasis on high-level project information.

Here are a few rules for satisfying the needs and tight schedules of executives:

- Be clear and concise at all times. Take time to prepare your materials and practice your delivery.

- Highlight project successes.

- Describe issues and risks and provide options for resolving them.

- Summarize project status including the schedule and cost.

- Present requests or recommendations persuasively. Back up your presentation with compelling facts and statistics.

Project Status Reports

Project status reports keep people informed about the progress that's being made on your project and what's happened in the recent past. These reports are important and can be chock-full of information, but brevity is a virtue. The key to reporting project status is to be concise while still delivering information that people need or want to hear. Here are some guidelines for producing effective project status reports:

- **Use a standard format**   The people in your audience can find the information they need more quickly if you deliver project status in the same format each time, as demonstrated by the project status report template in Figure 11-4. Develop a template for your project status report and include notes about how to fill it in.

- **Begin with a project status summary**   Key stakeholders appreciate a summary of status, so they can decide whether they must review the entire report in detail. Include major accomplishments, issues, risks, and plans for the next period.

- **Review the budget and project schedule**   Summarize the budgeted and actual costs and the planned and actual dates for the status period, and explain significant variances (more than 10 percent).

> **NOTE**   As project manager, be sure to define the meaning of significant variance during project planning. A 2 percent variance on the backyard remodel project might be insignificant. The same 2 percent variance could be catastrophic if your project has a hard deadline.

- **Focus on accomplishments**   Achieving goals and handing over deliverables is more important than the detailed tasks that led up to them. Publicize successes, such as effective practices, shortcuts, clever solutions, and so on.

- **Document lessons learned**   By publicizing effective techniques or ill-advised approaches, other team members can be more productive.

- **Report the status of significant issues and risks**   Describe the progress made toward resolving issues and managing risks during the last status period. Identify issues that have been closed and risks that have been successfully resolved. Also, document the risks that were avoided by implementing plans to circumvent those risks or because the work packages that were at risk have been delivered without issue.

- **Create and distribute status reports on schedule**   If a status report isn't important enough for you to send it out on time, your readers might not consider it important enough to read.

FIGURE 11-4 By using a template for your project status report, you won't forget to include important information, and readers can find the information they need more easily.

PROJECT FILE   The file Project_Status_Report.dotx in the Chapter11 folder on the companion website can serve as a foundation for your project status report.

BEST PRACTICES

Poorly written project status reports can raise more questions than they answer. Here are some tips for producing status reports that truly inform your audience:

- If you include activities that are in progress, also include when they will be complete.

- Include the results of meetings, discussions, training sessions, and so on.

- Include specific, quantitative results. Use numbers rather than terms, such as few or numerous.

- Take the time to correct typographical errors and grammatical errors.

- Proofread the report for errors that Word doesn't catch.

- Include links to a project repository, so readers who want more information can locate it without calling you.

SEE ALSO   Chapter 18, "Archiving Historical Information," describes several methods for storing project documents.

Taming Email

Email is usually a vital part of a project environment; it is fast and convenient to send messages when you have time and for others to read when they have time. However, email has several shortcomings. Some of email's failings are technical issues that you might work around but never truly control. However, the effectiveness of what you communicate in your email is something that you *can* control. Some good email messages do take time to write, but you can improve the effectiveness of your email with a few simple guidelines:

- **Be concise and clear**   Everyone receives a lot of email. Make your point quickly and simply, so the reader can easily understand your message and get on to something else. Because email isn't interactive, taking the time to make your point in the first message can prevent a series of email exchanges containing questions and answers.

■ **Add informative subject lines**   Some email doesn't need anything more than a subject line. For example, if you want feedback on a document you posted to the shared site, send an email with the subject "Please provide feedback on the project plan by this Friday." Subjects like "For your information" don't tell recipients whether the messages are worth opening and make finding information difficult later.

■ **Present your request and the deadline in the beginning**   Start your email messages with what you want from readers and when you want it. Once you have their attention, you can fill them in with the details.

■ **Don't assume your email arrived or was read**   Email is lost, caught in spam filters, deleted by mistake, and have other results that mean your message wasn't received. Follow up with a polite request if you don't receive a response by the deadline. If you prefer email, follow up with another email, but then switch to the telephone or a personal visit.

■ **Avoid humor**   Without facial expressions to go by, readers might interpret your humor as insults.

■ **Set a schedule for responding to email and keep it**   Publicize your window for responding to email and honor that response time.

TIP   If you will be traveling or in meetings and won't be able to respond in your normal time frame, tell your team that as well.

■ **Check the spelling and grammar in your messages**   Proofread your messages carefully to find errors that Outlook didn't catch.

■ **Set up a mechanism for handling low-priority email**   To prevent hundreds of low-priority email messages from swamping a project team, set up a distribution list or standard subject prefix to identify email that is for readers' information, not action. People can filter this email into different folders to delete or read at their leisure.

Here's an example of an effective email:

From: Juan-Carlos Rivas
To: Project Team
Subject: Action Required - Feedback on New Search Web Page

The search web page is complete and available for your review at http://www.adatum.com/search_temp. This web page includes the feedback from our initial review. We will finalize this web page on Tuesday, so I need your feedback by 5:00 P.M. on Thursday, 10/13/2011. You can send me an email or deliver a marked-up copy to my office.

Thanks, Juan-Carlos

Summary

Project management and communication are inseparable. Every project manager must tell people what they need to know; when they need to know it; and most important, in the way that helps them understand it. This chapter introduced the communication plan, which identifies who, what, when, and how for your project communications.

You also learned guidelines for good communication to ensure that you get your messages across and that you understand what other people are trying to tell you. The chapter explained techniques for conducting productive meetings, which help you achieve project objectives without wasting time or your project's budget. It described the information to include in project status reports and how to produce reports that your audiences will appreciate. And finally, it concluded with some guidelines on how to make the most of email for project communication.

4 Controlling Projects

CHAPTER 12

Managing Project Changes

> " *Change is one thing. Progress is another.* "
> —BERTRAND RUSSELL

YOU'RE STANDING on a ski slope and your friend asks you to hold her ski poles while she unzips her jacket. No problem. You take the poles in your right hand. Then, she asks you to hold her gloves so she can scratch her nose. The gloves go in your left hand. It sure is warm, so you hold out your arms to hold her hat, backpack, and jacket. She cheerily says, "OK, I'm ready to go," and skis off as you stand there eyeing your load. There's no way you can ski down the hill. Change requests in projects often have the same sort of effect. Each one seems quite manageable, but at some point you realize they've made your project objectives completely impossible. To make matters worse, stakeholders are likely to forget the changes you obligingly added when the schedule runs long and the budget runs over.

Saying no to every change request is one option, but it's not realistic. People have new ideas or come up with a better approach once they understand the project a little better. Competing products introduce exciting new features, or components you're using are no longer available. You must accept that change is inevitable. The only sensible solution is to *manage* the changes that affect your project.

This chapter describes the basic steps for change management and also discusses who should be part of the *change review board*—the group that decides whether changes that are requested will be added to the project. You'll also learn about simple methods for tracking changes using Microsoft applications.

An Overview of the Change Management Process

Change management is the process of identifying and documenting potential changes, determining whether the changes are beneficial and necessary, analyzing the scope and impact of the changes, estimating the effort and cost of the changes, deciding whether to make the changes, and finally managing the changes after they're added to the project.

Boiled down to the basics, you need only two things to manage change:

- **The original plan**   As you learned in "What Is Project Planning?" on 58, you can't gauge progress unless you know where you started. Before you can manage changes, you must identify the items you want to control, usually referred to as *baseline documents* (aka the project plan or project notebook), and the version that constitutes the baseline. Otherwise, you can't tell what the changes are (called *change requests*, or CRs) and what was supposed to be there all along. For example, if you don't identify a set of requirements as the original to work from, you won't notice that a dozen new requirements crept in during design.

- **A process for tracking and managing changes**   The change management process doesn't have to be complicated, although in large projects the basic steps can comprise several detailed procedures. At its core, the process has to identify the items that you control with the process, who is responsible for deciding whether changes are made, and some steps for getting change requests from the requesters through approval or rejection by the decision makers to ultimate action. The best change management process is one that balances the need for tracking and controlling changes with the need for some flexibility and responsiveness.

Figure 12-1 shows the basic components of change management. On the left side of the diagram are the steps to build the original project documents: the project plan, requirements, specifications, and so on. When the stakeholders approve the project documents, they become baseline documents under the control of change management. The right side of the diagram shows the steps for processing change requests, which, if approved, result in changes to the baseline documents.

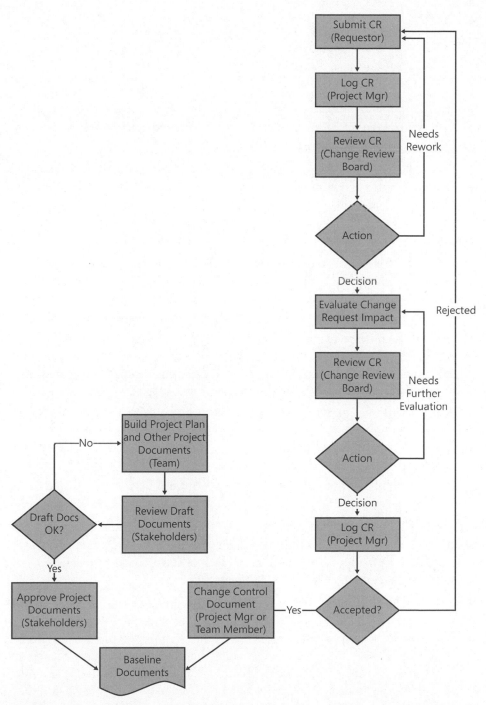

FIGURE 12-1 Change management is about deciding which changes will be made to items you control and tracking the progress of those changes.

NOTE   Your change management process has to be ready to go by the time stakeholders approve the project plan because the plan is one of the items that you must control.

What Do You Control with the Change Management Process?

In project management, control documents include your project planning deliverables, such as the project scope and objectives, the project schedule, and the remaining sections of the project plan. As the project progresses, you add additional deliverables, such as requirements and specifications, schematics, design drawings, system architecture diagrams, style sheets—anything that you use to guide the results for the project.

When you first develop documents and other kinds of deliverables, you constantly make changes until you produce the final result that you submit to the stakeholders for approval. The important point is that these deliverables aren't control documents *until stakeholders sign off on them*. Until you reach that state, you can use features, such as Track Changes in Microsoft Word or a revision table within the file, to keep track of changes you make.

When stakeholders review these draft deliverables, they may ask you to rework them to correct mistakes or fine-tune the content. For example, if stakeholders want you to pull the final date back in, you'll have to rework your project schedule to fast-track or crash the project. The other possibility is the one you're waiting for—stakeholders approve the deliverables, which triggers several actions. Besides a big sigh of relief, you distribute the deliverables to team members who need them to do their project work, *and* you place the deliverables under control of the change management process.

The Change Request Form

Changes may sound simple and straightforward, but the safest approach is to treat every change as significant. That means that your customers (or stakeholders or team members) must document each change they request with a change request.

A change request document helps the project team understand the change being requested so they can evaluate the change. Someone requesting a change uses a change request form to describe the change in detail, the results desired, and the business justification. The change review board reviews the requests and either accepts the change request or asks the requestor to rework it and resubmit. After a change request is accepted by the board, the project manager and team members use the detailed information to evaluate the change.

PROJECT FILE   The Word template shown in Figure 12-2, Change_Request.dotx, is available in the Chapter12 folder on the companion website.

You can use different tools to set up a change request form. For example, a Word template is one solution. You can store the template in a shared folder for the project, so requesters can create a change request form and email it or print it. If you manage a large project with a geographically distributed team, a web page with an online form is another option. Depending on the technology that's available, you might also use a database with submittal forms, a Microsoft Windows SharePoint Services website, or other software solutions.

<Project Name>   **Change Request Form**

Date submitted:
Change requested by:

To be filled in by person requesting change:
Describe the change and resulting deliverables.

Business justification for change.

To be filled in by project manager:
CR number:
Action: (approved or not approved)

Approved by _____   Date _____

FIGURE 12-2 A change request form stores details about each change request.

The Change Request Impact Statement

A change request impact statement describes the alternatives for handling the change request that the project manager has identified, as shown in Figure 12-3. The statement also spells out the impact of each alternative. For example, one way to handle the change request may not affect the project schedule and budget. But more often than not, a change request increases the duration of the schedule, requires more resources, or requires a combination of the two. Optionally, the change request impact statement can include a recommendation for the best way to address the change.

When a change request is accepted by the change review board, the project manager and other team members dive in to evaluate the impact of the change. The project customer or executive management review the impact statement. Similar to an initial change request, the impact statement may come back to the project manager for further evaluation. If the impact statement is approved, the project manager adds the request to the project plan. If it's rejected, the project manager gives the requestor the bad news.

<Project Name>   Change Request Impact Statement

CR number:

Evaluation approval required: Yes   No

Estimate to evaluate the change request:

Hours	Cost	Duration	Change to project end date

Approved by _____   Date _____

Change request evaluation

Estimate impact to project:

Hours	Cost	Duration	Change to project end date

Describe analysis, alternatives, and recommendation.

Change request approved by _____   Date _____

FIGURE 12-3 A change request impact statement documents the evaluation and response to a change request.

> **PROJECT FILE** The Word template shown in Figure 12-3, Change_Request_Impact.dotx, is available in the Chapter12 folder on the companion website.

The Change Request Log

Keeping track of change requests as they work their way through your process is crucial, but it doesn't require sophisticated tools. A change request log can act as a repository for tracking the status of submitted change requests, including who is responsible, status dates, and the estimated and actual impact of change requests on the project. As a change request moves from step to step in the change management process, be sure to update the log with its status.

> **PROJECT FILE** The Microsoft Excel workbook, Change_Request_Log.xlsx, is available in the Chapter12 folder on the companion website.

Managing Change Requests

Now that you have control documents under the jurisdiction of change management, here's the basic approach to handling change requests:

1. When a requestor submits a change request, you add the change request to a change request log. In this step, you document who submitted the request, the date it was submitted, and a brief description of the request. The change request log is a summary of the status or final disposition of every change requested.

2. The change review board considers the change requests you've submitted. Change review boards may require that the requestor or someone who fully understands the change request be present to answer questions as the board deliberates whether to approve the change request for further analysis. If the change review board accepts the request, you begin the impact analysis. The board might also ask the requestor to do some more work on the change request.

3. You launch the analysis of the change request impact. You choose the best person to evaluate the change request. For instance, if the customer requests an extension to a deck, you might assign the change request to the structural engineer, who can determine whether the design can handle the extra load or requires stronger supports. Add the person responsible for evaluating the request to the log. You work with the person assigned to evaluate the request. In addition, the evaluation should take into account whether the change request introduces any new risks to the project and how you would handle them.

4. The change review board considers the change request impact statements you've submitted. Most change review boards require that the requestor or someone who understands the change request be present to answer questions the board may have.

5. If the change review board accepts the request, you document its decision in the change request log. Then take the steps necessary to add the change to your project.

   If the change review board rejects a change request, you document the decision and notify the requestor. The board might also ask you to do some more work on the change request impact.

6. For accepted change requests, you update the control documents and begin tracking the work that the change entails. You might have to adjust the effort on an existing task in your project schedule or add new tasks. Of course, you must also assign the change to someone to perform. When the change is complete, you make a final update to the change request log to show the actual results of the change in hours, cost, and change to the project finish date.

> **NOTE**   For large projects, you might have several levels of change review boards. For instance, a major project with subprojects could have change review boards within each subproject with a top-level change review board for requests that affect the entire project scope.

BEST PRACTICES

You don't have to push *every* change request through *every* step of the change management process. Channeling even the most miniscule requests through the change management process could introduce weeks of delay before a change request receives approval. Change management is necessary, but at the same time you have to keep things moving on projects. One solution to this dilemma is to set thresholds for who can approve changes to a project.

Some change requests are so bizarre you might not assign them to a team member to evaluate. You simply notify the requestor that his change is rejected. If people don't provide enough information, you can ask them to rework their requests and try again.

Changes that don't affect the schedule or budget don't have to go to the change review board. You can work out a plan with the project team and make the change, although you still track the change in the change request log.

However, when schedule, cost, quality, and other objectives are affected, change requests need to go through the change review board for approval. Even the change review board has its limits. For changes that affect the business case for the project, the customer and project sponsor must have a say in the decision. Alternatively, you can define an emergency change process to handle sudden yet substantial changes to business needs.

Another way to manage small changes is to save them until you have enough to work on as a collection. Then you can see whether you have the time and budget to perform them. The full impact of all the changes is more obvious than the innocuous small requests. What's more, team members can be more productive by working on several small changes at once than to switch between their assigned tasks and change requests. However, this approach comes with a risk of rework if the parts of the project in which the changes lie are finalized while the change requests wait for their go-ahead.

Who Belongs on the Change Review Board?

Change review boards typically include the key stakeholders for the project. The customer, representatives from all the groups involved in the project, and project team leads are likely candidates for the board. Functional managers for people working on the project might participate. And project managers are always a part of the board because they submit the requests and have the most in-depth knowledge of the project. For example, in the backyard remodel project, the customer belongs on the change review board. Although the customer may submit the majority of the change requests, he or she also must review the impact and cost of those requests. The contractor is on the change review board to evaluate the feasibility of change requests, as well as their impact on the schedule and budget. In this example, the contractor acts as the project manager and may distribute change requests to other resources, such as the lead carpenter, to evaluate.

Summary

Change management is essential if you want to make good business decisions about the change requests that you receive during a project. Many people fear that the change management process can turn projects into slow-moving bureaucratic nightmares, but change management doesn't have to be that way. The first step is to decide the balance between managing change and allowing the flexibility to respond quickly. Then develop a process that specifies who approves changes and how you make approved changes part of your project plan.

CHAPTER 13

Modifying the Project Schedule

> *The more alternatives, the more difficult the choice.*—Abbe D'Allanival

GETTING THE PROJECT schedule just the way stakeholders want it is like juggling chainsaws. You have to pay attention to every detail or the results could be disastrous. One of the challenges is that you have so many alternatives from which to choose. Do you shorten the schedule and increase the cost? Do you sacrifice quality or reduce the scope? Do you look for more resources or look at how you can use the ones you already have more effectively?

But you have to start somewhere. This chapter reviews different alternatives for optimizing your project schedule and how they affect duration, cost, scope, and quality (and whether the people who work on your project ever get to go home). Each section explains how to apply these alternatives to your project schedule using Microsoft Project features.

SEE ALSO   Chapter 14, "Balancing the Budget and Other Project Variables," looks at the options you have from a business perspective. You must take into account the effects changes have on every aspect of your project and, in many cases, other projects or business objectives at higher levels in your organization.

TIP   This chapter is meant to introduce you to Project features that can help you adjust your schedule. These features include options and all kinds of handy behaviors to tweak your schedule just so. To get to the nitty-gritty details of Project features, look at the book by Teresa Stover, *Microsoft Office Project 2010 Inside Out* (Microsoft Press, 2011).

Simplifying Solution Hunting

Setting up views and selecting options can make your search for solutions easier. Here are some setup tasks to complete before you start looking for ways to improve your schedule.

Here are the steps for displaying summary tasks and the project summary task:

- **Display summary tasks**   On the Format tab, in the Show/Hide group, select the Summary tasks check box, and then the Project Summary Task check box. Whether you're trying to shorten duration or cut costs, summary tasks make it easy to see if you're getting the results you want. The project summary task shows start and finish dates, total duration, work, and cost for your project. Summary tasks show similar fields for portions of your project. As you make changes, you can check these fields to see whether you are obtaining the results you want.

- **Display the critical path and the baseline**   The Tracking Gantt view displays gray taskbars for your baseline schedule (as shown in Figure 13-1), blue taskbars for noncritical tasks in your current schedule, and red taskbars for critical path tasks in your current schedule.

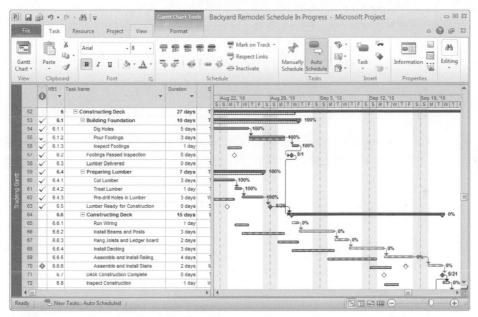

FIGURE 13-1 The Tracking Gantt view displays the critical path and includes taskbars for the base-line so you can compare actual progress to your plan.

Shortening a Project Schedule

If the project duration expands beyond the desired finish date, you can shorten it in several ways:

- **Shortening lag time between tasks**   If tasks on the critical path include lag time between them, reducing that lag time is an easy way to shorten the project duration. It won't cost any more; resources don't have to work harder; and risk is low. The difficulty with this approach is that the lag time is often due to a dependency on other groups. For example, lag time might indicate the delay until stakeholders meet to approve documents. Or a vendor requires two months between your equipment order and delivery. If you can convince the stakeholders to hold an emergency meeting or expedite shipping, you can reduce the lag time in Project by following these steps:

SEE ALSO   Lag time is a delay you can add between tasks, as described in the sidebar "Lag and Lead," on page 127.

1. Double-click the link line between two tasks in the Gantt Chart view.

2. In the Task Dependency dialog box, in the Lag box, change the number of hours, days, or other time period to the new lag time you obtained. For example, if the lag has decreased from 30 days to 20, type 20d.

3. Click OK.

- **Fast-tracking a project compresses the schedule by running tasks concurrently instead of in sequence**   Fast-tracking can introduce risk because you start some tasks before their predecessors finish. However, fast-tracking can often shorten a schedule without increasing cost.

> **SEE ALSO**   To learn how to fast-track a project, see the section "A Fast Track to an Early Finish," on page 150.

- **Crashing is a technique in which you spend additional money to reduce duration**   The trick is to reduce the duration as much as possible for the least amount of money.

> **SEE ALSO**   The section "A Crash Course on Project Crashing," on page 154, describes how to choose tasks to reduce duration cost-effectively.

- **Reducing scope**   If stakeholders decide to reduce the project scope, you might think that the solution is simply to delete the tasks for the scope you're removing. But that's not a good idea because you probably know that decisions that go one way on Monday are as likely to go the other way by Friday. In Project 2010, the Inactivate command leaves task values in place but removes them for inactivated tasks from the project's rolled-up duration and cost and removes resource assignments from the assigned resources' availability.

> **SEE ALSO**   To learn how to use the Inactivate command, see the section "Reducing Scope," on page 157.

Splitting Long Tasks into Short Ones

You might be able to improve your schedule and reduce cost by splitting a long task into several shorter tasks. Instead of the same person performing the entire task, you might be able to assign different resources to the shorter tasks, so you can overlap the tasks. And if you can assign less expensive people to some of the shorter tasks, you can reduce the overall cost. Figure 13-2 demonstrates breaking up a long task to achieve both of these benefits. The original task in the top window takes 30 days and costs $24,000. By splitting the task into work that a designer and drafter can do, as illustrated in the bottom window, the new duration is 25 days and the cost is $18,000.

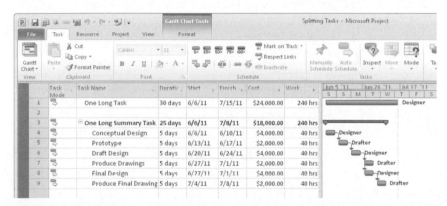

FIGURE 13-2 By breaking up long tasks into several shorter ones, you might be able to reduce the duration and the cost of the work.

To change a long task into several shorter ones, the easiest approach is to treat the original long task as a summary task and create the shorter tasks as subordinate tasks. Here are the steps:

1. Insert a blank row below the long task by clicking the Task Name cell immediately *below* the long task in the Task Sheet. For example, in Figure 13-2, you click the Task Name cell in row 4.

2. To insert blank rows for the new subtasks, press Insert as many times as needed.

3. The insertion point appears in the Task Name cell for the first blank task below the summary task, so you can type the name for the first subordinate task.

4. Press Enter to save the name.

5. Select the task you just created and, on the Task tab, in the Schedule group, click the Indent Task button.

6. After the first subordinate task is indented, add the remaining subordinate tasks by pressing the down arrow and typing the task names.

7. Link the subordinate tasks based on the dependencies between the smaller packages of work and assign resources to the smaller tasks.

> **SEE ALSO** To learn how to create links between tasks, read the section "Creating Task Dependencies," on page 127.

8. To remove the resource assigned to the summary task, double-click the summary task to open the Task Information dialog box.

> **NOTE** If you don't remove the resource assigned to the summary task, your summary task will double up on hours and cost—some from the resource assigned to the summary task and some from the resources assigned to the subordinate tasks.

9. Click the Resource tab.

10. Click the cell with the original resource name in it and press Delete to remove the resource assignment from the summary task.

11. Click OK to close the dialog box.

Adjusting Resource Allocation

Changing the percentage that you allocate resources to tasks may change the schedule duration and cost, depending on whether you reduce the percentage to remove resource overallocations or increase the percentage to shorten duration. In Project, you can take two approaches to modifying the allocation of people to tasks, and the following sections explain how to do both:

■ **Changing the units that resources are assigned to a task**   This approach changes the number of hours that resources work on that task each day. If you increase the units, the task takes fewer days to complete. Increasing units is easy in Project, but in the real world, it only works for so long. People get tired of working long hours and they begin to make mistakes. And if they don't earn overtime pay, morale decreases even faster still.

- **Contouring resource assignments**   Contours adjust how much people work on their assignments at different times during the task duration, such as starting off slow, working full time in the middle, and tapering off near the end. These contours are often a more realistic model of the time that people spend on tasks than all or nothing.

Changing Units

Modifying resource assignments can be a game of hide-and-seek with Project if you don't understand how the program calculates resource assignment fields. If you create a task with the Task Type set to Fixed Units, you can type a task name and duration, choose a resource, and click OK. Project sets the units to the resource's maximum units (for example, 100 percent for full time) and calculates the work. If you want to change units (or make other modifications), assignments may seem less cooperative. This section explains how Project calculates the fields for resource assignments, so you can change units or other values and get the results you want.

Resource calculations depend on the relationships among task duration, work, and units. You can calculate any one of the values as long as the other two fields are set:

Duration = Work / Units

Work = Duration x Units

Units = Work / Duration

> **NOTE**   But how do you know which one Project calculates? Hidden inside the program is a bias for which value it changes. Project tries to change duration before changing work. Because stakeholders almost always want a project finished sooner, duration is always a good guess at the value you want to change. Besides, the work that a task requires doesn't change that often (unless it increases as you learn more about what is required), and the allocation of resources tends to stay the same as well.

Most of the time, deciding what to do is easy. If you specify duration and units, Project uses them to calculate work. If you specify work and units, Project uses them to calculate duration. You can even leave units blank and specify a value for work; Project simply sets the units to 100 percent and then calculates the duration.

> **NOTE**   Project 2010 keeps track of the original assignment units and the peak units. When you first assign a resource to a task, you set the units or Project calculates the units based on the work and duration. Project uses this value if you reschedule the task later on. Peak units come into play if the actual work that a resource performs translates into higher units. For example, suppose a resource works several 10-hour days, which represents units of 120 percent. Project sets peak units to 120 percent. However, if you initially assigned a resource at 100 percent and later increase the task duration, Project uses 100 percent for the additional duration, even though peak units are 120 percent.

Sometimes, you want to change values for a task assignment in a way that conflicts with Project's bias. In these situations, the Task Type field tells Project which field to keep fixed when you assign resources. For example, a Task Type of Fixed Duration tells Project to change work or peak units. For fixed-work tasks, Project keeps the value for work the same and instead recalculates duration or peak units. Table 13-1 shows the relationship between task types and field calculations.

TABLE 13-1 Project Recalculates Different Fields Depending on the Task Type

TASK TYPE	CHANGE DURATION	CHANGE ASSIGNMENT UNITS	CHANGE WORK
Fixed Units	Work	Duration	Duration
Fixed Work	Peak Units	Duration	Duration
Fixed Duration	Work	Work	Peak Units

Armed with this newfound knowledge, you can now change assignment units on a task with ease. Here are the steps:

 Details

1. If necessary, display the Task Form in the bottom pane of the Gantt Chart view. (If the Gantt Chart view shows only one pane, on the View tab, in the Split View group, select the Details check box. In the drop-down list, choose Task Form.)

2. In the top pane of the Gantt Chart view, select the task you want to modify.

3. In the Task Form, in the Task Type list, choose the task type for the field you want to keep. For example, if you want the number of work hours to stay the same and the duration to change, choose Fixed Work.

4. In the section of the Task Form that shows resource assignments, select the person's Units cell, and change the value to the new percentage that the person is available. For example, if someone was assigned at 50 percent, type 100% to change it to full time.

5. Click OK. For a fixed-work task, Project recalculates the task duration.

6. To keep your tasks consistent, change the Task Type back to Fixed Units.

In the top window in Figure 13-3, the crew member works half-time (50 percent) for 8 days to complete 32 hours of work. In the bottom window, by setting the Task Type to Fixed Work and changing the units to 100 percent, the crew member performs 32 hours of work in only 4 days.

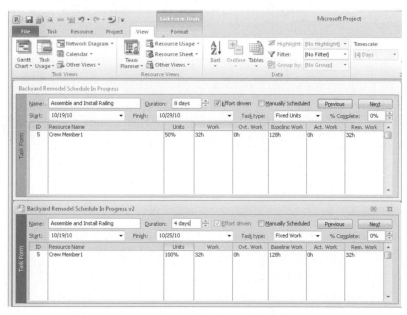

FIGURE 13-3 Change the Task Type to tell Project which field you want to keep the same value.

Adjusting Work Contours

The Work Contour feature in Project changes the allocation of resources over the course of their assignments. For example, you can apply the Bell work contour, which starts someone's assignment slowly, increases to a higher allocation in the middle and then tapers off the assignment at the end, as demonstrated in Figure 13-4. Contouring tasks can help you optimize your schedule by modeling assigned time more realistically. For example, the work that people have to do on a task often dwindles at the end, so you might be able to start a new assignment before the previous one is complete without overallocating anyone.

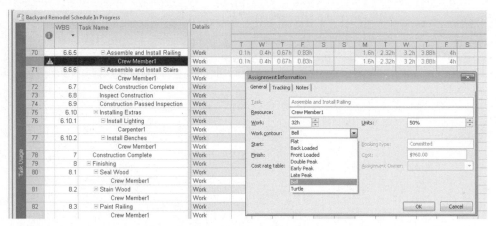

FIGURE 13-4 Work contours adjust the allocation of work for resources over the duration of their assignment.

Here are the steps for applying a work contour to a resource assignment:

1. On the View tab, in the Task Views group, choose Task Usage. (Or in the Resource Views group, choose Resource Usage.) These are the only two views that show detailed assignment information.

2. For the task whose assignment you want to contour, double-click the name of the resource, Crew Member in Figure 13-4.

3. In the Assignment Information dialog box, in the Work Contour list, choose the contour that you want. For example, Back Loaded adds more time at the end of the assignment, which is similar to a crunch at the end. Front Loaded adds more time up front.

4. Click OK to contour the hours.

Assigning Overtime

Asking people to work longer hours is another strategy for shortening a project schedule. By working beyond the normal day, they can complete tasks in fewer days. If people earn a salary and don't earn any extra for working longer hours, the project price tag doesn't go up. However, this sort of overtime abuse won't work for long. Employees get tired of long hours. Morale decreases and employee turnover increases—both of which negatively affect your project. If people are paid overtime rates, your project costs do increase. In addition, you have to consider whether people could do more beneficial work with that time.

TIP   Don't resort to assigning overtime during planning. If you plan for overtime and the project runs into trouble, more overtime probably isn't an option.

You can assign resources to work overtime in a couple of ways. You use the Overtime Work field only when you pay resources more for overtime hours. Here are some of the techniques you can use:

- **Increase work hours for a period**   If resources don't earn premium overtime rates, you can assign longer hours for a period of time. To do this, in the Resource Sheet view, double-click the resource you want to set up for overtime. In the Resource Information dialog box, in the Resource Availability section, specify the start and end date for the overtime and the units, as shown in Figure 13-5.

    NOTE   If you assign percentages in the Resource Availability section, the resource's availability for all other time periods remains at the Max. Units value you specify in the Resource Sheet.

- **Modify the working hours in a resource's calendar**   For example, you could specify the work hours for one Monday to start at 7:00 A.M. and end at 7:00 P.M.

    SEE ALSO   The section "Scheduling Around Nonworking Time," on page 147, describes how to set working and nonworking times in a calendar.

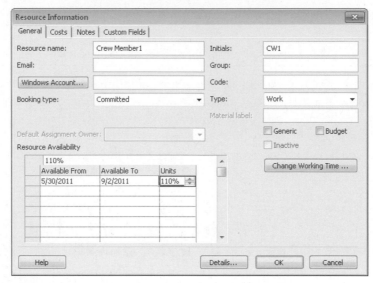

FIGURE 13-5 You can specify a resource's availability at different times.

- **Assign overtime hours paid at an overtime rate**   If you pay more for overtime hours, you use overtime hours and the overtime rate in Project to calculate labor costs correctly. You set a resource's overtime rate in the Resource Sheet's Overtime Rate field.

OVERTIME HOURS PAID AT AN OVERTIME RATE

Project doesn't automatically assign hours that people work as overtime hours. If people receive premium pay for overtime hours, you must set up a few things before Project can calculate the cost accurately. In the Resource Sheet, be sure to fill in the Ovt. Rate cell with the amount that the person is paid for overtime. For example, resources with a standard rate (Std. Rate) of $50 an hour might receive $60 an hour for overtime.

Then, for each assignment, you must specify the number of overtime hours. To do this, follow these steps:

1. If the Task Form isn't visible in the bottom pane, on the View tab, in the Split View group, select the Details check box, and then in the drop-down menu, choose Task Form.

2. Right-click the Task Form pane and select Work on the shortcut menu.

    In the resource assignment table, Project displays the Units, Work, and Ovt. Work fields along with a few others.

3. Type the number of overtime hours for the assignment in the Ovt. Work field, as shown in Figure 13-6.

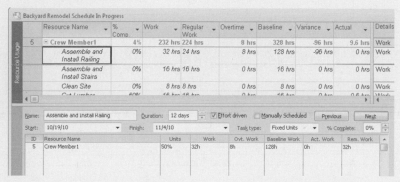

FIGURE 13-6 The Work value equals the hours of regular and overtime work.

The Work field represents the total work hours for the assignment, both regular and overtime work. Project subtracts the overtime hours from the hours in the Regular Work field for the assignment. For example, if a task's Work equals 32 hours, and you assign 8 hours of overtime, the Overtime Work field changes to 8 hours, and the Regular Work field changes to 24 hours.

Substituting Resources

Whether you have to replace a resource who can't work on your project anymore or you're looking to assign less expensive resources to cut costs, you can replace resources in assignments.

If you know the resource that you want to replace, you can simply choose a new resource in the Task Form. In the Resource Name section, select the name of the resource you want to replace and then, in the Resource Name list, select the new resource you want to assign. Project changes the resource assigned, but keeps the units, work, and duration the same. If you selected a person with more or less experience or who works faster or slower, you should consider changing the values in the Work and Duration fields to reflect the new person's productivity. In the background, Project recalculates the cost with the new resource's Std. Rate in the Resource Sheet.

To substitute a resource with someone similar, the Assign Resources dialog box provides several features for finding suitable replacements. Here are the steps for replacing a resource using the Assign Resources dialog box:

SEE ALSO The section "Using the Assign Resources Dialog Box," on page 142, describes how to find replacement resources with the characteristics you want.

Assign
Resources

1. In the Gantt Chart view, select the task in which you want to replace a resource.

2. On the Resource tab, in the Assignments group, click Assign Resources.

3. To replace a resource, in the Assign Resources dialog box, select the resource and then click Replace.

4. In the Replace Resource dialog box, shown in Figure 13-7, in the Units field for the resource you want to use as a replacement, type the percentage you want and click OK.

   Project adds a check mark to the left of the resource name and moves the assigned resource above all the unassigned resources in the list.

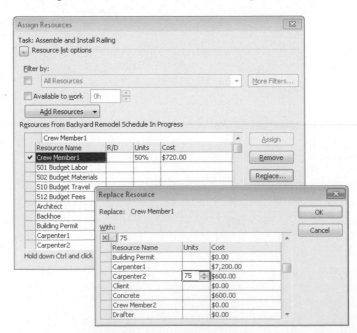

FIGURE 13-7 You can select a replacement and assign the units in the Replace Resource dialog box.

Modifying Baselines

The typical approach to baselines in project management is to save one when the stakeholders approve the project plan and compare project performance to that baseline from then on. However, one of the reasons you might be reading this chapter is because something significant has happened to your project, and you've had to adjust the schedule in response. The original baseline is still important, but it might not be as helpful for measuring performance now that you've fast-tracked some tasks, crashed a few others, and removed some scope as well. In situations such as these, you can save a new baseline after you make major revisions to your Project schedule.

Saving Additional Baselines

Set
Baseline ▾

In Project, you can tell if you have an initial baseline saved in the Set Baseline dialog box. On the Project tab, in the Schedule group, click Set Baseline, and then choose Set Baseline on the drop-down menu. A saved baseline displays text such as *(last saved on 11/1/2011)* after the baseline name. Because the Variance table displays value for only the first baseline in the list (named Baseline), saving additional baselines requires a couple of steps:

1.   On the Project tab, in the Schedule group, click Set Baseline, and then choose Set Baseline on the drop-down menu.

2.   In the Set Baseline dialog box, make sure that the Set Baseline option is selected.

3.   In the Set Baseline list, choose the first baseline name *without* a last saved on date, such as Baseline 1 (see Figure 13-8).

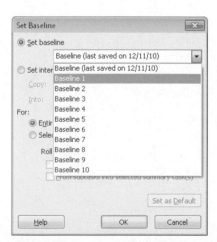

FIGURE 13-8 You can set up to 11 baselines, including Baseline, Baseline1 through Baseline10.

4. Under the For heading, select the Entire Project option.

5. Click OK. Project stores the current scheduled values in baseline fields, such as Baseline1 Duration.

6. Before you do anything else, open the Set Baseline dialog box once more (see step 1).

7. In the Set Baseline list, choose Baseline, and then click OK to store the same baseline values in Baseline. By doing this, values you see in the Variance table compare the scheduled values to your current baseline.

8. A message box appears, warning that you are about to overwrite a baseline that you've already saved. Click Yes.

Clearing a Baseline

If you decide that you want to remove a baseline that you've saved, do the following:

1. On the Project tab, in the Schedule group, click Set Baseline, and then choose Clear Baseline.

2. In the Clear Baseline dialog box, make sure that the Clear Baseline Plan option is selected.

3. In the Clear Baseline list, choose the baseline name you want to remove.

4. Under the For heading, select the Entire Project option.

5. Click OK. Project removes the values in the fields for the baseline you selected.

Viewing Multiple Baselines

If you want to see several baselines, the Multiple Baselines Gantt view shows taskbars in different colors for Baseline, Baseline 1, and Baseline 2, as shown in Figure 13-9. On the View tab, in the Task Views group, click Other Views, and then choose More Views. In the More Views dialog box, double-click Multiple Baselines Gantt.

FIGURE 13-9 Compare the schedules for three baselines in the Multiple Baselines Gantt view.

TIP   If you want to modify the Multiple Baselines Gantt view to show different baselines, such as Baseline 4, right-click the Gantt Chart and choose Bar Styles on the shortcut menu. In the Bar Styles dialog box, you can replace the baseline start and finish date fields with the fields for the baseline you want to display.

Summary

Tweaking a project schedule to deliver the combination of scope, schedule, and budget is a balancing act. Depending on which measures are more important, you can choose different techniques for modifying the schedule. Some techniques focus on rearranging tasks, whereas others look at reassigning resources. This chapter explained the alternatives and showed how to apply them using features in Project.

CHAPTER 14

Balancing the Budget and Other Project Variables

> ❝*There is such a choice of difficulties that I am myself at a loss how to determine.*❞—JAMES WOLFE

TO BE A PROJECT MANAGER, you had better be able to juggle. Your aim is to balance the project's objectives and scope with the constraints of time, money, scope, and quality; and the realities of change requests, risks, and the ebb and flow of day-to-day progress. At the same time, you must temper the moods of your project team—from organizational inertia, when you need to plead for seemingly every bit of work, to a kind of euphoria in which team members become so absorbed in their work that time and money seem not to matter at all.

Regardless of the unfortunate circumstances that arise—a key resource's unexpected three-week Tahitian honeymoon, the pay rate of the person you find as a replacement, or the radical scope change when the customer wants clogs, not blogs—you must find a way to remedy the situation. Sometimes, you can adjust your project plan to complete the project within the original constraints. At other times, an infusion of additional funds or additional time is required. More likely, you'll juggle *all* variables of your project to achieve as much as you can while sacrificing as little as possible. The options from which you can choose are as numerous as your project objectives and as varied as the personalities of your team members. Balancing all the factors is a talent that takes time to develop, so this chapter introduces some of the strategies you can use to bring a project back into balance.

Cost, Scope, Quality, and Schedule

Although managing a project successfully is an art, the foundation is pure math. Cost is a function of project scope, desired level of quality, and schedule. In other words, how *much* depends on how *many*, how *good*, and how *long*. If you change one of these factors, something else has to give. So, you must evaluate your choices to decide which solution best fits the priorities for your particular project. For example, if quality is the key to differentiating a product from the competition, taking more time and increasing the budget might be the preferred choice. However, if getting that same product to market before the competition is critical, reducing the product features (scope) or accepting a slightly higher level of errors (quality) might be better.

As the project manager, you might be asked to compile recommendations for stakeholders to consider for getting a project back on track. If your budget is running out, and that's all you have to spend, should you sacrifice scope, schedule, or quality? Will adding resources shorten the schedule or simply increase cost? And how will these changes affect the risks you take for the project? Following the money is one way to remain objective through these complicated decisions. Go back to the benefits and monetary results you and the stakeholders forecast for the capital budget analysis.

> **SEE ALSO**   The section "Understanding Capital Budgets," on page 165, describes how to use capital budgeting to analyze the financial benefits of a project.

Balancing Acts

The good news is that you can bring a project back into balance in any number of ways. Of course, that's the bad news as well. With so many options, how do you separate optimal solutions from the also-rans?

You can pare down the options by starting with the ones within the realm of your authority; that is, what the project sponsor gave you authority over in the project charter. If your course correction doesn't affect anything or anyone outside of your project team, you can push on without having to ask permission.

SEE ALSO   The section "The Project Charter: Publicizing a Project," on page 51, describes how the project chart communicates your authority as the project manager.

If internal changes aren't enough, you can expand your options to those that require stakeholder permission, such as increasing the schedule, increasing the budget, reducing scope, or modifying the business objectives. And if your organization manages a portfolio of projects, the final step is to see whether your project is important enough to warrant pulling resources from other projects.

BEST PRACTICES

When you ask stakeholders to decide what to do, it's a good idea to come with a list of the options that you recommend, including the pros and cons for each. Be sure to emphasize the advantages of your recommended option and any disadvantages it has. Be prepared to answer the stakeholders' questions. They'll want to know what other solutions you looked at and why they won't work. And they'll want to know why you recommend the options you provide.

SEE ALSO   Chapter 9, "Evaluating Project Performance," describes how you determine how far the project is off track. Chapter 6, "Building a Project Schedule," and Chapter 13, "Modifying the Project Schedule," describe techniques to improve project performance.

Unless the problems that derailed your project are obvious when you check project status, review your project plan and the assumptions within it. If something has changed that skewed your project plan—the objectives, scope, schedule, and budget no longer align—you can see how much ground you'll be able to regain by optimizing the remainder of the project. By determining the sources of problems and trying different solutions before you go to the stakeholders, you're more likely to receive the support you request.

Reassigning Resources

Changing which resources do what and where resources come from can help you rein in the project schedule, cost, or both. Depending on the resource strategy you choose, you might need stakeholder permission or the go-ahead from the project sponsor. Here are several ways to improve performance with resource changes:

- **Reassigning resources to the critical path**   This shortens the schedule with no change to labor cost. In fact, if the project pays for overhead charges or the rent on extra office space, a shorter schedule could reduce overall costs. If you have the right kind of resources to spare working on noncritical path tasks, you can move them to the critical path and shorten the remaining duration. Sounds great, but this approach comes with a lot of caveats. You've probably heard the saying "Too many cooks can spoil the broth." Adding more people can backfire. For example, when tasks aren't interrelated, you can assign more people to them, such as different houses in a development, but only so many surgeons can work at the same operating table. In addition, resources you add to a project may require time to become familiar with the project or may not have the exact skill set you need. In these situations, adding resources could extend the project duration more than working with the original team.

SEE ALSO	The section "A Crash Course on Project Crashing," on page 154, describes the technique known as crashing and how to apply it effectively to shorten a project's duration.

The other challenge with shortening the critical path is that the critical path can change. As you reassign resources from one task to another, the changes in duration can add tasks to the critical path that weren't on it before. Moreover, reassigning resources takes time and effort, so the decrease in duration you can achieve should be long enough to be worth your attention.

> **NOTE** Suppose you can crash the project, but you don't have the resources within your team to do it. Depending on the resources you need, the solution might be as simple as hiring other resources or as difficult as prying specialized resources away from another project.

- **Using less expensive resources**   This can reduce costs, but the effect on the schedule depends on the resources. Perhaps a vendor is anxious to add your company's name to its client list and is willing to work at a discount. However, you usually get what you pay for. Resources that cost less are typically less experienced, so the trade-off is lower cost versus a longer schedule—and you might have to accept lower quality as well.

- **Working overtime**   This is another way to shorten the schedule, often at the expense of cost and possibly quality. You use the resources you have, so no groveling to managers is required. If resources aren't paid overtime, you seem to obtain a shorter schedule at no extra cost. But that works for only so long. Eventually, your people burn out, and the quality of their work might suffer. On the other hand, if you must pay overtime, the cost increases. Furthermore, salaried employees who work overtime hours carry an opportunity cost.

> **SEE ALSO** Chapter 7, "Working with a Budget," explains the cost of using resources on a project whether you pay them a set amount, by the hour, or with a premium for overtime.

- **Outsourcing some or all of the work**   This can sometimes reduce cost and duration. Specialists or vendors might be able to complete work faster or at a lower cost. For example, if you have trouble hanging a picture straight, a professional carpenter is probably faster, less expensive, and better than you are for framing a house. One disadvantage to outsourcing is an increase in risk because you have less control over the outsourced work. In addition, setting up outsourcing takes time and effort. If the subcontractor you choose turns out to be less experienced than you expected, chances are you won't have time to switch to another vendor without slipping the schedule.

TIP   Sometimes, you can negotiate better rates if you commit to a volume of work with the same vendor. Furthermore, negotiating fixed fees removes some of your risk of cost overruns.

- **Working with customer resources**   This is another option, particularly if the project objectives are very important to the customer. For example, in the backyard remodel project, the homeowners might decide to do some of the work to keep the budget within their means. Of course, this approach works only if the customer has resources with the right skills.

- **Increasing productivity with faster or more experienced resources**   This is an attractive strategy. For example, a more experienced engineer, even one whose hourly rate is higher, might accomplish work in significantly less time and with less direction. An experienced engineer might work more quickly and introduce fewer errors, so testing takes less time as well. The difficulty is that more productive resources cost more and are in higher demand.

Optimizing the Schedule

When the project schedule runs off course, project managers tend to revisit their original estimates. In fact, stakeholders have been known to apply pressure to improve estimates so that the project comes in on time and within budget. The problem with this approach is that estimates tend to be optimistic, which could be why the project needs rework. If you succumb to revising your original estimates, you might be telling stakeholders what they want to hear—at least until the project is over and the results are only too obvious. Instead of playing games with numbers, you can try the following techniques to improve your project schedule:

- **Fast-tracking a project shortens the schedule by overlapping tasks that normally run in sequence**   As long as tasks don't use the same resources, you can reduce duration without increasing cost by paying closer attention to when work can occur. Unfortunately, fast-tracking can increase risk because you start some tasks before the ones they depend on are complete.

> **SEE ALSO**   The section "The Fast-Track to an Early Finish," on page 150, describes how to fast-track tasks in a project to shorten duration.

- **Breaking a project into phases to control costs**   This approach often complements a decision to reduce or alter the scope of a project because scope removed in the first phase can be added back in later when more money is available. The risk is that the later phases might never receive funding or approval.

- **Progressively increasing scope and quality**   In this strategy, also called incremental development or agile development, the project delivers a rough product that does most of the job. Then work continues to add the rest of the scope and improve quality until all the project objectives are met. Because customers sometimes can't articulate what they want, this approach has an added advantage of giving the customer something to look at. The feedback you get about the first delivery can help the project produce results closer to what the customer has in mind.

> **SEE ALSO**   Chapter 20, "Other Project Management Approaches," describes a few ways to manage projects that deliver incremental results.

PRIORITIZING COST-RELATED CHANGES

Some cost changes have little effect on your project. For example, if your project includes a contingency fund, it can cover some additional work hours or the extended rental on a backhoe. More expensive or more influential budget changes can affect a project's goals and its financial health. However, for changes that are critical to achieving the project's benefits, adding money to pay for those changes might be more advantageous than sticking to the budget.

Project managers often have authority to approve additional costs up to a preset limit (for instance, increases that total less than 5 percent of the overall budget). Typically, stakeholders decide whether to approve changes when the cost increase on the project is significant. The project charter usually specifies the extent of a project manager's financial authority.

> **SEE ALSO**   The section "The Project Charter: Publicizing a Project" on page 51, describes the project charter and how it documents a project manager's authority.

Business Decisions

When everything you try isn't enough to correct your project's course, you have to reconsider the balance between cost, scope, quality, and schedule. And that means that you have to get stakeholders involved. Here are some guidelines when considering a change to project variables:

- **Reducing scope**   This option might be necessary when all other methods for controlling the project fail. The best way to reduce scope is to eliminate the least important requirements first. For example, if the homeowners for the backyard re-model want lighting, the lights around the deck and stairs are important for safety, but the aesthetic spotlights that shine on the trees might be eliminated without too much difficulty. As project manager, you can recommend the scope items that can be eliminated based on your overall understanding of the project's objectives. However, when deep cuts are needed, additional interviews to understand what the customer really needs are in order.

- **Changing financial goals such as ROI**   This option might be an option, for instance, if your organization is willing to sacrifice some profit to beat the competition to market, to increase market share, or to achieve other strategic business objectives.

- **Increasing the duration of the schedule**   This option might be acceptable from a business standpoint, but increased duration often comes with increased cost. If stakeholders decide to increase the schedule, you must evaluate the financial measures to ensure that they are still acceptable as well.

> **NOTE** Sacrificing quality is rarely a good idea. The phrase "Close enough for government work" conveys that feeling of resignation from results that are functional but less than what they could be. Reduced quality often ends up costing more in rework, repairs, team morale, and irretrievably damaged reputations.

Summary

Money is important, but it isn't the only project characteristic that counts. As circumstances change, you must continually weigh cost against schedule, scope, quality, and risk to make sure the project achieves its goals within the constraints placed upon it. You can recover from some changes by fine-tuning your project. Although fine-tuning takes time, you can make the changes you need without obtaining permission from anyone else. For more dramatic changes, you have to work with project stakeholders, and sometimes top management, to choose the right approach.

CHAPTER 15

Managing Risk

> ❝The pessimist sees difficulty in every opportunity. The optimist sees the opportunity in every difficulty.❞—*WINSTON CHURCHILL*

PROJECTS ARE often tied to opportunities—everything from bringing a new product to market to improving your home for more enjoyment or resale. But opportunities invite risks—large and small—and risks can threaten a project's budget, its schedule, and the quality of its results. Some risks are more likely to occur than others, and some risks produce more damage, in terms of time and money, if they occur. *Risk management* is about identifying risks, estimating the effect each risk could have, reducing the chances that risks will happen, and planning actions to take in response if they do. Like cutting costs by foregoing insurance coverage, you can choose to go without managing risk. But if risks occur, the risk planning you do and the risk responses you put into action are indispensable for keeping a project on schedule, its budget on track, and its stakeholders happy.

In this chapter, you'll learn some practices for managing risks. As you'll see, risk management is not a one-time task. It is a way of project management life that you begin during project initiation and then repeat continuously until the project is complete. Risk-management processes help you systematically track risks, assess their potential impact, and develop and evaluate plans to handle them. You'll learn more about each of these processes in the sections that follow. But first, you'll learn about some of the advantages that risk-management practices provide.

The Benefits of Managing Risk

Projects—like life—are grounded in uncertainty. Risks that come to fruition can undo carefully laid plans because dealing with unexpected or challenging conditions requires more time, more energy, and more money than you'd expect. Learning how to manage risk helps reduce the number of times you're caught off guard, and when you are, lessens the effect of what went wrong.

Risk management can help a project team accomplish its goals with less trouble and anxiety. Sure, discussion of risk and uncertainty might dampen the mood of the team members at the start, when their eyes are bright with enthusiasm. But the potential effect of many risks increases over time, so identifying risks early is well worth a small and short-lived letdown. You and the team will be ready to monitor and deal with risks before they take on a life of their own.

Consider risk management as an approach to avoiding issues that could have a detrimental (or catastrophic) effect on your project. It can increase your and other participants' understanding of the project. For example, risk management provides a catalyst for measuring less risky solutions that offer the same level of quality or results. You can make stakeholders and managers aware of risks that they had not yet considered. And you can help everyone appreciate the implications of decisions that introduce a higher level of risk. In short, a realistic assessment of risks helps set expectations for project performance. Identifying and analyzing risks have a number of other benefits as well, such as the following:

- Providing clarity of project objectives

- Providing better schedule and cost estimates

- Helping you and the team proceed with confidence, knowing that risks are recognized and shared

- Documenting the need for contingency in the budget and schedule, and providing the information needed for allocating a contingency allowance

The Risk-Management Plan

Risk planning—similar to budget and schedule planning—involves some guesswork. You can't, for example, identify or anticipate every risk a project might face. In risk management, these risks are called *unknown unknowns*—events you simply can't foresee with unknown impact to your project. For instance, if you don't realize that life exists beyond the solar system, you can't anticipate the destruction of your construction project by the Galactic Department of Transportation. So you start by identifying risks that you know might happen (called *known unknowns*), such as a stretch of bad weather that keeps you from pouring concrete. You define each risk that might occur and assess its effect on, say, the project's budget, schedule, scope, or resources. Then you develop plans for how to handle those risks and who will handle them if they should occur.

Risks can pop up at any point in a project's life. Some risks are present before work on a project begins. You might be handed a project whose scope and objectives are unclear. Financial assumptions might be too optimistic; resources once committed to the project might have taken new jobs, with new responsibilities and goals; organizational conflicts and department politics could threaten to divide the loyalties and the motivation of the project team. During project planning, you consider these risks as you build estimates, assign resources, and make other decisions.

Here are some of the factors that introduce risk:

- **Insufficient project management processes**   If your organization doesn't have project management processes in place, improper planning, management, and project control put your project's budget and schedule at risk. Issues with resources or funding can arise due to poor prioritization of projects.

- **Vague timing of future activities and events**   There's less certainty (and hence more risk) when a contractor says, "Yeah, I think I can fit you in come June. Probably take me a couple of weeks," instead of "I'll be there the morning of the 15th. I'll finish on the 21st because I start another job the next day."

- **Stakeholders aren't involved**   Suppose your design team has come up with creative new packaging. The trouble is that the materials are no longer available from any of your preferred suppliers, which you would have known if the procurement group had been involved. Identifying all the stakeholders for a project and including them in discussions can prevent surprise issues.

- **Technology issues**   Technology can be expensive, and hidden costs often crop up when you begin to implement the tools. Some projects also require technology that is new, complex, hard to come by, or all of the above.

- **Geographically dispersed teams**   When team members are located in different areas around the globe, differences in cultures and time zones can dramatically increase risk due to communication issues. Different time zones make it difficult for team members to collaborate effectively and introduce delays in handing off work from one team member to another. In addition, geographic separation can make it difficult for team members to develop effective working relationships with one another.

- **Options are limited**   Watch out for work that depends on people with rare combinations of skills or materials that are available from only a small number of sources.

- **Experience is limited**   Perhaps resources in key roles are new to the team or this is your first time working with a client. Responding to risks introduced by a lack of experience requires instinct as much as a well-crafted plan.

- **Unpredictable external events**   Risks like these fall into the category of environmental factors; for example:

  - A regulatory agency or city department changes permitting requirements or cancels your contract after the mayor's new budget is passed.

  - A rock slide closes the interstate to traffic, which means the supplies you're waiting for must be rerouted, delaying completion of some critical tasks.

  - Workers you hire for your project go on strike.

TIP

Events that appear to be small risks are as important to evaluate as larger ones. Risks can crop up within the details of specific tasks such as the hours allocated or the estimated costs. As isolated events, these risks are easy to manage, but small-scale risks that mount up task by task can have a significant effect on schedule, budget, and, ultimately, on project scope and quality.

The good news is that risk-management processes don't need to be complex. A small set of documents will do, starting with a *risk-management plan*, which you prepare along with the project's communication plan and other planning documents. It can be quite simple on small projects: a list of risks, an estimate of their impact, and a summary of actions you'll take if they occur. For more complex projects, your risk-management plan might include a separate information sheet or risk assessment form for each risk you've identified, as illustrated by the risk information sample form in Figure 15-1. Later, as you monitor and respond to risks that occur, you track what goes on risk-wise in a risk log.

Simply having systematic procedures in place makes it easier to jump to action and make good decisions when risks occur.

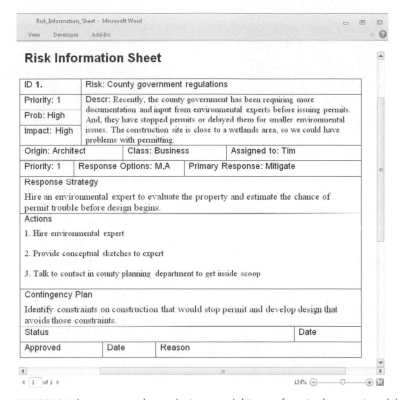

FIGURE 15-1 In more complex projects, you might use a form to document each identified risk.

PROJECT FILE   The form in Figure 15-1, Risk_Information_Sheet.docx, is available in the Chapter15 folder on the companion website.

For projects of any size, putting together a simple risk-management plan helps team members think about what they will do about risk *before* they need to do it. A plan forges a common understanding of the nature of each risk and sets out the steps to control and reduce a risk's probability and impact. A risk-management document typically includes the following sections:

- **Identified risks**   Include a list of *all* risks you've identified for the project with brief descriptions. You reserve your assessment of significance and decisions about risk response for other sections of the document.

- **Risk assessment**   Estimate the likelihood of the risk occurring and the potential impact to the project. Team members and stakeholders must agree on which issues pose the greatest threat because you usually can't manage every risk you face. To limit the number of risks to a manageable number, the assessment section includes a prioritized list of risks.

- **Risk response**   Formulate the strategies you plan to use to avoid some risks completely, reduce the probability that risks occur, and lessen the impact if they do occur. This section identifies which risks you will respond to and which ones you will accept. Moreover, you can identify the money (and time) you keep in reserve to implement your risk responses.

- **Monitoring plan and metrics**   List the processes you plan to use to monitor risks and the metrics you use to evaluate risks.

- **Risk triggers**   Make a list of the risk triggers, events, and circumstances that provide early warning of risks that are in danger of occurring. For instance, if one of your risks is that a critical resource is in short supply, missing a task deadline might indicate that the risk is coming to fruition—or has already occurred—and you must take action.

- **Risk documents**   Include the risk information sheet and risk log you plan to use to manage risks.

Identifying and Describing Risks

Most of the time, you can't manage risks with one-on-one conversations in the hallway. The processes you follow to identify and describe risks (and later to assess and plan how to respond to risks) need to be more systematic. Resistance to formal risk management is more common than you'd expect. Someone might say, "We know every project has risks. We could spend the duration of the project trying to define them all. Let's just deal with them as they come up." That approach, of course, earns the award as the first risk for your project.

TIP

The formality and sophistication of your risk-management processes depend on the size and complexity of the project; how many groups, departments, or organizations are involved; and the expectation and needs of stakeholders. Yes, more formal risk-management processes require more time. However, you'll also realize greater benefits. For example, documenting your approach to managing risks on one project is great information to have when you're planning and making estimates for future projects.

From the beginning, you know at least some of the areas that present risks to manage: making changes or additions to project scope, meeting quality and performance benchmarks, controlling costs, and meeting the schedule. Begin by identifying risks you might encounter for each of these areas. For example, discussing task durations as you refine estimates often raises potential problems. Add those to your list of risks.

SEE ALSO

What better way is there to reduce and control schedule risks than by developing a realistic schedule in the first place—one with durations that take into account the possibility of risks occurring? Chapter 6, "Building a Project Schedule," describes how to estimate projects more accurately and develop more realistic schedules.

Think beyond your project when identifying risks. Meet with key project resources and ask them about risks they foresee. Ask experienced project managers to review your plan and talk to people who are experts in specific areas of the project. If you're working with a vendor for the first time, for example, talk to the vendor's other clients.

BEST PRACTICES CONTRIBUTED BY MAX DUFOUR

To identify as many unknown risks as possible, explore what-if scenarios for timelines and deliverables that are not clearly defined. Consider potential changes in the timing of tasks or changes in deliverables that could impact your project. If any what-if scenarios are likely to affect the project, document them as risks.

To obtain a more complete understanding of project risk, go beyond assessing the probability that a risk will occur. In addition, assess the probabilities of different potential outcomes, such when a deliverable is completed. For example, if your construction project is scheduled during hurricane season, delays are more likely than construction during the dry season.

Be as specific as possible when identifying and describing risks. Identify the roles or re-sources whose work would be affected, the related tasks, and the deliverables and goals that might be jeopardized. Also, be as precise as possible in describing the consequences, such as the time added to the schedule or the extra cost if a risk occurs.

You might stop short of adding a risk when you see your lead engineer pull away on her new Kawasaki motorcycle without a helmet, but consider the risks that resources present. Which resources are booked to the maximum? Whose skills are vital to the completion of key tasks? Are hard-to-find resources assigned to the longest tasks on your critical path?

In a simple risk-management plan, the risk assessment includes a summary of the risks you've identified, probability and impact, and background for your assessment. This information helps you prioritize the risks you monitor because most projects have too many risks to watch them all. Table 15-1 illustrates a simple risk-assessment summary.

> **SEE ALSO**   You can learn more about determining the ratings for probability and impact in the section "Choosing the Risks You'll Manage," on page 346.

TABLE 15-1 A Simple Risk Assessment Summary

NO.	RISK EVENT	PROBABILITY/IMPACT	ASSESSMENT
1	Availability of appropriate conference facility	High/Very High	Most conferences are scheduled one to two years in advance, so it is very likely that the higher-quality conference facilities are already booked. In addition, a two-week window makes availability at the right time unlikely. To make a good impression on industry heavy hitters, it is imperative to have a high-quality facility.
12	Marketing initiative is late	Medium/Very High	A major marketing initiative will have management backing, so it should not suffer for funds or resources as much as other projects. If the marketing initiative runs late and comes after the conference, the impact is catastrophic.
2	Availability of appropriate lodging for several hundred executives	High/Medium	Because conference facilities are often connected with a hotel, it is very likely that the hotels with conference facilities have blocks of rooms reserved. However, the impact is not as great because there are usually multiple hotels nearby.

> **NOTE**   Microsoft Office Online (*www.microsoft.com/office*) offers templates related to project risk management, including a sample risk-management plan (in Microsoft Word), as well as a risk-assessment questionnaire and a risk-identification questionnaire. Distribute the questionnaires to stakeholders and team members to identify risks and to collect information you need to assess and quantify the impact of the risks.

Assessing Risks

Assessing risks can be subjective. But for some risks, you'll have some details to work with. If you're managing a project to produce this year's hottest toy, a large percentage of initial revenue depends on seasonal sales. What are the prime risks of missing the release date? What happens to the revenue forecast if you miss the release date by 30 days or even one week? You can often quantify a specific risk (the late completion of a task or the decrease in manufacturing capacity), but you also need to understand the broader effects of the risk if it occurs: What other tasks depend on the task that is late, and what risks does that heighten or introduce?

Assessing risks boils down to two big questions:

- How likely is this risk to occur?
- How much damage might it do if it does?

The answers to these questions aren't easy to come by. You often have to rely on rough tools such as your experience and the collective wisdom of the team. Sometimes, you can obtain harder evidence. Based on the information that you can gather and analyze, set up a scheme for classifying risks. You can go with low, medium, and high; or work with numerical ratings (1 for low, 2 for medium, and 3 for high). Bottom line: you want a convention that lets you record the probability and impact of a risk consistently and that helps you evaluate the significance of risks, given the number of risks and the size and complexity of the project.

Whether you go the analytical route or trust your gut, assessing risks in terms of time and money is essential. Without an estimate of the impact of a risk, how can you decide how much money and time to spend addressing it? For example, you can correlate thresholds of time and money to levels of impact. Less than $25,000 is low impact, $25,000 to $50,000 is medium impact, and anything over $50,000 is high impact. Similarly, you could assign the number of months of delay to represent low, medium, and high impact.

■ **WARNING** Tasks that are difficult to estimate are red flags for risk. Work with the people assigned to those tasks to determine why the estimates are so uncertain. You can then determine how to manage the associated risks.

Choosing the Risks You'll Manage

You'll find risks under almost every stone that you, stakeholders, and the project team turn over. You simply can't manage every project risk you identify, including those that result from factors largely out of your control. Risk management entails not only identifying and assessing the risks you might encounter but also determining whether you should bother monitoring them at all. Clearly, you have to prioritize risks, and the probability, impact, and cost (called the *risk value*) are your tools.

For risks with low probability and little impact, you might simply ignore them (that is, accept the consequences if the risk occurs). Or you might use some money from contingency funds to cover the cost. There's no reason to devise intricate response plans to risks that pose little danger to your project. They aren't likely to happen, and they don't hurt very much if they do. The ones to watch are those with a high probability of occurring and a significant effect.

SEE ALSO   The section "Setting Up Contingency Funds," on page 351, explains what contingency funds are for and how to decide when to use them.

Sorting by probability and ranking risks makes Microsoft Excel an ideal tool for evaluating probability and impact. After you add risks and their probability and impact to a worksheet, you can calculate risk value by multiplying probability and impact, as demonstrated in the Excel worksheet in Figure 15-2. Risk value represents the consequences (the costs) of each risk should it occur.

| | File | Home | Insert | Page Layout | Formulas | Data | Review | View | Add-Ins | | | Risk_Graph |

N20

	A	B	C	D	E	F
1	Risk ID	Risk	Impact	Probability	Risk Value	
2	10	The main resource on the project wears many hats.	1.0	1.0	1.0	
3	1	We might have to replace a developer	0.8	1.0	0.8	
4	6	The existing requirements must be extracted by reverse-engineering the code of the existing system.	0.8	0.8	0.6	
5	8	Production demands could impact testing.	0.8	0.8	0.6	
6	3	The software is not well documented.	0.6	0.8	0.5	
7	5	The requirements must satisfy conflicting stakeholder needs.	0.6	0.6	0.4	
8	2	The level of management support and commitment is not proven.	0.6	0.6	0.4	
9	13	Groups are accustomed to working independently and developing processes specific to their business.	0.5	0.6	0.3	
10	7	Resources are already working 60-hour weeks on production.	0.5	0.6	0.3	
11	14	Software is lacking productivity features.	0.6	0.5	0.3	
12	4	Project cost, schedule, and scope could all become critical.	0.5	0.5	0.3	
13	9	The database, with which the application integrates, is not complete.	0.5	0.3	0.2	
14	11	A major upgrade has been released.	0.3	0.5	0.2	
15	12	The client is only experienced with in-house programming using obsolete software tools	0.3	0.3	0.1	
16						

FIGURE 15-2 With risks in an Excel worksheet, you can calculate risk value and sort risks by probability and impact.

For a visual indication of how many risks you should monitor, you can turn the tabular information into a chart in Excel, as shown in Figure 15-3. For this chart, the legend correlates risk value with the duration of potential schedule delays. With a set of calculations such as these, you can prioritize risks and start developing plans for how to respond. For example, any risks in the lower-left portion of the graph are innocuous enough to ignore. The risks in the middle of the graph warrant analysis to determine whether you want to track them. And the risks at the top right are the ones you definitely want to keep your eye on.

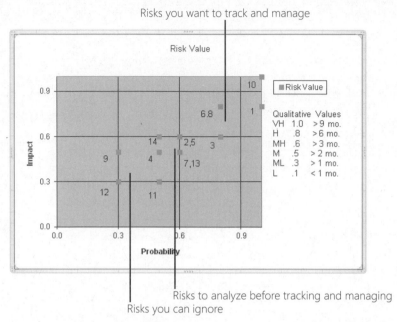

FIGURE 15-3 You can chart the probability and impact of risks (the risk value) to see how many fall in the quadrant of high probability and high impact.

TIP	Impact and probability of a risk event are not one-time measures. You must reevaluate risks and adjust these measures as work progresses.

PROJECT FILE	The Excel workbook shown in Figure 15-3, Risk_Graph.xlsx, is available in the Chapter15 folder on the companion website.

BEST PRACTICES

Similar projects share similar risks, which means you can learn about risks you're likely to encounter by studying what happened to other projects and by talking to people who were on those teams. If your organization doesn't record historical information about projects, show your manager the time and money at risk as an incentive to start.

When you hold a post-project review or lessons-learned session, be sure to discuss the risks that occurred and the risk responses that worked—or not. In particular, talk about the risks that occurred that no one saw coming, so the next project manager and project team won't be blindsided.

SEE ALSO	Chapter 18, "Archiving Historical Information," describes how to record information about projects you've completed. Chapter 16, "Learning Lessons," provides tips and guidelines for finding out what went well and not so well on projects.

Responding to Risks

After you have decided which risks are significant enough to manage, you need a response for each one. For example, if your project includes a helicopter delivery of a hot tub, you might consider an insurance policy to cover the damage if the hot tub falls on the house. Or if your resources are completely booked, you might mitigate the risk of unavailable resources with a plan to line up subcontractors ahead of time.

Identify the metrics you'll use to measure the success of the response if you have to carry it out. For instance, the schedule variance is one measure you might use to see whether your resource response is working. Because risks have different probabilities and impact, responses must be appropriate for the magnitude of the risk. For example, a response that costs $100,000 is overkill if the price of delivering the project late is only $10,000.

In general, the best options are the ones that prevent a risk from occurring. But reducing impact or preventing impact from snowballing will work, too. Here are some methods you can use to respond to risks to your project:

- **Accept the risk**   If risks are negligible in probability or impact, the easiest option is to accept the consequences. Your hard disk might crash, but you'll be willing to accept the time it will take to restore your files from your company backups. You don't have to plan any other actions. In effect, it's less expensive to accept the consequences than to respond to the risk.

- **Avoid the risk**   If one portion of your project poses huge risks to completing the rest of the project, you might avoid the risk by eliminating the risky portion from the scope. Of course, this option works only if the scope change doesn't irreparably damage the business case for the project.

- **Limit the impact**   Often called *risk mitigation*, this option entails taking steps to lessen whatever consequences a risk might pose. For example, if team members are unfamiliar with a new tool, but that tool must be used to prepare project deliverables, sending the team to a training session mitigates that risk.

- **Transfer the risk**   Transferring risk means that you put the majority of the burden of the risk on someone else. The most common example is purchasing insurance policies, which transfer risks to the insurance companies. You don't set aside project money to rebuild should a fire destroy your construction; instead, you pay a small premium for fire insurance. If a fire starts, however, your project will still suffer a setback to the schedule.

TIP   Asking vendors for fixed-price bids is another example of transferring risk. With a fixed-price bid, the subcontractor faces the risk of cost overruns if the work takes more time than allocated. (You might decide to share the risk by specifying the percentage of cost overruns that the subcontractor must absorb.)

- **Use contingency plans**   Contingency plans are alternative courses of action you can take if a risk occurs. They often rely on additional funds set aside to handle unanticipated costs. For instance, you might plan a conference in a reasonably priced hotel with a great conference room layout. Your contingency plan if that hotel is unavailable could be to choose another more expensive hotel and increase the conference registration fee. The next section discusses how to gauge the size of a contingency fund and the processes for using one.

For any approach to risk response, you should evaluate your ability to implement a particular option. Here are some questions you can ask to help you decide whether a response is feasible:

- Do you have the resources for the response?

- How will the response affect resources on other tasks and other projects?

- Do you need to purchase or provide additional equipment? For example, would you need to purchase another computer or outfit another workstation to bring a new resource on board?

- How does the response affect performance expectations for the project?

- How quickly can you implement the response strategy?

Keep in mind that scope, schedule, budget, quality, and risk are interconnected. If a risk occurs, the response might entail scope changes or schedule changes, which need to be tracked through your change-management process.

> **SEE ALSO**   Chapter 12, "Managing Project Changes," describes the steps for a typical change-management process.

Setting Up Contingency Funds

Living hand to mouth, without any budget or time set aside to handle unexpected events, is no way to run a project. Experienced project managers build some buffer into project schedules and establish contingency funds in their budgets as a way to respond to risks that occur. The question with contingency funds is "How much?"

You can determine an amount for a contingency fund in several ways, although the method is often part calculation and part negotiation with management. Some organizations use a percentage of the project budget and duration to calculate contingency, basing the percentage on prior experience. Still another approach is to use a percentage of the target profit margin. In other words, project sponsors might agree to give up one percentage point of the expected return to cover the costs of uncertainty.

Most organizations ask project managers to estimate the cost of likely risk events. You can multiply the cost by the probability as a start for the amount of contingency funds you need to set aside. Here's an example:

- Design has run over budget on two of the last three projects, so you set the probability of cost overrun at 66 percent.

- The average overrun is 10 percent, and your design cost is $50,000. You set the impact at $5,000.

- The risk value is the probability multiplied by the impact: 66% × $5,000, or $3,300.

You typically don't add the entire risk value to a contingency fund, however, because there's a low probability that *all* your risks will occur.

 TIP Sometimes budgets are based on cost ranges instead of single numbers. Budgeting to a cost range is a type of basic contingency, so adding a contingency fund is redundant.

A contingency budget handles the *costs* of risks. As the project manager, you might be given a threshold for authorizing expenditures from the contingency fund. For amounts above that limit, you have to get approval of management, customers, or stakeholders.

You might also have what's sometimes referred to as a *management reserve*, which is money set aside by project sponsors and stakeholders to address unanticipated risks and other situations. This reserve, if it exists at all, is usually a percentage of the total project budget. In addition to dealing with the occurrence of unknown risks, a management reserve can be used to fund significant change requests that happen to provide significant value. Project sponsors often control the management reserve.

 TIP Another component of contingency planning is to identify any nice-to-have requirements that everyone agrees can be abandoned if necessary. The time and budget allocated to these requirements could be shifted to cover work related to key requirements if issues arise.

You can spread a contingency allowance over all the phases of a project, with a percentage designated for each phase (with the unspent portion carried over to the next phase). Or you could spread the funds over major areas of responsibility (design, production, and testing, for example). Another approach is to hold the contingency allowance in a single pot and disperse it through a request and approval process.

NOTE Publicize the conditions under which contingency funds are available. By doing so, you don't have to worry about team members relying on those funds to correct schedule and budget mistakes or stakeholders trying to grab their share before the contingency pot is gone.

Tracking Risks

The overall risk to a project varies as work progresses. Risk is high early on when uncertainty is at its peak. As the amount of work on the project is completed, the overall risk decreases. Your risk-management documentation should include a risk log that you use to track and update the status of each risk.

A risk log includes some of the same information as a risk-management plan, but in condensed form. Here are items to include in a risk log for each risk you track:

- **ID number**   Each risk receives a unique ID number whether or not the risk has occurred.

- **Description**   A brief description of the risk.

- **Planned response**   The actions you plan to take to respond to the risk if it occurs.

- **Risk owner**   The person responsible for monitoring the risk. Monitoring the risk includes evaluating its status and the effectiveness of the response. You must assign someone who understands the task or the area of the project in which the risk might occur.

- **Outcome**   If the risk occurs, include the result of the planned response.

Because of the rise and fall in the probability and impact of risks, risk management is a continuous activity. Updating the risk log regularly is part and parcel to managing a project. In other words, don't wake up on day 83 of the project and decide it's as good a time as any to check risk status.

As you pass milestones in a project, you can close some risks. For example, if resource availability was a risk, but your project just obtained five more people because of another project's delay, you might close that risk. (Of course, the risk could return if the other project gets back on track.) Closing a risk may free up contingency funds you need for other risks.

On the other hand, you're likely to add risks as a project progresses. Perhaps a component that is vital to quality has turned out to be a tougher design problem than you thought. As you identify new risks and add them to the risk log, you assess their probability and impact, calculate risk value, and develop response strategies as you did for the risks identified at the beginning of the project.

Managing risk involves modifying your assessment and approach to active risks, looking ahead at future tasks to find ways to make up time and reduce costs, dipping into reserves when a clear need arises, and then repeating these steps periodically.

Here are some practices to keep in mind for conducting risk management as work on a project progresses:

- **Regularly update the risk log so that it reflects the current status and performance of the project**   Close risks that are no longer an issue and adjust the probability and impact of risks you're monitoring. Update the status of each risk that has occurred and document the steps you've taken in your response plans.

> **NOTE**   Some project managers refer to risks that occur as *issues* and log them in an issue-tracking log. Other project managers use the term *issues* to refer to small obstacles that arise and track risks, both potential and real, in a risk log. Either approach is fine as long as you identify the difference up front.

- **Ask team members about risks in project status meetings**   Besides keeping the risk log current, this process helps educate the project team about your risk-management procedures.

- **Follow your risk-management processes for each new risk**   Assign someone to assess each risk and develop a response plan.

- **Report risk status with other project status**   The way you update and report risk status depends on the size and scope of a project, the budget, and the way you communicate. You might include a section in your regular status report. You also need formal risk-review meetings, in which stakeholders discuss options for addressing risks, learn about the status and success of responses, and approve contingency funds if the stakeholders' say-so is required.

Summary

You've successfully established an approach to managing risks when the processes you use can be repeated, measured, and demonstrated with pride to stakeholders. You don't have time to monitor every risk, so risk management includes prioritizing risks and monitoring only the most significant ones. By planning ahead, you can prevent some risks completely and limit the consequences of others. Risk changes throughout the life of a project, so risk management is an ongoing activity. You monitor risks and keep people informed about project risks in status reports, project status meetings, and regular risk-review meetings.

5

Closing Projects

CHAPTER 16

Learning Lessons

IN THIS CHAPTER, YOU WILL:

- Understand the benefits of identifying and documenting lessons learned

- Identify techniques for obtaining lessons learned

- Learn how to document lessons learned so they can benefit others

> "*The essence of success is that it is never necessary to think of a new idea oneself. It is far better to wait until somebody else does it, and then to copy him in every detail, except his mistakes.*"—*AUBREY MENEN*

"I HOPE YOU'VE LEARNED YOUR LESSON!" Unless you were different from most children, you probably heard that admonishment more than once while growing up. Unfortunately, that statement has made many people think of lessons as negative and mistakes as something to hide. As an adult and a project manager, not repeating the mistakes of the past is an important part of improving performance for your projects.

Improving performance isn't just about avoiding past mistakes. Progress comes from continually building on the successes of others. After the Wright brothers got the first airplane airborne, the path to today's jumbo jets was nothing more than a lot of enhancements.

This chapter focuses on how you learn from past performance to improve future results, which covers more about psychology than it does project management. Few people like to admit mistakes. Some don't like to advertise their success—either for fear of boasting or in a misguided attempt to keep the glory to themselves. Others keep quiet about successes because they think they're insignificant. You'll learn some techniques to draw out the successes that people have achieved as well as effective yet gentle ways to identify the mistakes that you don't want to repeat. More important, you'll learn how to take advantage of your lessons learned by documenting them and publicizing them so that everyone else in your organization can put them into practice.

The Importance of Lessons Learned

> *"The only real mistake is the one from which we learn nothing."*
> —JOHN POWELL

Documenting performance and other information about past projects and making a point of reviewing that information *before* beginning new projects is the most effective way to improve project performance. Nothing is as disheartening as making the same mistakes you made once before. And why should anyone else have to suffer the frustration of repeating a mistake when you've already paid that price? Remembering and repeating a project's successes is just as important. Best practices are effective because they help people move forward instead of reinventing what someone else already discovered. Here are some of the ways that you can put lessons learned—positive and negative—to use:

- **Apply proven effective techniques**   If you've used a document template to produce a document, you already know how reuse can speed up and increase the accuracy of your work. Proven practices, processes, and documents work the same way for projects. Successful strategies, powerful approaches, time-saving techniques, shortcuts, checklists, and well-designed documents help future project teams start where past teams left off. For example, suppose you discover that the usually recalcitrant sales team calls you back when you leave messages that tell it which sales won't go through until it resolves an issue with you. By sharing this nugget with other team members and project managers, you can improve the performance of more projects than your own, increase the results of the entire organization, and spread joy to people around you.

Although every project is unique, many projects share tasks, types of resources, typical costs, and potential risks. If a completed project is similar to the one you're managing, you can reuse that project's documents as templates to save time and increase accuracy.

- **Eliminate the costs of past mistakes**   Mistakes can be costly in so many ways: overspent budgets, delays, missed deadlines, poor quality, reduced scope, unmet objectives, and damaged reputations, to name a few. Your organization has paid for past mistakes. It would just as soon not pay for them again. By reviewing the mistakes that others have made and taking steps to prevent them, you can avoid a second round of tuition.

- **Build better estimates**   Every project struggles with the unceasing optimism of the people who estimate project time, money, and other resource requirements. You can build more realistic estimates for your projects by evaluating actual values from completed projects. For example, if past projects underestimated the time and resources needed, you can increase your future estimates. If those projects ran into problems, you can estimate a shorter schedule and lower costs because you've learned how to prevent similar problems.

TIP   Past performance is equally helpful if you're being pressured to set unrealistic dates or budgets. By showing stakeholders historical data, you have a better chance of convincing them that your estimates are realistic.

- **Educate project managers and team members**   Educating team members can make your job as project manager easier. Using lessons from past projects, you can show team members why you ask them to perform the tasks that you do. They'll realize that you're trying to help rather than annoy. And, they'll work more autonomously so you have more time to keep projects on track.

NOTE   Project management grows more popular every year, so organizations continually require more project managers and more project-savvy workers. Lessons from past projects are a great teaching aid when you show others how to manage projects of their own.

BEST PRACTICES

Some people don't take anything on faith. Past performance can help you convince others that your plans will work, whether you're trying to build a schedule that the team can meet or prove the benefits of project management to your company's executives. For example, if previous projects couldn't meet the deadlines and budget you're being asked to accept, you can push for more realistic numbers. Or you could show that the time spent on quality assurance and control actually saves money instead of costing extra.

Lessons learned can also demonstrate how project management helps improve performance—or how the lack of project management hurts. Folks who are new to projects might not understand the value of project management practices. Lessons learned provide real-life examples that can be persuasive. For instance, suppose you've had trouble with scope creep in the past. If documented lessons learned identify the lack of change management as the culprit, you'll have an easier time convincing your executives to support a change management system. Knowing how much scope creep cost other projects or how much money a preliminary change management process has saved can be even more compelling to cost-conscious executives.

SEE ALSO Chapter 18, "Archiving Historical Information," discusses how to store project performance data so that you can justify process improvement.

Collecting Lessons Learned

Status updates, code reviews, and other project meetings can be convenient opportunities for gathering suggestions for what to do and what not to do in the future. But scheduling meetings regularly and specifically for identifying lessons learned is a better idea. Extracting lessons learned from reticent team members requires a delicate balance of honesty and tact. Getting the attendees into a productive mindset and laying out the ground rules for these meetings takes some extra care.

There's enough work to do on projects that no one has time to attend unnecessary meetings. If people think a meeting is about finding fault, they'd just as soon see the dentist for a root canal. The following sections provide some suggestions for getting the most out of lessons learned sessions.

TIP   You can initially present these lessons learned meetings as informal project reviews. You collect valuable information for future projects and educate team members on better project processes at the same time.

Meeting Participants and What They Do

Lessons learned sessions can be quiet—too quiet, if people don't want to expose their mistakes or worry that others might make fun of their discoveries. To the contrary, a troubled project could lead to chaotic sessions of finger pointing as everyone tries to place the spotlight on someone else. Effective project reviews and lessons learned meetings don't just happen. They need a few participants to play special roles and the other attendees to interact in productive ways. The following sections describe each type of participant and how they contribute to running a worthwhile lessons learned meeting.

TIP   Sometimes, the same person can play multiple roles, depending on the size of your project, the number of meeting participants, and perhaps the openness you expect during the meeting. For example, the project manager could also act as facilitator, or a team member could double as the scribe. If you think that team members might be reticent about discussing lessons learned with a manager in the room, you can set up a meeting without managers to be run by an impartial facilitator.

Project Manager

Project managers initiate lessons learned meetings, so most of the meeting preparation falls into their hands. Here are the meeting responsibilities that a project manager usually performs:

- **Preparing for the meeting**   The project manager puts together any materials to be used during the meeting, such as project status, issues list, or items that team members have identified since the previous meeting. The project manager can set up the meeting or delegate those tasks to the meeting facilitator. Setting up a lessons learned meeting includes the following:

    - Planning the agenda

    - Estimating the length of the meeting

    - Scheduling the meeting date, time, and location

    - Distributing the meeting materials (at least a few days prior to the meeting)

TIP   As project manager, stay on the lookout for successes and fruitful lessons learned as you read status reports or talk to team members. Then, you can jump-start the discussion if the meeting gets off to a slow start.

- **During the meeting**   The project manager kicks off the session with an overview of the project status; for example, the phase or milestone that prompted the lessons learned meeting, and the materials distributed before the meeting. The project manager also helps control the meeting interactions; participates in the discussions; and takes notes about accomplishments, problems, action items assigned, and decisions made.

TIP   Because of project managers' thorough knowledge of their projects, they are likely to catch important points that the facilitator or scribe might miss.

- **After the meeting is over**   The project manager works with the facilitator to write a lessons learned report and distributes the report according to the communication plan. For example, you probably don't want external stakeholders to see your lessons learned unless the lessons affect them directly. The project manager also tracks any action items to ensure that the people responsible complete them.

SEE ALSO   The section "Documenting Lessons Learned," on page 369, describes what goes into a lessons learned report. Chapter 11, "Communicating Information," explains the components of a communication plan and identifies the attendees and stakeholders who should receive information.

Lessons Learned Facilitator

The facilitator can assist the project manager by setting up the meeting, or she can focus strictly on ensuring a productive session. Here are the tasks that a facilitator performs to run an effective meeting:

- Describe the goals of the meeting, such as identifying lessons learned for the project design phase.

- Explain the ground rules for the meeting and the responsibilities of the participants.

SEE ALSO   The section "Ground Rules," on page 364, describes rules that help run an effective lessons learned meeting.

- Control the meeting interaction.

- Keep the meeting focused on the agenda topics and progressing according to the set schedule.

- Suggest methods for setting priorities, promoting discussion, and making decisions.

- Help the group resolve interaction issues, discussion logjams, and meeting conflicts.

- Support discussions by making notes on a flip chart or white board.

INITIATE DISCUSSION WITH OPEN-ENDED QUESTIONS

Like some parties, feedback sessions can take some effort to get started. Meeting attendees often hang back and let someone else be the first to talk. Ask the wrong kind of question, such as "Are things okay?" and your team members are likely to answer with "Yes." That is not the way to kick off discussion about lessons learned.

Open-ended questions (the ones that you can't answer with one word) are perfect for initiating discussions. For example, if you ask a team member "What worked well?" she might tell you about how she obtained a timely response from the sales team.

SEE ALSO   See "Accentuating the Positive," on page 364, and "Analyzing Problems" on page 366, for more examples of open-ended questions you can try.

Scribe

The project manager and the facilitator are typically too busy with their other responsibilities to take thorough notes. Appoint someone who is familiar with the project to take notes about discussions, accomplishments, problems, action items, and decisions.

TIP A person who is fast on a keyboard or has legible handwriting is important, but familiarity with the project is more so. Outsiders might not recognize acronyms and project-specific terminology, and they could struggle with which points are pertinent.

Team Members

Team members play simple roles, but they're not necessarily easy. Before the meeting, team members make notes about the lessons they've learned and review the materials that the project manager distributed. During the meeting, they share their discoveries and participate in the discussion. What's difficult about being a team member in these meetings is overcoming psychological obstacles and bad meeting habits, both of which are described in the next section.

Ground Rules

Surviving a meeting that spotlights some people's successes and other people's disappointments is a challenge. Egos and reputations are on the line. If you don't handle them with care, you won't learn as much as you had hoped. As the project manager, you have to manage more than your own personal interactions. If emotions run high, the productive discussions can quickly deteriorate to "That's the stupidest thing I've ever heard!"; "What planet are you from?"; or worse, a deafening silence.

Every good meeting needs ground rules, but lessons learned sessions need them more than most. Analyzing successes and failures is tough work, so repeating the rules is in order. Printing them on the agenda is a start. But the facilitator should review the rules at the beginning of the meeting and should jump in to redirect attendees if they go off track.

Accentuating the Positive

Rousing some initial discussion is much easier when you ask people about their successes: the tips, tricks, and other successful techniques they've discovered recently. People are more willing to talk about what they've done right. In fact, all but the quietest (or most secretive) team members enjoy sharing their successes.

Unless your meeting time is very limited or your attendees are unusually boastful, make a point of asking each person if they've found a tip or technique they recommend. If your team members aren't jumping in with suggestions, here are some open-ended questions to help launch the exchange:

- Have you found techniques that save time (money, rework, patience, and so on)?

- What is your most exciting discovery on this project?

- Have you solved any tough problems recently? How did you solve them?

- Have you had any "Aha!" moments? Tell us about them.

- What are the benefits of your approach?

- What do you recommend for future projects?

BEST PRACTICES

Many people think there isn't enough time for KaiZen (continuous improvement). However, a small amount of effort up front can often lead to big improvements. By taking time to identify positive lessons learned, you can repeatedly boost quality and save time.

As an example, Jeff Furman, a PMP instructor and author, managed an initiative to correct problems in a large quality assurance testing environment. At the start of the project, each software tool was tested by the programmer who supported the tool. Tests were inconsistent, performed manually, and not shared with other programmers.

Mr. Furman's team started by collecting all the existing tests. They documented the tests, analyzed them, and stored them in a single repository. By doing so, the team assembled a well-organized and robust set of tests of product features. The repository ensured that the tests were easy to find and available to everyone, including new personnel. The newly organized test suite also enabled the team to set up automated tests that could be run with or without human intervention. The tests ran on a schedule, and the results were sent directly to test owners and management.

This simple approach combined with automated tools both reduced the time to run tests and increased quality by ensuring that the same comprehensive set of tests were run for each upgrade. The company received an unanticipated benefit by using the tests as part of hardware and system software upgrades and business continuation testing.

Analyzing Problems

The hardest part of collecting lessons learned is getting people to admit mistakes. Hiding mistakes is the worst response, but the one chosen most often. Although most people would agree that making mistakes is okay as long as you learn from them, convincing them to share their own gaffes is another matter. It's no surprise that team members don't want to be labeled as the one who triggered a cost overrun or a missed deadline. They worry that they'll lose their jobs or their chances for promotion. And sadly, in some work environments, their concerns are justified.

Your task as project manager and lessons learned detective depends on your organization's perception of mistakes. In organizations that recognize the value of learning from mistakes, your job is a little easier. Yet, even in proactive environments, people are hesitant to admit mistakes. The most important step that you can take to make people comfortable discussing failure is to focus on the problem, not the people. For example, if the discussion begins with "Mary didn't check the purchase orders and we received the wrong equipment," chances are that Mary will withdraw from the conversation, grow defensive, try to blame someone else, or choose one of many other unproductive responses. Instead, focus on the problem—we received the wrong equipment. Ask questions like "How can we improve our procurement process?" or "What can we change to ensure that we receive the right equipment next time?"

Here are a few open-ended questions to help identify problems in a non-accusatory way:

- What would you do differently on the next project like this?

- What can we do better?

- How can we improve?

- What obstacles have you run into? What was your solution?

GETTING BETTER, NOT BLAMED

Focusing on improvement instead of blame can take getting used to. Personal and professional life is as rife with blame as projects are. And the same advice works in each of these environments. Talk about yourself instead of other people. Describe the problem you faced, how it affected you, and what you did about it. One way to frame a problem from your perspective is to begin your sentences with "I." For example, "I couldn't tell which servers were delivered." Admitting to mistakes that you've made or improvements you've discovered sets an example that your team members can follow.

The wrong approach is describing someone else's mistake. For example, if the answer to how to improve is "Make sure Mary checks the purchase orders," you'll be back where you started. You and the meeting facilitator have to help team members from reverting to old habits. If someone starts a sentence with "You" or someone's name, get ready to jump in and redirect the discussion. If you have the misfortune of working where the preferred approach is to find and punish scapegoats, don't expect to hear about mistakes right away. You must first earn the trust of team members. And that could take longer than your project lasts. However, you can take steps to break down the barriers.

In a punitive environment, you have to show team members that it's safe to admit mistakes. You might need a process that doesn't publicize the raw notes of lessons learned meetings; only the recommendations for improvement that come out of the meeting. In addition, taking notes that don't include people's names might help attendees feel more comfortable about talking. Use small problems and recommendations to demonstrate that they can report issues without repercussions.

> **NOTE** Some people don't like to say anything negative in public. At the beginning of the project, set up and publicize a method for team members to submit anonymous feedback, such as a written questionnaire. In the email or memo announcing the lessons learned meeting, remind attendees that they can submit issues and suggestions via this alternative. You can rework the suggestions you receive into less threatening topics for the face-to-face session.

The Importance of an Agenda

Distribute an agenda for the lessons learned meeting a few days before it occurs. An agenda tells the attendees what they should be prepared to discuss and provides the first reminder of the meeting ground rules.

An agenda is even more important once the meeting begins. By following the agenda, you can be sure to cover all the important points, give each topic its fair share of time, bring wayward discussions back to the topic at hand, and otherwise rein in meetings run amok. Figure 16-1 shows an example of an agenda for a lessons learned meeting.

PROJECT FILE A Word template, Lessons Learned Agenda.dotx, is available in the Chapter16 folder on the companion website.

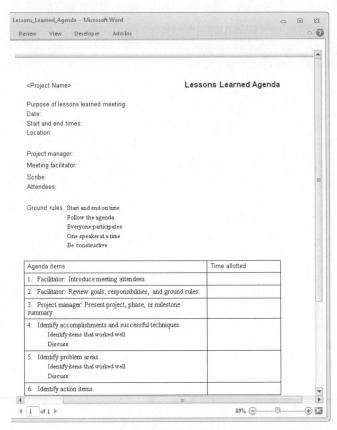

FIGURE 16-1 Distribute an agenda before the meeting so attendees can prepare to discuss their lessons learned.

BEST PRACTICES

Many organizations never get around to collecting lessons learned on projects, and the ones that do often save that task for the end. But project teams don't learn their lessons in the final days of a project. If you wait until then, many valuable lessons learned are already long forgotten.

Setting aside some time regularly to identify lessons learned is the best way to capture ideas while they're fresh. New techniques tend to become habit quickly. By scheduling lessons learned meetings at regular intervals, you can catch those tips while they still provide some excitement or stress relief.

Mistakes, on the other hand, have more staying power. The people who make them aren't likely to forget. However, you still want to catch that information quickly, so you can disseminate it to others and prevent those same mistakes from occuring again.

Documenting Lessons Learned

Lessons don't realize their full potential unless everyone knows about them. Without some way to share lessons learned, other project managers and team members will make the same mistakes you made, solve the problems you've already solved, and rediscover the same effective techniques you're already using.

A lessons learned report is one way to publicize recent successes and problems that have been resolved. It describes what went well on a project and what could be improved. The report describes the corrective items that resolved previous problems or action items proposed to fix problems the next time they arise. Lessons learned reports go into the project notebook to become part of the historical archive for a project. Figure 16-2 shows an example of a lessons learned report for the backyard remodel project.

SEE ALSO   The section "Information to Store about Projects," on page 386, describes the components of a project notebook.

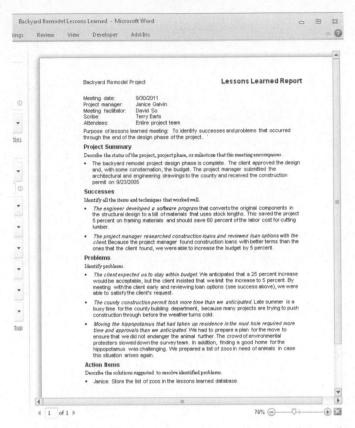

FIGURE 16-2 Distribute a lessons learned report after a meeting so others can take advantage of what you've discovered.

The problem with lessons learned reports is that they are quickly forgotten. A repository of lessons learned for all projects is a useful tool for project managers looking for solutions to pressing problems. The format that a repository takes depends on your organization and the technology that's available. For instance, a small company might develop a Microsoft Excel workbook to track lessons, whereas a large organization might use a Microsoft Access database or a Microsoft Windows SharePoint Services website.

PROJECT FILE   A sample lessons learned workbook, Backyard Remodel Lessons Learned Database.xlsx, is available in the Chapter16 folder on the companion website.

Summary

Learning from the past is the easiest way to improve performance in the future. Documenting lessons learned isn't difficult. But identifying lessons can be. Whether you're trying to identify what people did well or the mistakes that occurred from which you can learn, you must make people feel comfortable about sharing what they know. Running meetings that emphasize improvement rather than blame is the best approach. Written questionnaires are also effective, particularly in more difficult work environments.

CHAPTER 17

Closing a Project

> "All love affairs end. Eventually, the girl is gonna put curlers in her hair."—AL MCGUIRE

WHEN THE DELIVERABLES in a project are delivered, you might *think* the project is done. But you still have a few *project management* tasks to finish. Although the closing phase of a project is short, don't make the mistake of thinking it isn't important. The first key accomplishment during this phase is receiving formal acceptance from the project customer. After all, if the customer *doesn't* consider the project a done deal, you aren't really ready to close the project.

As long as you've been producing project reports *during* the project, generating closeout reports at the *end* of the project isn't a big deal, and the final results that the closeout reports show are valuable. They summarize what the project achieved and how you accomplished those achievements. Closeout reports are part of the project documentation you produce for posterity. These reports also act as educational tools for other project managers and project teams working on projects in the future. This chapter summarizes the reporting you perform at the end of a project and references other sections in this book that describe project reporting in detail.

SEE ALSO   See "Project Status Reports" on page 291, for information on how to gather and report during and at the end of the project. Chapter 16, "Learning Lessons," talks about documenting successes and needed improvements. Chapter 18, "Archiving Historical Information," describes techniques for storing your project information so you and others can find it in the future.

Another critical task in closing a project is ensuring that the transition to whatever should happen next runs smoothly. For example, with the backyard remodel project, you might provide the homeowners with the maintenance recommendations for the wood deck and the stone patio, and a quick review of how the electrical wiring works. If a project results in a new product, the closeout phase might include handing information over to manufacturing, operations, marketing, and other groups so they have what they need to build, sell, and support the product.

Obtaining Customer Acceptance

If only it were as easy to obtain customer acceptance as saying "Hey, we're done!" and the customer responding with "OK, great!" The risk with this friendly (and improbable) exchange is that the customer might come back a few months later, complaining that the results aren't really what the company had in mind or that someone just noticed that a deliverable was missing. The best way to close a project and make sure it stays closed is to get the customer (and other stakeholders) to formally accept that the project is complete.

For most projects, customer acceptance isn't a yes or no response. The deliverables and success criteria you documented in the project plan switch from being direction for the project team to standards that the project customer uses to determine whether the project is complete.

Deliverables are usually tangible, so customers can verify that they received them or not. For example, if the deliverable is a recommendation for the health insurance company your company will use, you simply make your recommendation and you're done.

Success criteria, on the other hand, require acceptance tests that must be completed successfully. For example, suppose you just completed a software project and one of the acceptance criteria is system availability of greater than 99.99 percent. Determining whether the system meets this criterion requires setting up a realistic test environment, determining the exact measurement process, running the system with test cases for a period of time, and processing the resulting data to calculate the availability. If the system doesn't pass the test, the project goes back into the execution phase until the problems are resolved and you run another test.

In many cases, the customer works with members of your project team to develop acceptance test procedures during project planning. These procedures spell out tests for every feature or specification that the project is supposed to deliver. When you and the customer run the acceptance tests during the closing phase, the customer signs off on each feature that is successfully demonstrated.

> **SEE ALSO** The section "Success Criteria," on page 33, describes success criteria and provides examples of effective criteria.

> **TIP** ✓ Good success criteria aren't open to interpretation. What if the customer requires that the same software system must have no critical or major defects and no more than 10 serious defects? Defects that corrupt data, computer systems that come to an abrupt halt, and anything that generates flames and smoke are typically recognized as critical. However, without clearly defined success criteria, the customer might categorize defects differently from everyone else. For instance, your customer might consider a crowded dialog box as a major defect because it could lead to data entry errors. Your team considers the same defect as cosmetic. By diligently defining success criteria up front, reviewing and obtaining acceptance on plans and prototypes throughout the project, and reviewing deliverables and preliminary test results, obtaining agreement that you have met the project's acceptance criteria is much easier.

Signing their names makes people think about the implication of their agreement, regardless of whether the signature is for a formal acceptance document of a project, the final project payment check, or the deed to the ranch. As with the sign-off on the project plan you produced some time ago, a meeting to sign off on customer acceptance emphasizes the significance of the event. If a face-to-face meeting with the project sponsor, customer, and other stakeholders isn't feasible, hold a conference call to verbally accept the project and send the project acceptance form to the customer and sponsor to sign (and return to you to store in your project notebook).

BEST PRACTICES

Meeting objectives and handing over deliverables is not the same as satisfying the customer. Sometimes, customers can't describe what they want, but they know when they see it—or know that what they're looking at *isn't* what they want. As well, you might have met the success criteria, but the process wasn't pretty to watch. Because everyone is different, success in your eyes might not impress the customer.

Organizations survey customers to find out what they think because it's better to learn about and correct a problem than to have customers complain to everyone they meet. Surveying the sponsor, customer, and other stakeholders to determine their satisfaction with results tells you much more than the signature on an acceptance form. Furthermore, you can ask them what they liked and what they thought could be improved to add to your lessons learned database. Include the survey results in the closeout report.

Documenting the Project

"The distance between insanity and genius is measured only by success."—BRUCE FEIRSTEIN

Maintaining information about past projects and making a point of reviewing that information before beginning new projects is the most effective way to improve project performance. Nothing is as disheartening as making the same mistakes you made once before. By reviewing past projects during planning, project managers and everyone else on the project team can improve on the past instead of experiencing the embarrassment and frustration of repeating past mistakes. Instead of reinventing what someone else has already discovered, you can use the experience of others to make your project more successful.

An historical record of the actual schedule, effort, and cost from completed projects is an invaluable resource for estimates you must produce for new projects. Every project struggles against the indestructible optimism of the people who estimate what the projects will require. You can circumvent the optimism of previous projects by reviewing how long similar projects in the past took and what they cost. You can also use project documentation to track statistics of project performance and evaluate project management proficiency and skills over time.

Likewise, historical data comes in handy, accounting for potential problems and changes that can increase time and cost. For example, if previous projects had problems that you now know how to prevent, you can make stakeholders happy with a shorter schedule and lower costs. If similar projects had to address the same change requests, you're better off including them in your plan at the beginning.

REUSING DOCUMENTS

Besides helping to prevent mistakes and putting proven best practices to work, starting with documents from a similar (and successful) project that's already complete is a big time-saver. Although every project is unique, similar projects are likely to include similar objectives and types of resources, familiar tasks, standard costs, and potential risks.

If you notice the same features repeating frequently from one project to the next, consider taking a few minutes to create a template from one of those projects. Existing documents that have worked well in the past are great candidates for templates. You can take advantage of a document's layout, headings, and even text that tends to stay the same from project to project (such as the project deliverables that your company typically provides). The only step that might take more than a minute is replacing project-specific text with either sample text or instructions about the kind of content to include.

You can also create a template for a Microsoft Project file and tell the program which types of data to remove:

1. With the schedule open in Project, on the File tab, select Save As.

2. In the Save As dialog box, from the Save As Type list box, select Project Template. Project automatically selects the folder for templates specified in Project options. (To see the location of your template folders, on the File tab, click Options, click Save, and look at the path in the Default User Template Location box.)

3. In the File name box, type a name, and then click Save.

4. In the Save As Template dialog box, select the check boxes for the types of data that you want to remove from the file before you save it as a template. For example, select Values Of All Baselines to remove the existing baselines because your next project will use different baseline values. Select Actual Values to remove the actual values from the previous project. On the other hand, you might keep the Resource Rates check box cleared if your resource rates don't change very often.

Project Closeout Reports

After you obtain the customer's acceptance, it's time to compare the actual project performance to the goals, objectives, and plans you laid out in the beginning. Were the project goals achieved? Did you successfully complete the project on schedule, within budget, and to the level of quality required? Is the customer happy with the results?

Project closeout reports are like status reports, only more robust because they sum up the final status of the project. The information they contain varies depending on the size of the project, what measures you've tracked during the project, and the deliverables and success criteria that the project is supposed to fulfill. For example, for the backyard remodel project, a constructed deck, a signed certificate of use from the county government, and a signed check for payment are good indications that the project is complete. The closeout report might identify those completed milestones along with a summary of the duration of the project, the final cost, and other information, as illustrated in Figure 17-1. Closeout reports for large projects typically include more information.

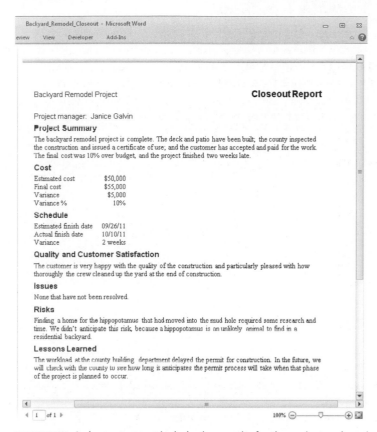

FIGURE 17-1 A closeout report includes key results for the project and can include useful information to improve future project performance.

PROJECT FILE   The file shown in Figure 17-1, Backyard_Remodel_Closeout.docx, is available in the Chapter17 folder on the companion website.

Project Summary

The last report you prepare for a project is the perfect place to sum up the endeavor. The closeout report starts with a high-level view of project performance, including the following items:

- **Was the project a success?**   After you review the project performance and measures of success, decide whether you think the project can be called a success.

- **Was project management effective?**   Now that the project is complete, would you do anything different in planning and managing the project?

- **What is worth repeating and what would you do differently?**   You might produce a separate lessons learned report and store lessons in a database for everyone to share. For the closeout report, include a high-level summary of what you and the project team did that delivered results and your recommendations for how to improve.

- **How did risks affect the project?**   Document the risks that occurred during the project, the risk response chosen, and whether it was successful. In particular, high-light any risks that arose that *weren't* identified in the risk management plan.

 TIP   Also consider documenting close calls—risks that didn't come to fruition, but were close to coming true, such as a resource short-age that was averted because team members worked double shifts for two weeks to meet a deliverable deadline.

Quantitative Results

Closeout reports include quantitative measures of project performance ranging from standard approaches, such as variance between estimated and actual finish dates, to project-specific measures like the reduction in telephone calls to customer support. Here are some typical quantitative results that appear in closeout reports:

- **Cost**   Customers usually want to know the final price tag of the entire project, the cost for each major phase, and other budget-related results, so it's no sur-prise that closeout reports contain these numbers. They also show the variance between the final cost and the estimated cost both in dollars and as a percent-age; they might include other financial results, such as profitability or return on investment (ROI). For large projects, you might break down reported costs in other ways, such as capital expense, labor costs, material costs, or cost of contractors versus employees.

SEE ALSO   The section "Understanding Financial Measures," on page 161, ex-plains commonly used financial measures, such as payback period, net present value, and internal rate of return.

- **Schedule**   Schedule results include the actual delivery date for the entire project and the variance between the final dates for key milestones compared to the forecast completion dates. You might document the variance as a percentage of the baseline duration to obtain a quantitative measure of project performance over time. For example, if the baseline duration was 100 days, and the project completed in 110 days, the schedule ran 10 percent longer than planned. You can compare this measure to schedule performance for other projects to see how you improve your future estimates.

- **Effort**   The number of work hours required to complete the project can be valuable for resource planning on future projects. Knowing the actual number of hours that people worked and when they worked them can help you assign resources more effectively in the future.

- **Completed scope**   A section for completed scope is particularly important if the project didn't fully deliver the items in the original scope or if the project scope expanded or shrank significantly due to change requests. In the closeout report, document the deliverables that the project did produce.

- **Changes**   Summarize the significant changes from the original scope or specifications.

- **Quality**   If the success criteria for the project include quality metrics, be sure to include the quality results in the closeout report. Without quality metrics to meet, you might include other types of quality-related results, such as the best practices that the team applied or the number of hours of rework on deliverables.

Closing Out Contracts

If you've had anything to do with contracts—negotiating, signing, or closing—you know that they mean paperwork. If your project involved a contract with the project customer, closing the contract offers the same degree of difficulty as obtaining customer acceptance. If the customer is happy and accepts the project as complete, ending the contract might be as simple as exchanging signed acceptance forms. In contrast, closing contracts can be difficult if parties disagree about whether the contractual terms have been met. Resolving these disagreements is best done without the lawyers involved—at least until a stalemate is obvious.

Enough.

TIP Most organizations don't close the financial books on a project until a few months after the final project delivery. By keeping the project open in the accounting system, additional charges, such as warranty repairs or support, are easy to add as project expenses. However, it's a good idea to close the project to additional labor hours so that people don't inadvertently charge time to your project.

Closing contracts also represents closure for the contracts you set up with vendors. You must review every contract for the project, whether for contract employees, subcontractors, service agreements, and so on, to determine the steps to close them. Then you diligently perform those steps.

Project Transitions

At the end of a project, you must handle two types of transitions: one for the team that worked on the project, and the other for the team that picks up where the project leaves off. Because projects are temporary, the members of the project team move on at the end of a project. Particularly with long projects, team members are bound to have some emotional reaction to leaving the project they worked on—sometimes relief, but in many cases, sadness or fear. Your job as project manager is to ensure that people's transitions proceed smoothly so that your project finishes without incident, and your team members are reasonably comfortable about the change. In most cases, you can complete this task by communicating the status of team members' availability to their managers, who then plan the transitions. The other transition is handing off information about the project to the people who take over the next steps—whatever they are. Fortunately, this transition is usually easier and less emotionally charged.

Transitioning Resources

The people and equipment that you assign to your project go on to something else after your project is complete. What resources do after they finish working for you might not seem like your responsibility, but planning these transitions is in everyone's best interest. When you work with your team members and their managers to plan their reassignments, you ensure that they finish the work they're supposed to do for your project. At the same time, you gain respect from the people and their managers as someone who is considerate of others and pays attention to detail. Furthermore, you might win points with the functional managers who have the team members lined up for their next assignments.

To plan resource transition, you need to know how long and how much you need the resources. If resources go back to their functional groups, their managers will appreciate knowing when their people are available, so they can line up additional work without worrying about overloading or benching them.

Knowing whether resources can start working on something else while cleaning up their assignments for you is important because assignments usually overlap. Assignments don't require the same level of intensity or time from start to finish, so it's common for people to start ramping up on a new assignment as work on the old one slowly trails off. Contractors and consultants appreciate knowing when they'll be done so they can start lining up new work without worrying about a gap between assignments, having to postpone another client, or working two full-time contracts simultaneously.

Handing Off Information

Although projects end, some part of them usually continues. Whether your project is a backyard remodel that the homeowner is going to maintain, a product that the sales team now has to sell, or a service that the technicians have to install and support, someone else needs to know what you did and what the status is. For example, construction projects typically hand over as-built drawings, which show how the resulting structure was built regardless of what the architect originally drew. As-built drawings might show a power line that was relocated because of a large buried rock or a framing detail that changed. Or a software development project turns over information to the team that will support the application once it's implemented at customer sites.

The information that you hand off depends on the project. Here are a few of the items you might want to provide to the team that takes over:

- The location of the archived project documents in case the team needs more information

- The closeout reports

- Any tasks that are incomplete, their status, and why they weren't completed

- Unresolved issues

- Test results

- Final specifications, as-built drawings, and product documentation

> **SEE ALSO**   Chapter 18 provides some examples of how to store archived project documents and where to keep them.

Summary

Closing a project is a combination of confirming that the project is, in fact, complete; recording what happened during the project; and tying up loose ends. Obtaining acceptance for a project may be simple and informal, or could require an acceptance test. Closeout reports document project performance and significant accomplishments. Finally, when everyone agrees that the project is over, the last task is to close any contracts that the project required, whether with the project customer or with vendors.

CHAPTER 18

Archiving Historical Information

IN THIS CHAPTER, YOU WILL:

- Identify information to archive about completed projects

- Discover several methods for building a project archive

- Learn about archival features in enterprise project management solutions

66*Insanity: Doing the same thing over and over again and expecting different results.*99—ALBERT EINSTEIN

IF AN ORGANIZATION wants to improve performance on projects in the future, it must learn from the projects in its past. Whether a project was a spectacular success or a dismal failure, there's valuable information in the documents from completed projects about what to do or what *not* to do the next time. Unfortunately, many project managers file away project documentation as soon as a project is complete and don't think to look at it when another project begins. If you're breaking ground as the first project manager in a company, project documentation for past projects are probably as rare as lips on chickens because no one realized that projects need documents like charters, plans, budgets, and status reports.

In the previous chapter, you learned how documentation for completed projects can help performance on future projects. This chapter describes the project information to store in a historical database. You'll also learn about a few ways to archive project information depending on the technology available in your organization.

Information to Store about Projects

If you have trouble getting enough time to plan a project, chances are good you won't have much time to study the project after it's finished. Fortunately, the project notebook you assemble during the life of a project contains much of the historical information you need. A *project notebook* is a comprehensive dossier of project plans and actual performance. Here is a list of information you typically include in a project notebook, which can also be stored in your project archive when the project is closed:

- Project contact list

> **NOTE** Contact lists become out of date quickly in organizations with frequent turnover. As an alternative, keep records of the organizations involved in the project and key people who may not change roles as quickly.

- Project overview
- Original project plan including the project schedule
- As-delivered plan
- Requirements
- Detail design specifications
- Change request log and documents
- Risk management plan and documents
- Issues log
- Deliverable acceptance log and forms
- Training
- Testing
- Correspondence

- Meeting minutes
- Status reports
- Project performance and variance reports
- Project close-out reports
- Lessons learned

SEE ALSO Chapter 2, "Obtaining Approval for a Project," and Chapter 3, "Planning to Achieve Success," describe the components of a project plan.

NOTE The information that you gather and store in a project notebook depends on the project type, the size of the project, and the maturity of your project management practices. For example, for the Backyard Remodel Project, the project notebook doesn't need a section for testing because the building inspections ensure that the construction conforms to code. And it doesn't need a section on training unless you intend to hold a class to teach your kids how to use the swings, your husband the grill, and the dog to keep his toenails off the redwood. However, the blueprints and as-built drawings for the remodel would go in the section on requirements.

After you add the final documents for a project to the project notebook, the project is ready to join the archive of other completed projects. If you work strictly electronically, archiving a project could be as simple as moving the electronic project folders to a new location for completed projects (and backing up all the files). If you also keep physical notebooks with hard copies of project documents, you'll have to store those on bookshelves reserved for project archives.

SEE ALSO Chapter 17, "Closing a Project," explains the value of project documentation and what goes into project close-out reports and other closure reports.

PROJECT FILE The Chapter18 folder on the companion website contains Project_Notebook_Contents.dotx, a Word template for keeping track of project documents and their electronic and hardcopy locations.

Shelf after shelf of identical three-ring binders is a daunting sight when you're trying to find a completed project to use as a guide. Navigating from folder to folder on the computer that holds files for completed projects and opening files with promising names can be equally tedious and time-consuming. Maintaining a file or small database of basic information about completed projects is one way to simplify finding similar projects.

The spreadsheet shown in Figure 18-1 is simplistic, but it's easy to maintain. You can filter the results by values in the Keywords column. For example, if you're working on a new project for marketing and want to find potential stakeholders, you can filter the Keywords column for "marketing" and start researching documents for marketing projects.

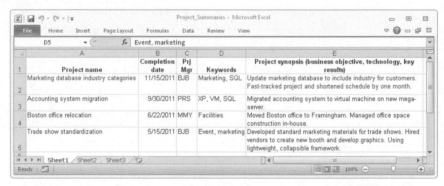

FIGURE 18-1 A file with brief descriptions of completed projects makes it easier to find projects similar to the one you're working on.

PROJECT FILE You can find the Microsoft Excel spreadsheet file for project summaries, Project_Summaries.xlsx, in the Chapter18 folder on the companion website.

Ways to Build a Project Archive

Customers, managers, team members, and project managers each require different types of project information. By organizing project documentation and storing it where it's easy to access, everyone can find the information they need when they need it.

If your company already has project management procedures and perhaps a centralized project office that manages the portfolio of projects, you're in luck. You don't have to worry about how to build a project archive. All you have to do is follow existing procedures to submit your completed project to the archive. However, if you want to start a project archive in your organization, start small. You can work with existing tools to determine what you need to store. Then, as the organization's needs and project sophistication grow, you'll have the information you need to propose a tool like Microsoft Project Server.

TIP Although you might still keep paper-based project notebooks (which might require one to dozens of binders), technology improves upon hardcopy storage, making it possible for people involved with a project to quickly find the information they need. If your organization is modest, you don't need to acquire tons of technology. Basic features included with your computer's operating system can satisfy your electronic storage need. But you can put other technology to work if it's available.

The best solution for a project archive is one that supports the size and quantity of projects you have and works within the limitations of your IT staff and budget. For instance, if you are the president, primary project manager, bookkeeper, and systems administrator, shared folders on a computer that everyone can access might be sufficient. The following are a few options for storing project information:

TIP A project archive doesn't do much good if no one knows about it. Project managers get the most mileage from project archives, so make sure they know where completed projects are stored. But anyone involved with projects can find helpful documents and information in an archive. You can notify everyone on your project team about the project archive resource when you kick off your project. Or if you prepare a welcome packet for new team members, be sure to include the location of the archive and a brief description of what it holds.

- **Shared Folder** Storing project documents on a shared network drive is a simple solution for accessing project documentation. You create a folder structure for projects on a drive that everyone can access. Team members connect to the network drive and review or work on the documents they need.

The big disadvantage of shared folders is that change management is difficult to control. Unless you have an IT staff to set up the appropriate shared folder permissions, anyone can copy, modify, or even delete project documents.

■ **Shared Workspace** Microsoft SharePoint 2010 is another solution for storing project documents. During project execution, you can use a SharePoint website as a repository for documents and a place for communicating with team members. When the project is complete, you can keep the site as an archive of the project. For example, the project team that worked on this book used this method to communicate between several people and sites across the United States. All someone needs to reach the site is a web browser and permissions to access its contents.

> **NOTE** If your organization has a document management system or another document storage solution, you can use it to archive project documents—as long as the people who work with the project archive can access the document management system.

Microsoft Enterprise Project Management Software

Microsoft Enterprise Project Management solutions are an option for organizations that manage many projects and want a tool to help manage their project portfolios, past and present. Enterprise Project Management software uses a project database to hold information about project schedules and resources and employs SharePoint to provide shared workspaces for document libraries, risk tracking, and issue management.

Summary

Creating an archive for completed projects helps project managers to improve project performance by reusing successful practices and avoiding past errors. Project archives don't have to be a huge undertaking. The information you need is assembled during project closeout. And you can use technology that's readily available in the smallest organization. After you've set up a project archive, make sure that people involved with projects know that it's available.

6

Beyond Projects

Selecting and Prioritizing Projects

> "*It's just as unpleasant to get more than you bargain for as to get less.*"—George Bernard Shaw

MANAGING PROJECTS WELL is a good start. But business is more complicated than that. Organizations have many projects from which to choose, but they usually don't have the resources to perform them all. So, they must pick. A dart board is expedient, but not the right approach if your organization cares about achieving its objectives. To consistently pick the right projects, you probably already know that you need a process and guidelines for selecting projects. The same process works equally well to stop projects that aren't delivering the desired results.

Organizational DNA is as unique as the human variety, which means that each organization uses different criteria to select projects and places different weight on the importance of each criterion. Project managers must learn what drives their organizations and then manage projects to meet those objectives. This chapter explains why you must understand the process and criteria that your organization uses to select projects.

Project Selection and the Project Manager

If you're a project manager and learn of a project only when you're assigned to manage it, project selection criteria might seem of little use to you. To the contrary, project selection criteria and the selection process can affect a project's fortunes at any time during its life cycle.

Like smart investors who monitor their investments to make sure that they're still delivering satisfactory returns with acceptable risk, most organizations evaluate projects as they progress to see whether they're delivering what they promised and still provide more benefit than other contenders. As a project manager, you must manage projects to deliver the results that stakeholders want. And if you can't deliver them all, focus on the results that stakeholders care about most. Although managing to deliver results is covered in Part 4, "Controlling Projects," those potential results are the reason you have a project to manage. Commit those results to your subconscious and make sure everything you do works toward achieving them. You must be able to respond to these business objectives.

BEST PRACTICES

You say that your organization isn't that organized, and you suspect a dart board plays a key role in project selection. Project selection criteria are still important tools in a project manager's toolbox. In fact, if your organization doesn't filter the list of projects it decides to take on, your competition for resources is tougher because the project portfolio is larger and more fluid.

By making sure that *your* project is aligned with the organization's goals and delivers impressive results in the areas that count, you'll have an easier time obtaining the resources you need—or assistance from management in removing obstacles.

Criteria for Selecting Projects

Project selection criteria vary by organization and situation. In a high-tech company, time to market and the number of new features could be the only criteria that matter. For a company that makes medical devices, safety and quality are of ultimate importance because patients don't want their pacemakers recalled due to design flaws. In addition to helping organizations choose projects, selection criteria help project sponsors and project managers decide whether a project is worth proposing. If a project doesn't meet the selection criteria, the team can bow out before wasting time proposing it to management. This section describes some of the criteria that organizations use to choose projects.

Criteria You Can't Ignore

Some project selection criteria represent automatic go or no-go decisions. Like income tax returns, projects need to satisfy regulatory requirements, such as the Sarbanes-Oxley Act. These projects must move forward if the organization wants to continue to be in business. Projects such as these move to the head of the project list, particularly if the government sets a deadline for compliance.

After the must do projects have been approved, an organization's mission, business objectives, and strategies are the most powerful factors in choosing projects. The fastest way to shorten a long list of projects is to ask, "Does this project support our mission and help achieve at least one of our business objectives?" If the answer is no, it's better to choose a project that is more in line with what the organization is trying to achieve. For example, if your company is focusing on improving quality and customer satisfaction, a project to reduce the cost of customer support is probably ill-timed. Table 19-1 includes types of objectives your project might have to achieve.

Another significant influence is the criteria by which the organization measures the project sponsor's performance. Ask yourself whether a project improves the project sponsor's perceived performance. If the answer is no, the project sponsor could disappear just when you need him most.

> **SEE ALSO** The section "Understanding Financial Measures," on page 161, describes several financial measures frequently used as criteria for selecting projects.

Linking Projects to Objectives

Linking a project to organizational objectives and strategies is the best way to show stakeholders the value that a project provides. Business objectives increase team members' commitment. And most important, the link to business objectives is crucial for evaluating change requests that increase or decrease project scope.

By understanding the business objectives that a project is supposed to support, it's much easier to prove the benefit of the project with hard numbers. For example, if your company spends $800,000 each year on support calls, the savings that a project produces is directly related to the number of calls it can eliminate. If an online knowledge base can cut calls in half and costs only $100,000 to implement, management will sit up and take notice.

> **NOTE** Projects that conflict with corporate culture and values should not make it through the selection process. If they do, employees begin to doubt that management means what it says. For example, a project to include bonuses for individual achievement in the payroll system is a bad idea for a company that emphasizes teamwork.

TABLE 19-1 Types of Objectives

CATEGORIES	OBJECTIVES
Sales and Marketing	Increase potential market
	Increase market share
	Reduce time to market
	Extend product life
	Increase customer satisfaction
	Increase quality or safety of products
	Improve reputation
	Decrease price to remain competitive
Production	Improve quality and safety of production process
	Reduce waste
	Decrease installation time
	Use more readily available materials
	Streamline production

Organizational Factors	Satisfy regulatory standards
	Provide value to stockholders
	Improve public perception
	Decrease labor skill level required
	Reduce training required
	Improve communication
	Improve employee morale
	Increase productivity
	Improve working conditions
Financial	Increase revenue
	Decrease costs
	Improve profitability
	Improve consistency of income

Risks and Opportunities

Despite great alignment with organizational objectives, some projects still struggle to gain approval because they represent substantial risks. For example, a project that offers outstanding benefits but plans to use untested new technology could be a huge failure if the technology doesn't work. Other projects might not win the top prize for organizational objective alignment, but they provide so much synergy with other projects that they rise a few rungs on the project selection ladder.

You must evaluate risks (and opportunities) to take into account the impact should the risk come to pass and the likelihood that it will occur. For example, a project that depends on highly specialized Venetian plasterers who are currently in high demand faces both a major setback if the resources are unavailable and an almost certain probability of a delay.

SEE ALSO   Chapter 15, "Managing Risk," describes how you identify, assess, track, and manage risks.

THE IMPORTANCE OF STAKEHOLDER SUPPORT

Alignment with organizational objectives is important for a project because *someone* has to care enough to push for the project to be selected and completed. If a project achieves a business objective, the stakeholder who benefits from that objective is more likely to sponsor the project and fight for it during the selection process.

Of course, stakeholder support is equally important once a project gets underway. Stakeholders can provide resources, eliminate obstacles, and resolve all sorts of problems. Stakeholder support often appears early in the project selection process, when a project review board or a similar entity evaluates the project. The next section describes how a project review board operates.

SEE ALSO   Chapter 2, "Obtaining Approval for a Project" provides techniques for obtaining and maintaining stakeholder support.

How a Project Review Board Works

Sponsors and project managers often become attached to their projects. They can lose sight of whether the projects make sense, pick the projects that are the most fun or the least trouble, or refuse to consider whether another project might be better for the entire organization. The solution to this problem is often a project review board, which can be a more objective judge of the merits of potential projects.

A project review board typically comprises high-level executives from every area in an organization. Here's how a project review board usually works:

- **Someone proposes a project.**   For the best chance of success, the person who wants his or her project to win a spot in the queue should evaluate the project using the same selection criteria that the project review board applies. And be prepared to answer questions that the board might ask.

- **The project review board analyzes the materials that the person proposing the project submits and asks questions about the proposal.**   If the proposal is unclear or incomplete, board members ask questions to clarify what they don't understand.

- **The project review board evaluates the project using the standard project selection criteria.**   Because the board includes executives from different areas, the group can identify issues or conflicts between business objectives. For example, if the company is trying to cut costs and increase customer satisfaction, the board could look for the projects that provide the most improvement in customer satisfaction for the least cost.

- **The board approves or rejects the project.**   The board communicates its decision to the proposer and explains the reasons for its decision. Telling proposers why a project wasn't chosen not only maintains morale but also helps them learn what the board looks for in projects.

Summary

Project managers must understand the project selection and prioritization process. Although a project manager might not influence the initial selection of a project, the selection criteria are useful to ensure that the project obtains the resources it needs and for measuring whether the project is delivering the right results at any point during the life of a project.

CHAPTER 20

Other Project Management Approaches

> "*Success is often the result of taking a misstep in the right direction.*"—AL BERNSTEIN

FOR YEARS, project managers have identified, tracked, and managed the critical path to deliver projects on time and within budget. Several years ago, the critical chain appeared on the project management scene. Unlike the critical path, the critical chain takes resource constraints into account to determine the most important path to manage. Managing the critical chain increases your chance of completing a project on time, often in less time than the duration of the critical path. This chapter provides a brief introduction to the concept of critical chain and how you implement it.

Traditional project management works well in familiar territory. When the goal and solution are clear, the scope and deliverables are easy to identify. The tools and technology you use have been around. Resources have the skills you need, and, ideally, are experienced with the work involved. So you document the project and build a plan for performing the work and achieving the project objectives.

But projects usually aren't that clear. Sometimes, the goal is known, but the solution isn't well defined. For example, suppose your customer wants a new business system, but the existing processes aren't documented and the customer can't give you a complete set of requirements. Say hello to agile project management. Following the lead of agile software development, agile project management uses iterations to deliver a successful solution; each iteration gets closer to what the customer requires. This chapter describes the basics of agile project management.

Managing the Critical Chain

The critical path for a project is the sequence of tasks with the longest duration. If a delay occurs in the critical path, the finish date for the project is delayed. The critical chain, in contrast, is the longest sequence in the project based on both task dependencies and resource constraints. Critical chain project management focuses on the tasks with the most constrained resources. You improve your chance of delivering the project on time, and possibly in less time because you apply your limited resources as effectively as possible. Critical chain project management uses buffers to reduce the probability of delayed tasks affecting the project finish date. This section provides an overview of how critical chain project management works.

> **SEE ALSO** To learn about critical chain project management in detail, read *Critical Chain Project Management,* Second Edition (Lawrence Leach, Artech House Publishers, 2005). *Critical Chain* (Eliyahu Goldratt, North River Press, 1997) is the book that introduced the underlying concept of critical chains.

Defining the Critical Chain

With critical path project management, you focus on the sequence of tasks with the longest duration and you schedule tasks to start as early as possible, as Figure 20-1 demonstrates. (The critical tasks are shaded with vertical stripes.) A critical chain considers task dependencies *and* resource constraints to determine the project schedule.

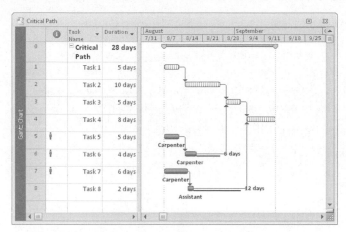

FIGURE 20-1 A simple project scheduled as early as possible based on the critical path.

Critical chain project management differs from critical path in that you schedule critical chain tasks as late as possible, instead of as early as possible for the critical path. Figure 20-2 shows the same simple project converted to as late as possible scheduling. Scheduling as late as possible has a few advantages. You don't incur project costs until you have to. The need for rework may be reduced because people perform tasks after they have gained experience and learned from earlier work.

> **NOTE**   Scheduling as late as possible is an option with critical chain because you add time buffers to protect the project from delays.

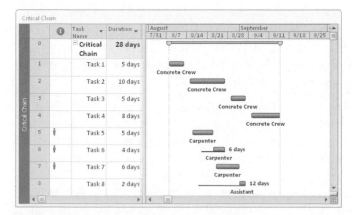

FIGURE 20-2 A project scheduled as late as possible.

With the critical chain approach, you eliminate resource overallocations beginning with the task sequences that have the least amount of slack. (The least amount of slack shows where resources are most limited.) In this example, tasks 1 through 4 don't have any slack. They appear as the critical path in Figure 20-1. Task 6 has 6 days of slack and uses the Carpenter resource. To eliminate the overallocation, you reschedule tasks 7 and 8, which have 12 days of slack, to occur earlier, as shown in Figure 20-3.

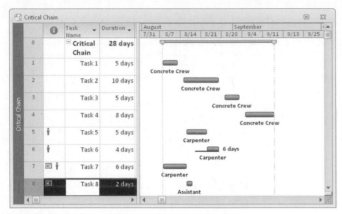

FIGURE 20-3 With critical chain, you resolve resource overallocations, starting with the tasks that have the least amount of slack.

Using Time Buffers Effectively

As you already know, you can't estimate task duration with total accuracy. If things go really well, a task may finish in record time. But if problems arise, the task could take much longer. If you build a project schedule using worst-case estimates for every task, your finish date is almost guaranteed to be later than the stakeholders want. However, even tasks that go well have a way of finishing according to their estimate. Perhaps the assigned resources work on something else or they work at a more leisurely pace. The bottom line: tasks almost never finish early, but they often finish late.

Critical chain project management doesn't give each task its own time buffer. Instead, a sequence of tasks shares a combined buffer, so that only the tasks that need the buffer actually use it. Because of the way statistical variance math works, the length of the buffer for an entire sequence of tasks is less than the total of all the individual task buffers. (The buffer for the sequence is equal to the square root of the sum of the squares of the individual task buffers.) Table 20-1 shows an example of the variances for a sequence of tasks. In this example, the buffer for the sequence of tasks decreases from the original total of 12 days to a shared buffer of 6.78 days.

TABLE 20-1 An Example of Individual Task Variances

TASK	PROBABLE DURATION	WORST CASE DURATION	DIFFERENCE
Task 1	5 days	7 days	4 days
Task 2	10 days	15 days	5 days
Task 3	5 days	6 days	1 day
Task 4	8 days	12 days	4 days
Total	28 days	40 days	12 days
Sequence Buffer			Square root(2²+5²+1²+4²) = 6.78 days

Buffers come in different flavors. A project buffer is tacked onto the end of the project to protect the overall project finish date. This buffer is calculated using all the tasks in the critical chain. You also add buffers at the end of each sequence of tasks, which are calculated based on the tasks in the sequence, as shown in Figure 20-1. Figure 20-4 shows the final critical chain project schedule. With the buffers added to the project and task sequences, the project duration is 34.78 days, a 13 percent decrease from the worst-case duration. However, you have also reduced the risk of delivering the project late.

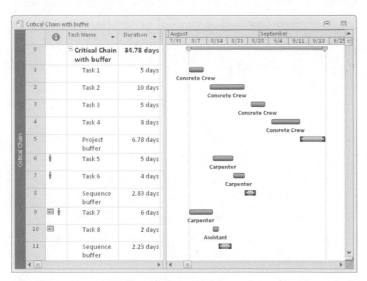

FIGURE 20-4 You add buffers to the end of the project and at the end of each sequence of tasks.

How to Use Buffers

Buffers in a critical chain are like the contingency funds you reserve to manage risk. If tasks take longer than estimated, and sequences of tasks begin to run late, you can dip into the time buffers without delaying the project finish date. One advantage to critical chain buffers is you don't have to respond to every delay that occurs. When you need to take action depends on the size of the delay and when it occurs:

- **First third of a sequence of tasks**   You take action when you have consumed one-third or more of the buffer. If you have consumed two-thirds of the buffer, you have a serious problem and need to look at aggressive solutions.

- **Second third of a sequence of tasks**   You take action when you have consumed one-third or more of the buffer.

- **Final third of a sequence of tasks**   You don't have to take any action unless the buffer is almost gone.

> **SEE ALSO**   The section "Setting Up Contingency Funds," on page 351, explains how you use contingency funds and management reserve to manage risks that turn into reality.

Agile Project Management

Agile project management is a good solution when you know what you are trying to achieve, but don't know how to achieve it. The processes you use are the same as the ones in traditional project management: define scope, plan, execute, control and monitor, and close. However, you repeat these processes until you have delivered a solution that meets the customer's requirements.

Because of the iterations in agile project management, each project management process works a little differently than in traditional project management:

- **Initiating (scope definition)**   The scope may change from iteration to iteration. For that reason, you should make sure to include some leeway in the high-level schedule to accommodate changes to scope.

- **Planning**   Your initial plan is at a high level and does not include much detail. One approach is to develop a partial plan based on the highest priority deliverables. As you iterate, you develop more detailed plans for additional work.

- **Executing**   Agile projects tend to use smaller teams of highly skilled people who work in the same location so they can collaborate easily.

- **Monitoring and controlling**   Status reporting occurs more frequently but is much more informal than in traditional project management.

- **Closing**   The closing process is similar to traditional project management, except that the customer accepts only the deliverables for the current iteration.

| SEE ALSO | To learn more about managing agile projects, see the book *Agile Project Management with Scrum* (Schwaber, Microsoft Press, 2004) or *Agile Project Management* (Highsmith, Addison-Wesley, 2004). |

Summary

Critical chain project management can shorten the overall duration of a project while improving your chances of delivering on time. If your project isn't as well defined, agile project management is a better alternative. With this methodology, you repeat the customary project management processes until you finally achieve the project objectives.

Glossary

accrual method When a project incurs actual costs for a resource, for example, as soon as the task starts, prorated as the task progresses, or after the task is complete.

activity Work performed by resources to achieve a result. Also called a *task*.

actual cost Cost that a project has actually incurred including labor, equipment, material, and indirect costs.

actual cost of work performed (ACWP) Total cost incurred for work completed on a task or tasks through the project status date (or the current date if no status date is defined). ACWP is used in earned value analysis to identify whether a project is on schedule and within budget. ACWP is also called *actual cost*.

actual duration The length of time between when a task started and the status date if the task is not yet complete.

actual finish date The actual date that a task was completed.

actual start date The actual date that a task started.

actual work The work that resources have actually performed on a task.

allocation The percentage of a resource's available working time that is assigned to a task.

assignment The work a resource is supposed to perform on a task, the resource's time that is allocated to the task, and the date range when the resource is supposed to work on the task.

baseline The original and stakeholder-approved plan for the schedule and cost for a project including any approved changes. Comparing the baseline to actual progress shows whether the project is on schedule and within budget.

baseline cost The project costs in the baseline plan, used to calculate earned value measures and project cost performance.

budget at completion (BAC) The estimated cost of the project at completion including actual costs to date and estimated costs from today until the finish date.

budgeted cost of work performed (BCWP) The baseline cost for completed work, calculated by multiplying the percentage of work complete by the total baseline cost. Also called *earned value*.

budgeted cost of work scheduled (BCWS) The baseline cost for work scheduled to be complete by the status date or the current date regardless of how much work is complete. Also called *planned value*.

calendar The working, nonworking (holidays and vacations), and special working days (overtime) used to schedule when work occurs on tasks.

change control board A group of project stakeholders who evaluate and approve or reject requested changes to project baselines.

change management The process of receiving, evaluating, and approving or rejecting requested changes to project baselines. Sometimes called *change control*.

change management plan A document that describes the change management process for a project.

change order A document authorizing a change for a project.

change request A document requesting a change for a project.

closing process The process of accepting the project as complete, documenting the performance, closing contracts, and releasing resources.

communication plan A document that describes the information that stakeholders require and the methods and procedures for communicating that information.

constraint A restriction on when a task can start or finish.

contingency plan A plan that identifies alternative approaches to be used if the corresponding risk events occur.

contingency reserve An amount of money, time, or both that is set aside for situations that can't be completely defined in advance, such as more time than originally planned to correct defects.

controlling process The process of comparing actual progress to the plan, analyzing the differences, evaluating alternatives, and taking corrective steps if necessary.

cost Project costs for people, equipment, and materials.

cost performance index (CPI) The ratio of budgeted costs to actual costs (BCWP/ACWP). To forecast the cost at completion, multiply the original cost baseline by CPI.

cost resource A resource type for expenses, such as travel, training, meeting room rentals, fees, and so on that aren't related to hours worked or quantities consumed.

cost variance The difference between the budgeted and actual costs of work performed. If the cost variance is positive, the project is under budget. In earned value analysis, cost variance is BCWP minus ACWP.

crashing Trying to reduce the duration of a task or entire project for the least amount of money.

critical path The tasks that determine the earliest possible finish date of a project. Each task in the critical path must be completed on time for the project to finish on schedule.

critical path method (CPM) A technique for determining the sequence of tasks (critical path) in a project with the least amount of float and therefore the least scheduling flexibility.

deliverable A tangible or measurable result for a project.

dependency Relationship of the start or finish of one task to the start or finish of another task: finish-to-start, start-to-start, finish-to-finish, or start-to-finish.

duration The length of working time between the start and finish of a task.

earned value The value of the worked performed (thus earned) up to the status date.

earned value analysis A method of measuring project performance by comparing baseline costs to how much of the budget has been spent and how much should have been spent for the completed work. See budgeted cost of work performed, budgeted cost of work scheduled, and actual cost of work performed.

effort The number of units of work to complete a task. Effort is not duration. For example, if two people work full time on a one-day task, the effort is two days.

effort-driven task A task whose total work doesn't vary as resources are added or removed.

estimate at completion (EAC) The forecast total cost at completion for a task or entire project.

executing process The process in which you launch the project and execute the plan.

fast-tracking Shortening the duration of a project by overlapping tasks that would normally be run sequentially, such as design and construction.

finish date The date that a task is scheduled to be completed, based on the task's start date, duration, work calendars, and constraints.

fixed cost A cost for a task that does not depend on the task duration.

float The maximum delay for a task that doesn't delay the finish date of the project. Also called *total slack*.

functional manager A department manager responsible for the people who work in that department. The project manager must work with functional managers to obtain and retain resources for a project.

Gantt chart A bar chart (named after Henry Gantt) that shows when tasks start and finish as well as the relationships between tasks.

implementation plan A plan that spells out the work to be done, when the work will be performed, who will do the work, and how much it will cost.

initiating process The project management process in which you officially commit to start a project.

internal rate of return (IRR) The annual return that a project delivers, taking into account the time value of money.

lag The delay between the completion of a predecessor task and the start of a successor task.

lead The amount of overlap between the end of one task and the beginning of another. For example, a lead time of two days means that the second task can begin two days before the first task ends.

leveling Delaying tasks to eliminate resource overallocations caused by two or more tasks using the same resource at the same time.

link A dependency between tasks: finish-to-start, start-to-start, finish-to-finish, or start-to-finish.

management reserve An amount of money or time that is set aside to allow for events that are impossible to predict, such as choosing a new vendor for materials due to a factory mishap.

material resource Materials consumed during a project, such as concrete or toner cartridges.

matrix organization An organization in which project managers and functional managers share responsibility for assigning resources to tasks and supervising their work.

milestone A significant event or accomplishment in a project, such as the completion of a phase or major deliverable.

net present value The value of the project expressed in today's dollars based on the percentage rate the organization uses for the time value of money.

network diagram A diagram that shows the dependencies between tasks. A network diagram shows tasks in chronological order from left to right.

outline A hierarchical representation of the tasks for a project. The Task Sheet in Microsoft Project is an outline that represents the work breakdown structure (WBS) for a project.

overtime The amount of work assigned beyond a resource's regular working time. Overtime costs are calculated by multiplying the overtime hours by the resource's overtime rate.

payback period The length of time it takes for a project to earn back what the organization pays to complete the project.

percent complete The percentage of task duration completed, calculated by dividing the actual duration by the scheduled duration.

percent work complete The percentage of work completed, calculated by dividing the actual work by the estimated work.

planned value The baseline cost up to the status date for tasks as they were originally scheduled in the project plan. *See budgeted cost of work scheduled*.

planning process The project management process in which you plan how you are going to complete the project.

predecessor A task that controls the start or finish of another task. In Project, predecessor does not necessarily indicate a task that occurs earlier in a schedule.

Program Evaluation and Review Technique (PERT) Evaluates the probable duration of a project by calculating a weighted average of the best-case estimate, most likely case estimate, and worst-case estimate.

project A unique job with a specific goal, clear-cut starting and ending dates, and—in most cases—a budget.

project charter A document issued by an executive, project sponsor, or customer, announcing a project and delegating authority to the project manager.

project organization chart A document that shows the reporting structure for people involved with a project.

project overview A short document that identifies why the project will be performed, the business value it provides, and what work it entails.

project plan A document that describes a project and the plan for completing it and achieving its objectives. The project plan guides the execution and control of the project.

project sponsor A person who has formal authority in the organization and is interested in seeing the project succeed.

quality assurance A process for evaluating project performance in relation to the specified standard of quality.

quality control Monitoring project performance for quality and identifying sources of unsatisfactory quality measures.

resource pool A set of resources available to work on project tasks, whether used by only one project or shared by several projects.

responsibility matrix A document that identifies who is responsible for different parts of a project and who has authority to make or approve decisions.

risk management The process of identifying what can go wrong, determining how to respond to risks should they occur, monitoring a project for risks that do occur, and taking steps to respond to the events that do occur.

schedule The overall timeline for a project including task dates, durations, relationships, costs, and resource assignments.

schedule performance index (SPI) The ratio of work performed compared to the work scheduled (BCWP/BCWS).

schedule variance (SV) The budgeted cost of work performed (BCWP or earned value) minus the budgeted cost of work scheduled (BCWS or planned value).

scope The extent of work that must be performed to complete a project.

slack The amount of time a task can slip without affecting the finish date of the project. Also called *float*. *Free slack* is the amount of time a task can slip without delaying another task. *Total slack* is the amount of time a task and its successors can slip without delaying the project finish date.

stakeholders People interested in, involved in, or affected by a project, such as customers, management, and project team members.

standard rate The rate charged by a resource for regular work hours.

start date The date that a task is scheduled to start, based on its predecessors.

statement of work A description of the work to be performed for a project, usually included in a contract.

success criteria A measurable result the project has to deliver in order for the customer to say the project is a success.

successor A task with a start or finish date that depends on another task. In Project, successor does not necessarily indicate a task that occurs later in a schedule.

summary task A task that summarizes the dates, duration, and work of all its subordinate tasks.

task A portion of work in a project with a start and finish date.

variance The difference between the baseline and estimated dates, work, or cost in a project.

work The time units required to complete a task. Work is different from task duration.

work breakdown structure (WBS) A hierarchical diagram showing work broken down into smaller packages to facilitate estimating work and costs, and tracking progress.

work package A task that represents actual work that resources do; it appears at the lowest level of the WBS.

work resource A resource, such as a person or equipment, that you schedule by the time worked on a project.

Index

What do you think of this book?

We want to hear from you!

To participate in a brief online survey, please visit:

microsoft.com/learning/booksurvey

Tell us how well this book meets your needs—what works effectively, and what we can do better. Your feedback will help us continually improve our books and learning resources for you.

Thank you in advance for your input!

Stay in touch!

To subscribe to the *Microsoft Press® Book Connection Newsletter*—for news on upcoming books, events, and special offers—please visit:

microsoft.com/learning/books/newsletter